PIONEER CONSERVATIONISTS
OF EASTERN AMERICA

PIONEER CONSERVATIONISTS OF EASTERN AMERICA

Peter Wild

MOUNTAIN PRESS PUBLISHING COMPANY
MISSOULA, 1986

Much of the material in this book originally appeared in *High Country News*. The chapter on Rachel Carson was first published by *Backpacker Magazine*.

Library of Congress Cataloging in Publication Data

Wild, Peter.
  Pioneer conservationists of eastern America.

  Bibliography: p.
  Includes index.
  1. Conservationists—United States—Biography.
2. Conservation of natural resources—United States—
History. 3. United States—Biography. I. Title.
S926.A2W53   333.95'092'2[B]   80-10354
ISBN 0-87842-126-2
ISBN 0-87842-149-1 pbk.

MOUNTAIN PRESS PUBLISHING COMPANY
MISSOULA, MONTANA

For my parents

Also by Peter Wild

Pioneer Conservationists of Western America
Chihuahua
The Cloning
Cochise
New and Selected Poems
Wild's Magical Book of Cranial Effusions
Peligros
Terms and Renewals
Fat Man Poems
The Afternoon in Dismay
Enos Mills
Wilderness
The Peaceable Kingdom

Contents

Illustrations

Preface

Not long ago I sat on a mountaintop overlooking one of those views that have made New England famous. Far below lay the village of Woodstock, Vermont, comfortably nestled with its town square and white steeple in a narrow valley. The cornfields and pastures surrounding the town gave way, as they should in such postcard scenes, to hilly woodlands rising to an intense, early spring sky. The last of winter's snow lay in the furrows of the higher fields; from somewhere came the putt-putt-putt of a farmer's tractor. My own sense of well-being heightened the charm of the place. Months before, the University of Arizona had granted me a sabbatical leave — that supposedly idyllic recess from academic cares — and after a winter of writing I was making my way across the country for a few weeks of backpacking in England.

The pause in mid-journey was also a coming home. Though not exactly a country boy, I had grown up in similar surroundings a few hours' drive to the south, milking cows after school, spending summers plowing and hoeing farm fields. Teenage visions of a more romantic future had drawn me away from New England; in the West I learned, as have many others before and since, that punching cows for $150 a month plus room and board or fighting fires for the U.S. Forest Service — at first vastly more exciting than spending all day shoveling out Bob Breyer's barn — eventually tapered off into its own brand of drudgery. In any case, as a result of such experiences I was, like many Americans, part Easterner and part Westerner.

Out of curiosity more than anything else, I had driven up from Massachusetts to visit the birthplace of George Perkins Marsh, the first figure in this book. As I was eating lunch on the huge quartz boulder that crowns Mt. Tom, a mountain rising directly behind the former Marsh home, two ideas came together in my mind. First, as a boy romping through the woods, Marsh certainly rested here to enjoy the view, even as I did. After years of thinking about Vermont's denuded hillsides and eroding streams, he sounded one of the first alarms about abuses to the planet with his book *Man and Nature*.

Secondly, my volume *Pioneer Conservationists of Western America* was then making its way through the presses. Beyond revealing the personalities of Western environmentalists, this book stresses that conservation really began, on a large scale at least, when an aroused public demanded that great swaths of still-unsettled Western lands be set aside for the enjoyment and economic well-being of future generations. Hence, most of our national parks, forests, and wildlife refuges lie in the West. But the cultural and family roots of most Westerners lead back to the East. Wasn't there another, somewhat different dimension to the conservation story, the growth of the initial Eastern concerns that led to our present nationwide movement? The question was rhetorical, of course, a stirring of what I already knew as I sat there atop George

Perkins Marsh's boulder. And so I determined to write a second book on conservation in the event that the response to the first volume indicated interest in it.

That this has proved the case is not all my doing. Explaining some changes in her publication, Frances Gendlin, editor of the Sierra Club's *Sierra* magazine, recently wrote me: "I'm more interested in the personalities these days than I was a few years ago — the magazine is finally getting more human, I think." Gendlin's thinking reflects a general shift in the environmental movement. Pollution, land preservation, and wildlife continue to be the central issues, as they should be in a cause linked directly to our hopes for the future, to our very survival. At the same time, however, as the movement, with its hundreds of thousands of volunteer supporters, has broadened, it also deepened, particularly in the last few years. There has been a realization that conservation is not an aberration, as its opponents would define it, but an integral part of the cultural and social development of a nation concerned with spiritual directions as well as with what goes into stomach and lungs. Ecology, the "subversive science," touches on all of life. To a large degree, conservation mirrors the nature of a culture as reflected in its novels, poetry, and social thought; in its history and politics; and in the collective ideal of its people. Hence, in this sense conservation never can be too "human."

A result of this realization is an awakened interest not only in the cultural sources of ecology but in the personalities who have come from those roots to give the movement its present shape. It goes without saying that these individuals are unique, variously blessed with literary skills, charisma, and a different vision of America's future — as well as sometimes cursed by egomania, even madness. Those who give their lives to extraordinary goals must to the same degree themselves be extraordinary people.

This observation is not an attempt on my part to revive the Great Man Theory of History. Rather, my hope is to make clear the richness and variety of the leaders of conservation, who in turn reflect the color and complexity of the movement itself. In its broadest sense, this book is for the person who time and again has heard references to John Burroughs, Rachel Carson, and Ralph Nader, and other conservationists, and who now wishes to know more about the figures behind the names, and about the movement these individuals have espoused.

Because of the intricacy of the subject, in all likelihood no one volume will ever adequately cover the history of conservation in America, though *Man's Dominion,* by Frank Graham, Jr., and *The Quiet Crisis,* by Stewart Udall, do yeoman's service in this direction. In any event, this book, along with my earlier Western volume, may be read as a history of the movement that places its emphasis on conservation's major personalities. Chapter 1 provides a general context for the concerns and themes developed by the figures who follow. The concluding chapter summarizes where conservation stands now and raises some questions about its future course. It is hoped that the bibliography will prove useful for readers who wish to explore further.

Peter Wild
Tucson, Arizona
January 1984

Acknowledgments

Every writer incurs personal and professional debts that never can be repaid. I should like to acknowledge these debts especially to the following:

As was true of the preceding volume on Western conservationists, most of the material originally appeared in *High Country News*. For a second time I thank Joan Nice and Marjane Ambler, the newspaper's editors, along with the staff, for their warmth and constancy. My appreciation extends to Joan's husband, Bruce Hamilton, the Sierra Club's representative for Wyoming and the northern Great Plains.

Librarians at the University of Arizona graciously lent focus to my often vague questionings. Among the many who helped, I am particularly grateful to Lois Olsrud, Mirene Hazebrouck, Charles Peters, Bob Gramer, Craig Hawbacker, and Jim Otterness. Also at the University of Arizona, Professors John McElroy, Art Kay, and L.D. Clark sharpened my perceptions of developing America. In all likelihood they didn't realize that our informal discussions were contributing to this book. However, research for the volume ranged beyond the walls of libraries and English departments and through several fields to individuals such as Anne Broome, Ed Zahniser, Paul T. Bryant, Alexis Parks, Neil Carmony, Mardy Murie, and Ellen Frank. I remember them here for their encouragement and guidance.

Close friends helped me over some shoals during the writing — another debt not easily discharged but at least publicly acknowledged here to Bill and Dorothy Livingston and to Doug and Pat Denniston.

Lastly, for repeatedly sharing their wilderness I thank Idaho ranchers Everett and Frederica Peirce — Everett, who teaches simply by being who he is; Freddie, who wakes singing in her sleeping bag.

In the beginning, all the world was America.

—John Locke

Childhood home of George Perkins Marsh, linguist, diplomat, conservationist.

Woodstock Historical Society, Woodstock, Vermont

Chapter 1

Wild America and "The Gobble Gobble School of Economics"

In 1831-1832 a curious and articulate French nobleman spent nine months touring the United States. From the brief visit of Alexis de Tocqueville came a book, *Democracy in America,* that still troubles Americans. Of a robust yeomanry turned loose on a wild land he wrote:

> In Europe people talk a great deal of the wilds of America, but the Americans themselves never think about them; they are insensible to the wonders of inanimate nature. Their eyes are fired with another sight; they march across these wilds, clearing swamps, turning the courses of rivers....

The fire in their eyes was an all-too-human greed. Some years later, after the Civil War, frontier wanderer John Muir grumbled about "the gobble gobble school of economics" that was indeed taking large bites out of his beloved Sierras. Most Americans rejected such unflattering views of development, which for years lay dormant, crowded back into the nation's popular consciousness by agreeable accounts of Bunyanesque heroics in a new land.

1

However, as with many of Tocqueville's analyses, this one has come forward with new vitality. Pollution, shortages of fuel, water, and lumber have brought with them the uneasy realization that the country is not the vast treasure house that the nation once imagined. And with environmental crises has come a less sanguine view of history. Our ancestors were not, it turns out, selfless heroes preparing the land for civilization. Now, without risk of being tarred and feathered, population expert Garrett Hardin can compare Americans to gorillas. According to him, they "make a new nest every night, crap all over everything, then move on." At least that has been our history. And considering the residue from long-forgotten chemical dumps bubbling out of the ground or the most recent warning about carcinogens turned loose in the nation's food, we nod sadly and helplessly admit the truth in Hardin's statement. We have, in short, run out of places to foul.

With varying degrees of rage and humor, modern authors have taken up the cudgel. Biologist Paul Shepard refers to the conquering spirit as "one of gold-hunting, root-hog-or-die, cut-out-and-get-out, where wilderness seemed to be civilization's worst enemy." In a more bilious mood, J. Frank Dobie comments: "The mass rule then, as now was: Conform and be dull." Edward Abbey, as usual squeezing fun mixed with bitterness out of our ecological plight, dubs the present legacy of the pioneer spirit "the replenish-and-forever multiply theology of the American Yahoo Church."

Some three hundred years ago, the English philosopher John Locke looked westward across the sea and mused: "In the beginning, all the world was America." Since then the nation has frittered away much of its natural heritage; in this light, the condemnation of a Dobie or an Abbey is not too harsh. We live in a paradise foolishly lost. Yet the truth of the indictments comes charged with emotionalism that obscures understanding of how we arrived at our present position — and more importantly, how we might deal with it if we are to survive.

The fact is that the wild lands confronting the colonists, in their view at least, were indeed civilization's worst enemy. With notable exceptions, early settlers were a poor and ignorant lot. Hoping to improve their fortunes, they spent their savings on miserable voyages across the Atlantic, only to find that they had exchanged the poverty left behind in crowded, resource-scarce Europe for another kind of economic desperation in America. Overnight they became displaced persons in a hostile land. George R. Steward sums up their plight in *American Ways of Life*:

> In considering the development of the United States, we are constantly inclined to forget one important fact — the utter and abysmal ignorance of the first colonists as how to cope with the wilderness. Transferred immediately, without experience or schooling, from the highly civilized countries of England and Holland, they can only be described as complete greenhorns. They were much more innocent and helpless, in fact, than the average American of today would be if placed in similar circumstances.

Failing to recognize, all around them, the potential for sturdy log houses, they erected pathetic brush shelters; they fumbled trying to adapt old-world farming techniques to frontier conditions; they clung to their traditional ways, refusing to exchange their tattered European clothes for the serviceable leather and fur dress of the Indians. Only half of the Pilgrims, we forget, survived their first winter. Many of the early arrivals starved and froze and sometimes went mad in a fruitful land.

The superstitions they brought with them, inspired by their native mythologies and the "howling wilderness" of the Bible, didn't help. As they stood awed before the wildness, they magnified real dangers into man-eating beasts, cannibals, and demons flickering through the forest gloom. No wonder that for decades they remained more European than American, scrabbling out a living as they clung to the coast.

Civilization eventually did take hold, not so much because of adaptive genius as by dint of the sheer numbers of immigrants throwing themselves against the battlements of nature. Meanwhile, any "root-hog-or-die, cut-out-and-get-out" method of survival that put food in their mouths was considered fair play in the hostile, endless place. Largely because of difficulties of survival, exploitive attitudes persisted long after the first waves of settlers made the Eastern seaboard safe from real or imagined threats of marauding wolves and hatchet-faced Algonquins. Having gained a secure foothold, Americans set out somewhat more enthusiastically to hack and plow their way across the continent.

For all their fears, the poor, the desperate, the uprooted make avid dreamers. Many newcomers believed stories about gold for the taking or — for the less credulous — about loamy soils and balmy climates that would produce crops without end or without labor. A classical mythology started that sort of fantasizing; it was elaborated by the wishful thinking of Europeans filled with hope while they groped their way across an unexplored land. Always, the fabled places — El Dorado or the New Zion — lay to the West. Not finding gold or an agricultural Eden over the horizon, the pioneers skimmed off whatever wealth in grass or timber or minerals came to their hands. For a while the earth seemed able to withstand these ravages.

But even before the results of this unscrupulous plunder were visited on pioneer descendants in the form of timber shortages, dust bowls, and plummeting water tables, a counter attitude began to emerge. Europeans crossing the Atlantic carried with them a complex and often contradictory cultural heritage, out of which came the seeds of the conservation movement.

Among other curious transformations, the Romantic Movement idealized nature — the wilder the better. In 1750, Frenchman Jean-Jacques Rousseau — lover from afar of wild savages, wild children, and wild landscapes — won a prize for an essay espousing the notion that nature blesses, civilization corrupts. With subsequent writings he brought into full revolutionary bloom a notion that had been germinating in Western Europe for centuries. By the nineteenth century, according to Paul Shepard, "the city had become the symbol of man's depravity." English poet William Wordsworth summed up the popular point of view in an 1806 sonnet:

The world is too much with us; late and soon,
Getting and spending, we lay waste our powers:
Little we see in Nature that is ours;
We have given our hearts away, a sordid boon!

It was a misty sentiment, one easily grasped by the sentimentally inclined public of the time. Yet in the practical affairs of life, economics remained a far more powerful force, and the exploitation of nature continued with only an occasional twinge of romantic regret.

One might marvel how not only individuals but entire nations plunge into the future girded with contradictory beliefs. New England philosopher Ralph Waldo Emerson looked upon nature as "raw material" to be molded "into what is useful." He blustered like some modern-day technocrat about "engineering for all America." Yet apparently unaware of what his other philosophic hand was doing, this nineteenth-century thinker also shaped the nature-worshipping vagaries of Romanticism into a more specific cast. Nature, his transcendentalism maintained, is a lens through which individuals can discover not only spiritual truth but even spiritual exhilaration. Morals and delights lie behind every bush. "I declare this world is so beautiful," he revealed while sitting by a Massachusetts pond, "that I can hardly believe it exists."

That pond happened to be Walden Pond. If Rousseau's ideas, spilling over as they did into politics, brought on the flood of the French Revolution, Emerson's became the main source of conservation in the United States. It should have followed from his teaching that friend nature — instead of being logged, plowed, blasted, and paved in the wholesale style of the day — should be protected, befriended in return for its spiritual gifts. Emerson's quirky, forest-loving crony Thoreau recognized this; he became one of the earliest advocates of setting aside woodlands in the wild state. Also, he stood alone. A great gap lay between the sentiment and the deed; actual preservation came only years later, after transcendental notions had worked their way from popular belief into demands for legislative action.

Meanwhile, Emerson's philosophy became the rage. No longer starving in the wilderness, Easterners tramped out of their dingy, crowded cities for weekend doses of wild delight. The badly needed fresh air and exercise buoyed many into believing that the philosophy delivered its promises. Thus, transcendental ideas became a main impetus for America's rediscovery of itself through nature. In addition, some of the picnickers and walkers formed organizations such as the Appalachian Mountain Club. Their purpose was hiking, not reform. But after individuals such as John Muir and Frederick Law Olmsted — both infused with Emerson's vision — led the way, the hiking clubs became bases for political power and change.

Americans like to believe they have always been a practical people. Sorting through the strands in the confused skein that forms the nation's changing collective attitudes, historians have found pragmatic motives for conservation, even in the early days of settlement. For one thing, resources were becoming scarce in Europe. To cite one well-known example, beginning in 1691 representatives of King William III cruised New England's wood-

lands to blaze the tallest white pines with the royal Broad
Arrow, thus reserving them for the masts of the English
navy.

More significantly, New England is a stony place, one
"better in growing character than in growing crops," in
one wit's words. Survival there was by necessity a community effort. A people with an organized approach to this
life as well as to the next, the Puritans parceled out land
according to community needs, making sure that each
individual had sufficient crop, pasture, and woodland.
Consequently, the staid farmers treasured what they had,
husbanding it as a trust for their children. Elsewhere in
the colonies, in Virginia for instance, settlement followed
a free-for-all course that was to be continued across the
continent. Yet the first New Englanders had set a precedent for land-use planning that their descendants would
revive.

In the meantime, their heads turned by high profits
from timber and wool, Puritan sons honored their fathers'
stewardship more in the breach than in the keeping. Two
hundred and fifty years after the landing of the *Mayflower*, however, it was precisely the lingering tradition
of care for an abused New England garden that moved
Vermonter George Perkins Marsh. He reawakened the
need for stewardship with the disturbing flourish of *Man
and Nature*. At about the same time, Connecticut-born
Frederick Law Olmsted was considering the frantic
sprawl of America's cities. Drawing on his family's New
England heritage that went back to 1632, his blueprints
for renewal imposed practical sense and transcendental
greenery on burgeoning urban areas. The Gilded Age dof-
fed its hat to Olmsted — then in its haste and greed
steamrolled over much of his vision. Yet restless Olmsted
carried his ideals to the other end of the continent.
Struggling to preserve California's park-like Yosemite
Valley, he championed a novel concept that would even-

tually bear fruit in our present system of national parks.

That system is now the most splendid series of preserves of any nation. But it did not become a reality until as late as 1916. Similarly, Congress did not create the national forests until 1905. In fact, nearly all such reserves — whether called parks, monuments, forests or wildlife refuges — are relative newcomers. They are the result of small bands of conservationists straining against exploitation. Their calling, as they saw it, was to throw up protective fences around the nature that an industrialized nation was rapidly turning into grist for its mills. That they succeeded at all in the predominant "gobble gobble" atmosphere of the times is remarkable — an indication of equally remarkable efforts and personalities. And their successes, if only partial, came just in time, around the turn of the century, when the country still had significant remnants of wild land to preserve.

It would make the job of historians easier if the conservation movement had sprung from more definite roots, if the early leaders had been better organized and more intellectually cohesive. Instead, once started, the move for preservation was backed by a bewildering array of motives: altruism and egomania, boosterism, greed, affectation, patriotism, sentimentalism, artistic sensitivity, and at times differences of opinion that set friends to tearing at each other's throats. Attempting to explain why a handful of Montana frontiersmen banded together to spend their time and money to establish Yellowstone, the country's first national park, one usually astute analyst throws up his hands. He concludes that the act creating Yellowstone, in 1872, "had something to do with vague qualities compounded of admiration for scenery and morality, as well as indifference and apathy. In short, the National Park Act had the insubstantial and obscure reference of an act of faith without apparent theology."

Despite the frustration of historians and of

environmental leaders seeking a consensus, diversity continues to be one of conservation's main strengths. And perhaps it's just as well that there was and is no single set of beliefs, no one true faith that like most true faiths can fall monolithically. However, perspective allows one to see how individuals joined their interests to found a broad movement. Hikers have already been mentioned, and there will be more to say of them later. Another group, argues John F. Reiger in *American Sportsmen and the Origins of Conservation,* has yet to receive its due.

While America was a wild land, hunting was a necessity, a means of putting meat on the table, not a sport. Yet in the nineteenth century a few Americans, especially better-off Easterners, emulated their English cousins by organizing into gentlemanly hunting clubs. According to Reiger, they developed their own esprit de corps, their own set of mores and taboos: "Increasingly, gunners and anglers looked upon themselves as members of a fraternity with a well-defined code of conduct and thinking. In order to obtain membership in this order of 'true sportsmen,' one had to practice proper etiquette in the field, give game a sporting chance, and possess an aesthetic appreciation of the whole context of sport that included a commitment to its perpetuation."

In contrast to their high ideals, they soon saw their sport suffering from overhunting, especially from commercial hunters, and from the rapid loss of game habitat to expanding industrialism. They were among the first to recognize the "myth of inexhaustibility." By the 1870s such periodicals as *Forest and Stream, American Sportsman,* and *Field and Stream* were spurring them to act. The magazines pointed to the strict game laws and well-managed hunting preserves in Europe that produced an unending supply of wildlife. To protect their pleasures, American sportsmen began buying up land around their clubhouses, thus establishing the start of our present refuge system. They stocked depleted Eastern streams with trout and lobbied for game-law reform. Many of them, concerned as much with the aesthetics of nature as with the chase, went beyond their own immediate interests to campaign for preservation of America's forests.

And forest preservation lay at the heart of early conservation. Powerful Eastern businessmen, some of them also hunters, backed efforts with the money and political muscle essential for success. Their motives were not always pure; and their public arguments were sometimes more addleheaded than scientific. Well before the turn of the century, the prolonged struggle for New York's upstate Adirondack Park set a precedent for similar battles across the country. The Manufacturer's Aid Association of Watertown applauded the Park's creation because of industry's dependence on a steady supply of water power, which only healthy forests could provide. Merchants counting on the hunting and tourist trades also saw their interests receiving protection along with the lands of the proposed park. Three hundred miles to the south, business leaders in New York recognized the link between the city's growth and nature. They fretted about sufficient drinking water but also about how to keep the Erie Canal full, their economic lifeline.

Once boosterism, based on fear and greed, developed, there seemed no end of supporting arguments for the park. If sparkling water could once again flow from the Adirondack Mountains, it would cleanse downstream marshes of malaria and "the malignant and deadly matter which now fills the atmosphere with intermittent and remittent fevers and diphtheria." Other campaigners insisted on the hygienic benefits of trees, which, they staunchly maintained, vacuumed free-floating disease germs from the air.

But there was much more than shirt-sleeve science in America at the time. During the Civil War period, the sciences, especially the natural sciences, gained a secure toehold in the culture, particularly in the growing federal bureaucracy. Often supported by the government, zoologists, botanists, and paleontologists scurried about collecting and classifying, beginning to understand the complexities of the natural world. They also protested when railroads cut through favorite Cenozoic boneyards; they strove, almost too late, to save at least a remnant of the American bison.

Taking their cue from Emerson, popular writers of the day — Thoreau, John Muir, and John Burroughs — saw their souls reflected in America's wildlife and woodlands. To them, setting aside forests as unexploited wholes often took on a religious imperative. Their books and articles in magazines stirred the public to re-evaluate its long-ignored wild heritage. Artists, too, were part of a zeitgeist favorably disposed toward unsullied nature. It was the painter George Catlin who as early as the 1830s first proposed the national park concept. Landscape artists Thomas Moran and Albert Bierstadt and wildlife painter John James Audubon helped the public to see nature with new eyes. In brief, conservation owes its origins to many influences that together caused a general shift in attitudes.

It was Easterners, of course, who explored and settled the West. While most of the pioneers scrambled to make a living, others — often the educated and well-off — brought notions of preservation with them. As noted earlier, it was Olmsted who campaigned for California's Yosemite. And it was a transplanted Easterner, Cornelius Hedges, a judge, former teacher, and graduate of Yale, who led his equally prominent friends — all transplanted from the East — in the crusade for Yellowstone. Such men gloried in the natural beauty and bounty that lay around them in the West; in contrast, they remembered their own depleted Eastern birthplaces. It took little imagination to see a similar wreckage visited on the West in the near future, unless large portions of the wild country could be set aside.

Yet today conservation means far more than providing a Glacier National Park as a summer pleasure ground for city people, far more than preserving a homeland for the California condor and the buffalo. In recent years the nation has begun to realize that the physical and spiritual health of its people depends on the health of the entire land. Because of this new concept, some years ago conservationists prodded Congress into buying up abused tracts in the East. Now, after decades of stewardship, these areas are restoring themselves to something of their former wholeness, setting the stage for a larger reinvasion of the East — an invasion not by axe but by healthy forests, beaches, clean water and air, one that, if successful, will partially restore the East's former ecological harmony and also renew our own hope for the future.

309 Madison   Hartley   Chicago.

George Perkins Marsh, linguist, diplomat, business failure. He observed nature as a sideline and wrote a book that became the fountainhead of the conservation movement.

Wilbur Collection, Bailey Library, University of Vermont

Chapter 2

George Perkins Marsh: The Prophet from Vermont

In the summer of 1800 startled villagers of Woodstock, Vermont, looked on as fire swept the top of Mt. Tom. Born a year later in the shadow of the local prominence, George Perkins Marsh grew up watching the woods slowly come back out of the ashes. In adulthood he would be praised as a distinguished ambassador and renowned linguist of his day. But a book on a much different subject was the lasting contribution of this shy, painfully bookish scholar from Vermont's backwoods. Ironically, he considered *Man and Nature* a mere sideline, the result of his lifelong curiosity over man's role in nature's changes.

In the early years of the nineteenth century, Vermont was still a frontier. According to one lawyer, the Green Mountains west of Woodstock remained a refuge for "all the rogues and runaways" of the former colonies, and Indians kept settlers on their guard in some remoter parts of the nation's newest state. Yet in the few decades since the first farmers tested the wilderness with plow and axe environmental changes were more than evident. The fire that seared the vegetation from Mt. Tom was a symptom of man's dismantling of the hinterland. In Vermont, as in other states, lumbermen had cleared much of the forest cover, leaving behind acres of debris to fuel forest fires. Sheep and cattle grazed over the eroding hillsides. Streams silted and fish disappeared. Reduced to trickles during droughts, rivers tore through villages during spring floods.

Bent on wresting a living from the frontier and convinced of nature's plenitude, few people stopped to consider the causes or consequences of the changes. One man did. In his youth, Marsh saw the Quechee River carry off his father's bridge and sawmill and turn neighbors' fields into useless mud flats. Years later, exploring deserts in the Middle East, he would note a few pitiful tribesmen scrambling after their goats to stay alive where cities had once prospered. Marsh's travels and historical studies eventually led to a volume that gave early environmentalists the first massive scientific evidence to document their concerns. Lewis Mumford rightly called it "the fountain-head of the conservation movement."

Viewed in retrospect, Marsh's life is a curious, if not melodramatic, blend of ingenious intellectual strokes and pathetic disappointments — a stereotype of the man who succeeds brilliantly in scholarship and government but fails again and again in the practical affairs of making a living. And it is likely that he would have foundered completely had it not been for his family's position and the efforts of friends. George's stern father came as close as one could on the raw frontier to being a gentleman farmer. A lawyer and successful businessman, Charles Marsh also served in the U.S. Congress. Among other allies with effective political connections, friends in Washington helped shield George Perkins Marsh from enemies during his career as ambassador. Building on this base, he went on to hobnob with some of the foremost intellectuals of the United States and Europe — John Quincy Adams, Louis

Agassiz, Robert Browning, and Matthew Arnold.

The boy who would become a robust man and an accomplished Alpine climber was a strange child. His head was large, and his face bore a dour expression. He preferred the family library to romping off to nearby Quaking Pogue swamp with the village children. By the time he was five, he was absorbing the family encyclopedia; by the age of six, he was learning Greek and Latin. He became so engrossed with study that his eyesight failed, the beginning of a painful malady that dogged the book lover throughout his life. Yet his family encouraged his leanings, and his father, an amateur scientist and an experimenter with farming techniques, often took young Marsh out to the countryside for informal nature lessons.

At the age of fifteen, the boy entered New Hampshire's Dartmouth College, located only a few miles from his home town. Withdrawn, though also known for flashes of wit, Marsh let his sometimes rowdy classmates divert themselves from the rigid curriculum taught by sharp-eyed but underpaid lecturers. For his part, he excelled in the limited college fare of the day: classical studies, mathematics, theology, and law. He used free time to absorb modern languages.

After graduating at the head of his class, he took a job teaching at Norwich Academy. The school subjected its students to high collars, guardhouses, and constant maneuverings across the parade ground in the belief that military discipline would immunize its charges against the evils of life. Distasteful as it was, Norwich offered one advantage to the young professor: just across the Connecticut River lay the Dartmouth Library, where Marsh spent nights learning Scandinavian and German. Still, he detested the atmosphere at Norwich; after a year he left. At a loss for a profession, he returned home to read law. Four years later he was admitted to the bar.

In 1825 he moved over the mountains to Burlington,

Vermont, where practicing law bored him as much — and paid little better — as had teaching. Suffering the dilemma of the scholar with no mind for business, he searched for a way to support his love of study. In the following years he tried everything from manufacturing to real estate. Everything seemed to go wrong: his wife died; a flood washed away his new woolen mill; foreign competition ruined his sheep business; and friends connived against him in railroad speculations. Creditors would plague him for most of his adult life.

Yet there were bright spots, indications of untested abilities and future successes. Voters sent him to the state legislature, and in 1829 he married his second wife, Caroline Crane. She was a sickly woman, fifteen years younger than he, but a person able to share his intellectual excitements. Learned journals applauded his translation of an Icelandic grammar and then went on to acclaim the 1843 publication of *The Goths in New England.* This essay reflected the popular enthusiasm of the day for things Nordic and mirrored Marsh's Calvinist background, with its tendency to divide the world neatly into good and evil. Marsh praised the Protestant peoples of northern Europe as the staunch bearers of democracy, industry, and true religion — contrasting them with the frivolous cultures of southern Europe. As simplistic and wrongheaded as the ideas seem today, it should be noted that few of the biases found their way into the book for which he is now remembered.

In the same year as the publication of *The Goths,* the conservative Whig party won Marsh a seat in the U.S. Congress. There he opposed slavery and the Mexican-American War. With a curious lack of foresight for a man sensitive to geography, he resisted acquisition of new territories in the West. Expressing the fears of his Vermont constituency, he saw the wild mountains and undeveloped deserts as financial burdens for the compact and industrialized East. More importantly, Marsh's wit and intellectual honesty attracted powerful friends. Side by side, John Quincy Adams and George Perkins Marsh nodded off during boring speeches. Marsh's help in establishing the Smithsonian Institution earned him alliances with the country's growing scientific bureaucracy.

Though stimulated and happy in Washington, Marsh yearned to travel. Yet his business ventures back in Vermont kept failing. At one point his finances reached such a low point that he sold part of his splendid private library. His chance to go abroad came with the election of Zachary Taylor. In return for Marsh's help in the campaign, the new President appointed him Minister to Turkey. It was the beginning of the travels throughout Europe and the Middle East that put the Vermonter in wider contact with Western civilization's most alert minds and provided additional firsthand evidence to support the conclusions put forth years later in *Man and Nature*.

As bookish and shy as Marsh might be, he was also incorruptible, fluent in languages, cool under pressure. In contrast to a host of lackluster officials representing the nation overseas at the time, Marsh made an outstanding ambassador, despite nearly impossible circumstances. In 1849, on the verge of the Crimean War, Turkey was suffering through turmoil, "full of villains of every description," in Marsh's words. Further, the U.S. Ambassador was unable to match the entertainments offered by European diplomats, whose salaries were often ten times greater than his, and whose palace fetes helped smooth the way for political objectives. Nevertheless, throughout the growing unrest he matched diplomatic skill with humanitarian concern by protecting foreign missionaries and winning asylum for distraught refugees. It was a thankless job for a conscientious man. Congress took years to repay his expenses, while back home Horace Greeley's New York *Tribune* falsely accused the threadbare ambassador of profli-

Marsh's wit and intellect made him an outstanding ambassador. In addition, his credentials as a painstaking scholar were impeccable. Wilbur Collection, Bailey Library, University of Vermont

gacy.

For all the handicaps and irritations, Marsh ran the embassy in Constantinople so smoothly that he found time for travel. He sailed to Cairo, then rode camels across the blistering Sinai Desert to Jerusalem. His later report to the Smithsonian, "The Camel" (1854), was a compendium of camel-lore, later forming a major basis for the U.S. Army's experimental use of camels in its Western campaigns. The weather, geology, flora, fauna, and remains of ancient Mediterranean civilizations all whetted the ambassador's intellectual appetite. He sent back crates of specimens to friends at the Smithsonian, discovered a new species of salamander, and scrambled happily over Greek ruins. In the words of his biographer, David Lowenthal, "Marsh sensed man's antiquity in every quarter.... It was here Marsh first realized that man had everywhere left his mark; in time he saw how far that touch had transformed nature." Marsh would eventually synthesize his wide experiences into *Man and Nature*.

With the election of President Franklin Pierce, however, Marsh lost political favor and the job that had sustained him both intellectually and financially. Returning to Burlington in 1854, he found his railroad stock worthless and his real estate gone. Cheated by enemies and supposed friends alike, and $50,000 in the red, he began the bleakest period of his life. He tried his hand at inventing scientific instruments — and managed to re-create devices that had been in use for years. He threw in with a cousin-in-law to establish the Winooski Marble Company, but the quarry failed because its stone was too hard for the tools of the day. For a while he traveled the lecture circuits but found the task an ill-paying nuisance. As before, every business he touched went sour.

Gradually, though, he worked his way out of despair. The governor of Vermont appointed him to the railroad and fish commissions. The former statesman used these opportunities to lash out at monopolies that had helped ruin him and to write a report pinpointing the environmental abuses that had nearly eliminated game fish from many of the state's streams. He taught briefly at New York's Columbia University and at Boston's Lowell Institute. The two resulting books, *Lectures on the English Language* (1860) and *The Origin and History of the English Language* (1862), became required texts of the day. He further solidified his scholarly reputation by contributing to national publications and by working on several important dictionaries. In the midst of these diverse activities, he started taking notes for *Man and Nature*.

The political climate changed with Abraham Lincoln's

election and with it Marsh's fortunes. Aided by his growing stature as a linguist — not to mention the influence of
friends — the scholar, now sixty, set sail as Ambassador to
Italy. He kept the post for the rest of his life. Severely
Protestant Marsh would never fully understand an ebullient and Roman Catholic country, but the personal circumstances of his new position, the lively intellectual
atmosphere, his improved finances, and the time to write
buoyed his spirits. His wife's health improved in the
balmy climate, and a circle of literati attracted to Italy
from all over Europe stimulated his energies. Though
aging, Marsh could work fourteen hours at a stretch —
most importantly at keeping Italian war materials flowing to the Union Army; and yet he found time to shoot with
King Victor Emmanuel and to spend summers studying
alpine glaciers. In the midst of these pleasant surroundings, he sat down in the winter of 1862-1863 to distill the
musings of a lifetime into one of the nineteenth century's
most influential observations on the environment.

The massive *Man and Nature* is an expanded discussion
of a simple view of the earth, yet one radically different for
its time. Marsh countered the prevailing enthusiasm for
development by proposing that "man is everywhere a disturbing agent," often unwittingly "a destructive power" in
nature. With convincing authority, again and again
Marsh pointed to ancient civilizations that had expanded
and then failed because they neglected to come to terms
with man's destructiveness. Nineteenth-century industrialism, he warned, was repeating old errors, "breaking
up the floor and wainscoting and doors and window frames
of our (natural) dwelling...." The consequences were obvious to anyone who cared to look into the future with clear
eyes: man will create a sterile legacy for his children
unless he stops the assault on the natural world. The book
discusses this thesis through chapters on forests, water,
and deserts — each supported by voluminous examples

drawn from the author's encyclopedic knowledge of ancient and modern history. Appropriately, Marsh's book concludes by weighing the benefits and disadvantages of such nineteenth-century schemes as the Suez Canal and the widespread drainage of coastal wetlands.

As the first scientific jeremiad on the environment, *Man and Nature* served as a catalyst for early environmentalists. Its conclusions were so irrefutable — and Marsh's credentials as a painstaking scholar so well known and impeccable — that the book became the rallying point for the conservationists who, in the late nineteenth and early twentieth century, laid the bases for today's continuing reforms. John Wesley Powell drew on Marsh's writings for support in his mighty but largely fruitless efforts to convince Congress that patterns of Eastern settlement wouldn't work in the arid West. Gifford Pinchot, first head of the U.S. Forest Service, called the volume "epoch-making."

Yet there is irony in the course of the volume's fame. After the turn of the century, the author was nearly forgotten, his reputation eclipsed by the activities of the reformers he had inspired. However, interest in *Man and Nature* revived during the 1930s — when the book's predictions of environmental disruptions became striking realities in the days of the Dust Bowl. Since then, a number of magazine articles have combined with Lowenthal's biography of Marsh to further a growing appreciation for the work's timeliness and accuracy.

In fact, some of Marsh's ideas were so far ahead of their day that they have received their due only in the last few decades. The early conservationists tended to see problems in isolation. For example, they launched separate campaigns for wildlife preservation and forest protection — failing to see the crucial relationships between the two. Anticipating the writings of Aldo Leopold, Rachel Carson, and Barry Commoner, *Man and Nature* viewed the natural world as an integrated whole. Nature, Marsh held, "knows no trifles." A society should first study all aspects of proposed actions, then proceed with the utmost caution toward the "unforeseen mischief" of disturbing the bio-sphere — a warning confirmed by present dilemmas resulting from reckless use of chemical pollutants. Addi-tionally, Marsh was prophetic in pointing to overpopula-tion and food shortages years before these subjects would appear as newspaper headlines. He advocated land-use planning, wilderness areas, game preserves, and solar power. He touched on the coming environmental crises of the cities long before they would be life-and-death issues for politicians.

Influential in Europe as well as in America, *Man and Nature* went through several printings. Marsh was able to take time out from his duties at the embassy to revise the book twice, reorganizing material and adding supporting evidence. The revisions appeared in 1874 and in a post-humous 1885 edition, both bearing the new title *The Earth As Modified by Human Action*. Today the book is most often known by its original title, the one used in a 1965 reprint by Harvard University Press.

While the aging ambassador revised earlier work and continued to write articles, he enjoyed a belated measure of peace. "The years passed tranquilly under Roman skies," according to Lowenthal. Prestigious societies in the United States and Europe honored Marsh, as the former debtor basked both in Italy's climate and in "an almost legendary" status of scholar and elder statesman.

During the summer of 1882 an Italian friend invited the American ambassador — now in his eighties — to take a holiday in Vallombrosa, a monastery converted into a forestry school. In the mountains around the ancient city of Florence, Marsh chatted warmly with the school's stu-dents and strolled through the hillsides that reminded him of his native Vermont. There he died suddenly, at peace with himself in the rural surroundings. Soon after, the forestry students carried his casket draped with an American flag down through the wooded hills, "a fitting end," writes Lowenthal, "to his long and distinguished life."

FREDERICK LAW OLMSTED.

Frederick Law Olmsted. He painted with rocks and trees.
Dualities warred within him throughout his visionary career,
leading at last to a tragic end.

Stokes Autograph Collection, Yale University Library

Chapter 3

Frederick Law Olmsted:
"Emerson With A Hoe"

Workmen leaned on their shovels and winked while their new superintendent, apparently a young gentleman, stepped over the runoff from pigsties. In theory their project was supposed to create a park out of a wasteland of swamps and ledges. But the site was so far north of the city that few believed it would receive much use. Many people looked upon the scheme, developing haphazardly for years, as a joke, just another opportunity for New York politicians to practice their traditional patronage and corruption.

Its new boss, though dapper in his cloak and cocked hat, was neither as youthful nor as effete as he appeared. By 1857 he had indeed devoted much of his thirty-five years to refining his aesthetic sensibilities, but he also knew the rough-and-tumble life of a sailor in the China trade, and he had parleyed with marauding Indians in Texas, while keeping a steady hand on his Colt. In the next few months, he not only engaged greedy politics in a running battle, he had thousands of men laboring purposefully to shape earth and trees in Central Park.

Drawing on his own thoughts and those of George Perkins Marsh, Carl Schurz, and other forward-looking men, he would offer to a young, rapidly growing, and often heedless nation a vision of what it might be — a land of humane cities surrounded by sweeps of national parks and forests. But though the public eventually hailed him as the master of the art he founded — landscape architecture — his vision failed to be implemented on a national scale. It lived, however, to be passed on to Teddy Roosevelt, Gifford Pinchot, Franklin Delano Roosevelt, and Benton MacKaye, who struggled to transform vision to reality during increasingly critical times.

Be that as it may, his successes are remarkable when considered against the odds. They arose from conflicts within his personality — a dreamy genius and a rash temper, indecision and strong drive, long periods of work followed by exhaustion. Opposing principles warred within him throughout his intense career, leading at last to a tragic end.

While George Perkins Marsh strained over his lawbooks in Woodstock, Vermont, Frederick Law Olmsted was growing up a hundred miles to the south, near Hartford, Connecticut. Like the Marsh family, the Olmsteds boasted a solid New England background, one of seafarers and Revolutionary War heroes, and they possessed sufficient wealth to provide contacts important to the careers of their sons. Yet for all his financial success as a dry-goods merchant, Frederick's father, John, was indecisive in some family matters. Uncertain of how to raise his son, he sent young Fred off to be schooled by a succession of inattentive country parsons.

If the boy's education suffered from this informal approach, he nonetheless enjoyed freedom to ramble over the wooded hills and rolling pastures of the Connecticut River Valley. His country pleasures were heightened on holidays, when John Olmsted loaded his family into a carriage and took them on lighthearted, lengthy, and — for their day — unusual excursions through New England, New York, and Canada. The peaceful countrysides with their small-town democracies formed the base of Frederick's future ideals.

But when the time came for him to think about a career, the indecision inherited from his father came to the fore. He had picked up some engineering skills while working as an apprentice surveyor, and his father's connections got him a job as a clerk in a New York importing firm; however, tallying figures in ledgers bored him. Next, he audited classes at Yale for a while; finally, seeking the romance of Richard Henry Dana's *Two Years before the Mast,* he broke off his desultory studies and signed on a ship bound for China.

A year later he was back, much sobered from rubbing shoulders with common sailors and ducking the abuses of a cruel captain. Still unable to settle down, he dabbled a bit further at Yale; then, eager to apply scientific techniques to agriculture, he persuaded his by now anxious father to finance a series of farming adventures.

All his undertakings failed to make money; Fred would continue to borrow from his father over the next twenty years. The first half of Frederick Law Olmsted's life, then, might seem to reflect the dallyings of a prosperous merchant's son. In reality the future city planner and champion of national parks was squeezing all the intellectual insights he could from each successive activity. The variety of experience would serve him well when he finally took fire and plunged into new disciplines demanding broad views both of nature and human nature.

At the age of twenty-eight, concerned about his lack of direction and nervous over prolonged dependence on his father's purse, restless Olmsted launched a series of travel and publishing ventures. Thinking back on an overseas trip, he wrote *Walks and Talks of an American Farmer in*

England (1852). The book reveals his developing interest in horticulture and his sharpening eye for the relationships between landscape and culture. In the meantime, the United States was seething over the perplexing slavery question. On assignment for the *New York Times*, Olmsted set off on two extended tours that took him through the Southern states and by horseback on into the wild Texas frontier. In three volumes over the next few years, he explained the social and economic conditions underlying antagonisms between the North and South. "Acclaimed," writes historian Theodora Hubbard, "as the most accurate picture of conditions in the South," the studies brought the late bloomer a heartening first fame.

His reputation now opened the doors to the literary world of New York City. For a time Olmsted felt he had at last found his profession, as a writer and publisher. Somewhat gingerly, he again turned to his father for support, and with the fresh enthusiasm that typified each new effort, he bought into the new management of *Pitnam's Magazine*. Buoyed by their expected successes — and Olmsted's borrowed money — the partners began a publishing firm — Dix, Edwards and Company. His brief but intense career in journalism brought editor Olmsted in contact with Thackeray, Washington Irving, and Herman Melville — heady acquaintances for a recently unknown writer. Of far greater importance for Olmsted's future, his ill-fated business career enlarged his circle of friendships with editors, journalists, politicians, and philanthropists, who later helped spread his concerns for the nation's land and rallied to support him under political attack.

With his business apparently going well, Olmsted took a break from office routine. In high spirits he boarded a ship for England to solicit manuscripts and publicize his firm's new books. A few months later, after he had taken time out to see the public parks of Florence and Rome, the bad news caught up with him. One of the partners had mismanaged funds; the company was going under. Olmsted wrote to a friend, "I can't tell how ashamed I am of being involved in such a mess." At the age of thirty-five, jobless and deeply in debt, Frederick Law Olmsted reflected on his series of enthusiasms turned to failures.

While he was back in New York mulling over his bleak prospects, a dinner companion happened to mention that the city fathers, weary of political delays, were looking for a man to push through the development of Central Park. Olmsted's interest in the position — and his success at winning it — are not as surprising as they may first seem. He possessed basic surveying skills from his apprentice days; as a former farmer, he had experience in organizing men and shaping the land; and as an admirer of public works, he had studied the major parks of England, France, Italy, and Germany. But what also swayed the park commissioners were Olmsted's letters of support — one of them bearing the signature of Washington Irving — from influential friends.

Olmsted's mastery in planning and building Central Park despite physical odds and political chicanery made him legendary, a kind of organizational wizard in the eyes of the public. And he remains a hero to many present-day New Yorkers, who consider the hundreds of acres of rolling hills, woods, and lakes the most precious land amid Manhattan's choked and corroding wealth. Now surrounded by skyscrapers, this rural remnant has won Frederick Law Olmsted the epithets "Hero of the Landscape" and "Playground Pioneer." Yet as is often the case with broad-gauge public praise, the labels tend to obscure the context of the accomplishment. Famous Central Park was but the first concrete result of Olmsted's slowly-evolving vision for America.

By the middle of the nineteenth century, Europe's cities had a few parks. Frequently these were laid out in straight lines of trees and paved walks leading to formal plazas

Now surrounded by skyscrapers, the precious rural remnant of Central Park makes Frederick Law Olmsted a hero to many present-day New Yorkers. New York Convention & Visitors Bureau

filled with bronze and marble statuary. In the United States, there were no large public parks. Rural towns emerging as population centers simply grew outward in widening circles of unplanned development. On holidays, the wealthy fled to Cape Cod or New Hampshire's White Mountains to forget the fetid, often disease-ridden cities. Ordinary people looking for greenery and fresh air picnicked in cemeteries.

The blind faith in America's laissez-faire growth, its bright dream that industrialization would somehow result in peace of mind and prosperity for all, represented only one side of a double standard. In its bones a century ago, as is true today, Americans also believed the opposite, that "God made the country; Man made the town," as the saying goes. Even as people boasted about their expanding cities, they felt that the truly good life was to be found among wooded hills laced by winding brooks, among the cows and chickens of Jefferson's rural democracy. This romantic view had as its most immediate philosophical authority Emerson's transcendentalism, which held that man can peer into nature and see the reflection of his highest moral and spiritual qualities.

Yet for all the cerebral niceties, the problem remained: What to do with the growing cities? To Olmsted, as well as to other intellectuals, the answer seemed simple: bring God's country back into Man's towns. Thus, as the nation's first large city park, Central Park was an innovative venture in city planning, but one having philosophical roots in the culture.

From the quagmire of pigsties and slaughterhouses that preceded Central Park ("a very nasty place" as Olmsted described it with reserve), he wanted to re-create what man had destroyed. He wanted to "make improvements by design which nature might by chance." And his purpose, inspired by the romanticism of the time, was as much moral as aesthetic. In fact, to him the two were the same:

the natural tranquility of his park would help make society good. Reflecting on his underlying social concerns, a writer for *Newsweek* has dubbed Olmsted "Emerson with a hoe."

He put his army of laborers to work moving tons of dirt to form "natural" hills and lakes and pastures; and he planted 17,000 trees to create the scenes that had pleased him as a boy hunting rabbits in Connecticut. But he was also a practical man, who realized that thousands of people would converge each day on his charming 843 acres of transplanted New England. To accommodate them, he laid out an extensive underground drainage system, rest stops, vistas, and pathways that wound through tunnels. And to strike a balance with the future transportation needs of the city, he allowed roads to cut across his park — roads screened by foliage or built below the general level of the land.

America's first park maker might have spent the rest of his life refining his unique urban creation, placing trees so that they would throw the proper transcendental shadows for the refreshment of city dwellers. But the Confederate fusillade against Fort Sumter changed his future, launching him into a series of endeavors that widened his intellectual horizons and eventually brought him national influence and fame.

To support the Union Army, unprepared militarily as well as medically for battle, Eastern philanthropists formed the United States Sanitary Commission, forerunner of today's Red Cross. Though he was reluctant to leave his park, patriotism moved Olmsted to accept the Commissioners' urgent invitation to direct their activities. For the next two years the nation's first landscape architect drove himself to bring order out of medical chaos. He directed a civilian corps of doctors and nurses, scurried back and forth between Washington and New York insuring delivery of tons of medical supplies, and organized the country's first fleet of hospital ships. Again combining high ideals with practical skills, he brought relief to thousands of soldiers — both Union and Confederate.

Short-tempered, plagued by insomnia and a variety of other real and imagined ills, Olmsted could be annoying in his penchant to have his own way. By middle age, though, he had developed a tough character of heroic proportions, often bewildering his admirers. One commissioner, worried about the General Secretary's health and mental stability, lamented to his diary that Olmsted worked with "feverish intensity till four in the morning, sleeps on a sofa in his clothes, and breakfasts on strong coffee and pickles!!!" He shouldn't have been surprised at such frantic commitment. A few years earlier, convalescing from a serious carriage accident that left him permanently lame, Olmsted had insisted he be carried around on a stretcher to direct the thousands of laborers in Central Park.

And he was a man of fierce public loyalties. Before the War broke out, he bought a brass cannon for Kansas abolitionists, to help them fend off proslavery marauders. And, more generally, throughout his life he supported various bills of social and environmental reforms. His personal loyalties were equally intense. Years later, when he finally achieved financial success, he took care to pass on architectural business to Calvert Vaux, his partner of Central Park days, who had fallen on hard times. And he knew his own mind. Arrogant and driving as he might be in professional matters, he had no desire for public acclaim in other areas. When a liberal splinter group nominated him for vice-president, he hid from the reporters knocking on his door, wanting only to be left to his work.

Characteristically, that same drive broke his health while he served on the Sanitary Commission, and to compound his troubles, his modest pay failed to keep pace with his debts. Again, a well-connected friend suggested an alternative. The Mariposa Estate, in the foothills of California's Sierras, needed a man to oversee its ranching and gold-mining enterprises. Olmsted searched his conscience, but by this time the Commission was on a firm footing and running smoothly. In the middle of the Civil War, Frederick Law Olmsted struck out for the West.

Originally carved out of the wilderness by the explorer General John C. Frémont, the estate was a vast feudal domain, its raw company towns isolated among thousands of acres. By the time the Easterner arrived, the ranch had been so badly abused — its riches of grass, timber, and gold skimmed off — that even Frederick Law Olmsted

Originally carved out of the wilderness by the explorer General John C. Frémont, the estate was a vast feudal domain, its raw company towns isolated among thousands of acres. By the time the Easterner arrived, the ranch had been so badly abused — its riches of grass, timber, and gold skimmed off — that even Frederick Law Olmsted couldn't save it. The two years of roaming over Mariposa, though, turned out to be the happiest of his life, and they proved to be a valuable interlude for Olmsted and the nation. For one thing, his salary allowed him finally to pay off his nagging debts. For another, the developing West offered him new perspectives on man's relationships to the land, for he saw not only rampant destruction but possibilities for stewardship. He studied the company's helter-skelter frontier towns and suggested they be rebuilt with the employees' health and welfare in mind — a radical proposal dismissed out-of-hand by the board of directors back East. But a seed that would flourish in a different situation had been planted in the foreman's mind.

During his stay, California was enjoying one of its periodic booms. Furthermore, it had acquired the sophistication — and wealth — that allowed enlightened citizens to worry about future growth. Occasionally staying in San Francisco where his firm did its banking, Olmsted, whose success with Central Park had preceded him, hobnobbed with the state's elite. They recruited him for various projects — designs for San Francisco's Golden Gate Park, plans for the new campuses of Stanford University and the University of California at Berkeley. Most entrepreneurs wanted to grace their California schemes with lush New England landscapes. To the contrary, Olmsted urged what few had thought of before: he recognized that man should respect the land as well as the climate. Anticipating the concepts of Frank Lloyd Wright, he planned buildings to fit in with natural surroundings and took advantage of the Mediterranean weather, suggesting landscaping with plants that would thrive in the hot climate without making demands on the limited water supply.

More significant for the future of conservation, he saw the havoc of hasty mining and timber development. Back East, Olmsted's family heard his sadness when he wrote: "All the big trees have been wasted — and still are being wasted, though I am checking it." On days off, he nosed his horse up into the Sierras to wonder and wander in unspoiled Yosemite Valley. With the practical concern he had always demonstrated for the wild land he loved, the ranch foreman lobbied with influential friends until the federal government ceded the valley to the state of California, thus creating the germ of the national park system.

Envisioning a "wild park" for posterity, Olmsted served as president of the commission governing the new reserve and drew up a management plan that left no doubt about his feelings for Yosemite. "The first point to be kept in mind," he reported to the California legislature, "is the preservation and maintenance as exactly as possible of the natural scenery: the restriction of all artificial constructions which would distort the dignity of the scenery."

Though the country would violate his ideals in Yosemite and future preserves, Olmsted helped set the stage for John Muir's strenuous campaigns to protect the Sierras. His views served as a basis for the nationwide effort fifty years later to create the national park system. It was in fact Frederick Law Olmsted, Jr., an activist following in his father's footsteps, who in 1916 wrote portions of the bill creating the National Park Service.

After the Civil War, the United States began a marked shift from a rural to an urban society. When Olmsted returned to New York City in 1865, he found himself beset by public officials and private individuals seeking his advice on construction projects funded by the country's new industrial wealth. For the next thirty years his architectural business prospered as he dashed back and forth across the country in a near monomaniacal effort to meet the demand.

Yet always at heart a New England country boy in his simple love of nature, he was troubled by the rapid growth. He feared that the newly industrialized nation was abusing the natural heritage which he considered essential for society's health. Looking beyond the practical affairs of his own business, the former president of the Yosemite Commission continued to pioneer not only the concept of preserving wilderness but of returning developed land back to its original wild state.

He became a prime mover in persuading the New York legislature to set aside hundreds of thousands of acres in the Adirondack Mountains — the first large state preserve of its kind in the East. Saddened by the claptrap of commercial exploitation around Niagara Falls, he lobbied until the United States and Canada agreed to tear down the eyesores and turn Niagara into an international park. Soon asked to draw up a plan to restore the area, Olmsted didn't mince words about the sanctity of the preserve. Beyond minimum facilities for the public's comfort, "nothing of an artificial character should be allowed a place on the property." Parks should be kept as special places where people could communicate with themselves through nature. To protect his ideals turned into reality, Olmsted constantly battled to keep out shooting galleries, race tracks, and the other paraphernalia that a nervous society proposed for his "wild parks."

His concepts also encompassed the economic needs of the nation. While drawing up blueprints for Biltmore, the palatial residence of financier George Vanderbilt near Asheville, North Carolina, Olmsted suggested that his young friend Gifford Pinchot oversee the estate's woodlands. Thus Pinchot, who later founded the U.S. Forest Service, had his first chance to harvest a forest scientifically — the first such experiment in the United States.

Olmsted's role in laying down these early gains for conservation tend to be forgotten, perhaps because his urban landscape work is more obvious to the pubic. Reaching his fame just when new colleges were springing up around the country, he helped design the grounds of Cornell University and the University of Massachusetts, as well as those of Stanford, the University of California, and others. He landscaped the National Zoo in Washington, D.C., worked on the design of the Chicago World's Fair, and laid out the grounds of the nation's Capitol building.

Busy as he was with such undertakings, Olmsted never found time to put his theories into a book. However, the basic ideas behind the projects may be seen today in Riverside, Illinois. Olmsted's plan for this Chicago suburb broke with the traditional grid-like pattern of most cities. Instead, Riverside is graced with curved roads following the contours of the land, open spaces, clusters of trees, mandated setbacks for homes, and a central meadow — all innovations for his day and all designed for appreciative people living in harmony with their surroundings. So great became the fame of such work that practically all the major cities of his time bear the rural signature of Frederick Law Olmsted. Among them, Boston, Montreal, St. Louis, Detroit, and Chicago owe the *rus in urbe* of their present parks to a man who established himself in his career well past the age of forty.

"He paints with lakes and wooded slopes, with lawns and banks and forest-covered hills," lauded one of his contemporaries. However, for all the accolades of his day, and for all his straining efforts, he could not counter the population growth that later demolished many of his exquisite plans. He could not turn aside the nation's preference for immediate gain through unplanned growth, which wrecked much of his careful designing. Yet, depressed as he became in later years, the failure was not in the scope of his vision but in the country's inability to fulfill it. Broken in mind and body, Frederick Law Olmsted died at the age of eighty-one, tragically watching ever fresh visions unwinding in his head while he was confined in an asylum he had helped design years before.

Carl Schurz. "I am going to have the luxury of doing what I think to be right." His enemies were dismayed.

Chapter 4

Carl Schurz:
A Sharp Tongue vs.
a Profligate Nation

Bayonets at the ready, sailors rushed ashore at Manistee, Michigan, and began seizing bewildered citizens. Earlier in 1853, the government had sent Isaac Willard to the backwoods town to investigate reports of timber thefts from public lands. When the agent impounded stolen logs, the populace threatened to hang the meddler from the Federal Land Office. Willard escaped, but one of his assistants lost his life in the brawl.

In turn the government took its measure of revenge by sending in the Navy to arrest the rioters. Despite its drama, the story is not one for the annals of conservation victories. The following outcry over government interference so rocked the nation's capital that Willard's boss, Commissioner Wilson of the Land Office, lost his job.

What makes the vignette extraordinary is that the government tried to enforce the law by sending Willard on his ill-fated mission. Up until the beginning of this century, settlers simply took what they wanted from the land. In the 1800s, timber corporations confirmed popular attitudes on a large scale as they cut swaths across Maine and the northern Lake States, then leapfrogged the plains to begin work on the thick growth of the Pacific Northwest. They are "not merely stealing trees, but stealing whole forests," despaired Carl Schurz.

The continental business was not without consequences. Farmlands eroded, silt filled rivers, and timber became scarce where it once had been so plentiful as to be a nuisance to agriculture. Deer, bear, and turkey all but disappeared from east of the Mississippi. Yet people ignored the radical changes in the face of their country—with some exceptions. President John Adams railed against those appropriating public resources "with the thirst of a tiger for blood." As early as the 1830s artist George Catlin proposed the idea of national parks to protect the "pristine beauty and wildness" of the frontier. Back in Massachusetts, Thoreau groused eloquently about abuses to his beloved woods. While the Civil War preoccupied the country, Vermonter George Perkins Marsh was warning that the nation would bring itself to economic ruin by dismantling the fabric of its land. But these isolated voices swayed few in a nation about to enter the freewheeling days of the Gilded Age. What was needed to put the ideas of Marsh and others into practice was a leader in a position to make sweeping changes. And the kind of leadership on the scale needed to succeed in a sprawling, developing land could come only from a government that was still winking at the devastation.

Estimates of Carl Schurz's role in this huge endeavor range to the extremes. One writer laments that he "got almost nowhere." Another offers him an accolade as "the father of the conservation movement." The difficulty arises because Schurz's contributions were unique yet not immediately successful. His tenure as Secretary of the Interior marks the first comprehensive attempt at government involvement, not only with a rational forest policy but with an ethic of care for all land. As with most first attempts at sweeping reforms, Schurz's did not at first take hold, but they outlined the pattern for the future of conservation.

The entire public career of German-born Schurz had a single aim: to bring the world around him in line with the democratic ideals and sense of justice learned in the violence of revolution against political oppression. The liberal spirit sweeping Germany during 1848-49 propelled him out of the classrooms of Bonn's Frederick William University and into the streets as a militant student leader. His adventures during the next few years of "wild, if somewhat aimless, enthusiasm" have comic opera aspects. Young Schurz escaped Prussian soldiers by dashing in and out of sewers while clutching an ancient pistol in one hand, a bottle of wine in the other. He connived intricate plots involving disguises and invisible inks, and in a breathtaking escapade, he rescued a beloved professor from gloomy Spandau prison. As others have observed, the exploits would make splendid material for Sigmund Romberg—if one ignores the tyrannies that caused them and the realities of busy firing squads.

The revolution failed, but not Schurz's deep commitment to ideals. He joined fellow forty-eighters, as they were called, in seeking a fresh start and political freedom in America. In 1852, at the age of twenty-three, he and his new wife sailed into New York harbor. "With the buoyant hopefulness of young hearts," as he later described his enthusiasm, "we saluted the new world." Schurz couldn't speak English, and he had no trade or profession. Yet, as was not the case with many immigrants disembarking full of hopes, the new world returned his salute. His revolutionary exploits, often told with emphasis on the swashbuckling details, had preceded him. Wherever he went, German-Americans welcomed him as a hero.

Fame gave a needed boost to a serious but amiable young man, who soon decided on a political career in his

Schurz's pleasures included literature, walks in the woods, and occasional dances. He was just what he appeared to be–a plain-living, high-thinking man.

The New York Historical Society, New York City

adopted land. And the advantage of his reputation didn't
go unnoticed by the newly formed Republican Party trying to woo converts to their cause. For a home base, Schurz
bought a farm in Watertown, Wisconsin, with the little
money he had and plunged into state politics. A year later,
in 1857—when Schurz was not yet thirty, not yet even a
U.S. citizen—he made a bid for lieutenant-governor. He
lost by a mere 107 votes, but the close race serves as a
measure of his early popularity and rapid climb up the
political ladder. Soon Schurz was a fiery orator—capable
of humor, irony, and moral earnestness in two
languages—on his way to becoming the arbiter of the
nation's large German-American vote.

Given his revolutionary background and dedication, it
is not surprising to find him embroiled in the anti-slavery
controversies that led to the Civil War. To the former
immigrant, Abraham Lincoln's candidacy took on a moral
imperative. Carl Schurz charged about the country, often
at his own expense, bolstering the anti-slavery cause as
the major issue in the Presidential race. Eastern newspapers reported his anti-slavery speeches and welcomed him
to national prominence. "We defy," he threw out his challenge to the nation's conscience, "the whole slave power
and the whole vassalage of hell." That ringing sense of
moral right was his political trademark, whether in the
issues of individual freedom, Indian policy, or conservation. In Schurz's mind, all concerns of government were
linked to the overall issue of justice.

Schurz's crusade probably turned the election Lincoln's
way. And for the rest of his life, the former revolutionary
remained a potent force in nearly every Presidential election. In the meantime, however, Abraham Lincoln appointed him minister to Spain. Actually, he wanted the
ambassadorship to Italy, but his revolutionary background lost him this sensitive post—happily taken, it
might be footnoted, by another future conservationist,

George Perkins Marsh. But the doddering court of portly Queen Isabella couldn't hold Schurz. With the news of Bull Run and subsequent Northern reversals, Schurz returned home to become a general in the Union Army. His regiments fought through some of the worst carnage of the War: the Second Battle of Bull Run, Chancellorsville, Gettysburg. Schurz's military courage matched his political toughness. To rally his troops he strolled along the front lines, puffing a cigar through the flying bullets. Yet he hated war and later refused to use his military service to political advantage.

In any case, by middle age he faced a secure future. For the rest of his life he served in important capacities, as a U.S. senator, then as editorial writer for such publications of national influence as the New York *Evening Post*, the *Nation*, and *Harper's Weekly*—all the while lecturing and analyzing American politics, "planning how society and the world could be improved." He contributed two outstanding books on American history, *Abraham Lincoln* and the *Life of Henry Clay*, as well as his own readable *Reminiscences*; and he fought for decades to establish the Civil Service in place of the patronage system.

As a reformer, Schurz was ahead of his time. The progressive impulse—the reaction against the Great Barbecue of America's resources—simmered under the surface of Amercan politics for years before coming to a boil in the popular movement led by President Theodore Roosevelt. In the meantime, fellow politicians gnashed their teeth over Schurz's dedication to issues rather than to party loyalty. The former revolutionary saw no inconsistency in bolting from one party to the other, even in supporting a third party. "I am," he said in opposing the corrupt administration of President Grant, "going to have the luxury of doing what I think to be right."

A sense of moral rightness, however, can set traps for the lone messiah. Schurz's tongue was sharp, too quickly stinging back at politicos who slurred him as a "cowardly Dutchman" and a "loud-mouthed" reformer. As would be true some years later of another forest lover, Gifford Pinchot, his self-confidence compelled him to give gratuitous and sometimes unwelcome advice. Yet in the balance, these were picayune flaws; for the most part he was a rare individual, capable of living according to the high standards he set for others. Mark Twain, an expert at sniffing out human pretense, praised his "blemishless honor," a quality that maddened his many enemies. At one point, they hired detectives to find some defect in his personality, some taint of scandal they could use to bring Schurz down to their level. The sleuths reported back that Schurz's pleasures included literature, walks in the woods, and occasional dances. He loved nothing more, however, than to spend an evening playing the piano while friends and family sang. He was, to his opponents' despair and dismay, just what he appeared to be, a "plain living and high thinking" man.

In 1877 honest but not brilliant President Hayes appointed Carl Schurz his Secretary of the Interior. For four years he grappled with the spoils system and fought for justice for the American Indian. As for conservation, concerns had been building for years, but so far they lacked focus. Such organizations as the American Forestry Association were sounding alarms for a rational woodlands policy. Individuals prominent in the public eye—the Sierra naturalist, John Muir; architect Frederick Law Olmsted; and the renowned explorer of the Grand Canyon, John Wesley Powell—were condemning the waste of the country's natural heritage. In Michael Frome's words, these conservation leaders found earnest support from a handful of "bird watchers and flower growers, scholars and poets afflicted with an irritating determination to nag the public conscience." Secretary Schurz's new policies shocked, and occasionally amused, a Congress still dedicated to dissipating the country's natural treasures, but they helped unite disparate voices. In one leap through public apathy, Schurz brought conservation to the fore as a national issue.

Conservationists often point to the enlightened forest programs he promoted while a Cabinet member. The praise is well aimed, but it falls short of the mark. What Schurz pushed to the center stage of national politics was not only the beginnings of a formal land use management plan for the entire public domain but a comprehensive ethic of care and appreciation for all nature. Further, as editor and lecturer he kept the issues before the public long after he had stopped nagging Congress with attempted policy changes and with annual gadfly messages from his office.

As to forestry, he had two specific goals: preservation and restoration. To stop rampant exploitation, he urged Congress to set aside, from public land, forest reserves. They would be administered by a professional, uniformed forest agency, which would select timber to be sold to private industry. At the time, millions of forest acres lay devastated—the result of the prevailing "cut and run" ethic. In addition, man-caused fires annually destroyed even more timber than was being stolen. Unchecked conflagrations often left frontier farms and communities in ashes. Schurz pointed out the necessity for fire protection and reseeding in order to stop the waste—to stop erosion, prevent floods, and insure steady supplies of water and timber for the future. He further urged that Congress amend the homestead laws so that the advantage would shift from the land-grabbing timber barons and ranching corporations to individual settlers. And, acknowledging that his proposals would move into a new area of government responsibility, he capped off the recommendations by asking for a commission to study how his plans might be changed to insure the greatest good for the nation.

*As activist Secretary of the Interior, Schurz fought for justice for
the American Indian. Here, he is addressing Indians on the
Rosebud River in Montana.*
The New York Historical Society, New York City

Schurz's background needs to be kept in mind. He had
grown up where forest husbandry had been a way of life
since the late middle ages, where abuse of the environment was considered murder of "future prosperity and
progress." Yet he was also a German romantic, a lover of
wild nature. At the time, the country had one national
park, Yellowstone—one place that excluded the hunter,
miner, and logger. Through some of the worst years of
waste, he helped keep the park idea alive by pleas to
preserve the redwoods "as an illustration of the magnifi-
cence of the grandest of primeval forests."

But Schurz's sensitivity is perhaps best shown by his
attitudes toward the country's arid regions—those vast
stretches making up most of the American West, but even

less understood than the country's forests. Explorer John Wesley Powell was on the verge of poking a large but not fatal hole in the myth—one of the most fantastic myths that modern man harbored—of the West as a bountiful garden requiring only the touch of the plow and a casual sprinkling of seeds to make it bloom. Powell told Congress what any sensible man not bent on swallowing his own delusions could see for himself—that the West was a dry place. Patterns of settlement successful in the humid East would not work there. Grasslands easily slipped into dust flats if not carefully managed; crops blew away, followed by the soil. Yet the land could be fruitful if Congress were to change the homestead laws, if agriculture were carried out on a cooperative basis, and if water were husbanded as a precious, life-giving resource.

As Powell's boss, Schurz signed the letter of transmittal recommending Powell's report to Congress. But more importantly, and perhaps coached by Powell, Schurz included the essentials of the Powell arguments in his message to Congress the year before the publication of Powell's *Report on the Lands of the Arid Region* in 1878. However, the attempt to soften the target failed. Congressmen—and the bankers, land speculators, and railroad men who supported them—howled their derision.

Despite frustrating failures, Schurz could show some practical results. Although Congress warily avoided passing new laws, under those already on the books Schurz sent agents into the field who either arrested astounded timber poachers or forced them to pay for stolen logs. His Department pressed legal action which, in the Secretary's words, "stopped the depredations on the public lands to a very great extent, and, if continued, will entirely arrest the evil." And what should have gladdened the hearts of Congressmen, his vigorous prosecutions brought in a net gain to the treasury. Congress, however, was not pleased by the fledgling forester. Instead, Speaker of the House

James G. Blaine—with one eye over his shoulder at the timber magnates, who kept his campaign coffers full— fumed at Schurz as "outrageous and un-American." Sensing the direction of the wind, Congress proceeded to cut the Department's budget for timber agents in proportion to their successes.

Time has vindicated Carl Schurz. Almost all his conservation programs have come—and are coming—to pass. In 1891 Congress authorized the first forest reserves, the foundation of our present National Forest System. In 1896 it funded the National Forest Commission. Urged by the progressive leader Theodore Roosevelt—who used arguments learned from Carl Schurz twenty-five years earlier—it created the Forest Service in 1905, a year before Schurz's death. Since then, reforestation has become an accepted, if still underfunded, program. The national parks have continued to expand in size and number, though only in 1978 did Schurz's beloved redwoods receive sufficient acreage for viable protection. As far as the desert heritage goes, the country is only now beginning to grasp the wisdom of what Powell and Schurz told the nation a hundred years ago.

Speaking of the early government campaigners, former Secretary of the Interior Stewart Udall observes that "As reformers, they lost. As land prophets, they won." Their prophecy sounded the call to arms for the younger politicians who set the course for today's conservation.

John Burroughs (second from left), a bit weary from the zany automobile excursions he shared with industrialists Thomas Edison, Henry Ford, and Harvey Firestone.

Ford Archives, Henry Ford Museum, Dearborn, Michigan

Chapter 5

John Burroughs:
The Harvest of a Quiet Eye

John Burroughs sits on a waterwheel flanked by Thomas Edison, Henry Ford, and Harvey Firestone. He looks as if he is about to cry, but that is not the case. He is old, the sun is in his eyes, and he's weary from a zany automobile excursion the industrialists were taking across the countryside as diversion from the strain of making their millions. Financially the rustic Burroughs did not qualify as part of this select group, but he was a celebrity in his own right—the most widely photographed American of his time.

As the rich often do, the industrialists liked to have a famous outsider along to add a charming dimension to their "traveling circus." Besides, as Harvey Firestone says in *Men and Rubber: The Story of Business*, Burroughs "could tell us about the birds and the flowers" as the caravan bounced along America's primitive roads, springs sagging from the tents, cots, electric lights, and portable kitchen that assuaged the hardships of camping out. For his part, Burroughs was no spoilsport on these boyish frolics. There he is, in the photographs of the Ford Museum archives, a woodsman well into his eighties blazing away at a target with a Winchester or taking on the younger Ford in a spontaneous tree-felling contest.

It would not be difficult to make a case for Burroughs as a conservation slacker. "I have picnicked all along the way," he said, reflecting somewhat guiltily on his long life, off "a-fishing while others were struggling and groaning." While he picnicked, such campaigners as Carl Schurz, Gifford Pinchot, and Teddy Roosevelt were risking their careers to stop the rapid wastage of America's wilderness and wildlife. Burroughs' activist record may be spotty at best, but his part in protecting the nature he loved was far greater than he imagined. Fulminating on the forefront of conservation, early activists succeeded only because of widespread sympathy and political support from a public made aware of nature's fragility by such writers as Burroughs. The writer's role has been one of the most essential, if uncelebrated, roles in the story of protecting the environment.

In any case, John Burroughs would have made a poor campaigner. He loved nature, and he loved to write. After that, the Devil could take the hindmost—at least that's how it appeared on the surface. While John Muir cajoled citizens into action from California's Sierras, Burroughs was holed up in his vineyard and celery patch on the banks of the Hudson River. When the two Johns—"John o' Mountains" and "John o' Birds"—met on camping trips, exuberant Muir had no end of poking fun at the stolid farmer. One critic compares buoyant Muir to a squirrel, Burroughs to a woodchuck—an observation not entirely off the mark. The lively Douglas squirrel was one of Muir's favorite creatures, while phlegmatic Burroughs had painted "Woodchuck Lodge" on the mailbox outside one of his writing retreats. And puzzling over the rural New Yorker's childlike lack of competitive drive, Harvey Firestone whimsically comments, "He was different from the rest of us." By "us," the rubber man of course meant

Edison, Ford, and other go-getters of American industry.
But the fact is that John Burroughs was different from the
go-getters of American conservation as well. In short, he
was his own man, a conservationist by default, and—
despite his appeal as a backwoods prophet to nostalgic
Victorians rattled by a changing world—not at all as pro-
saic or intellectually conservative as some have imagined.

In 1837 John Burroughs was born in an unpainted
farmhouse on the western slopes of New York's Catskill
Mountains. Of solid Yankee stock, the Burroughs family
was rustic, John's surroundings thoroughly rural. As was
the case with many families of the time, the Burroughs
were nearly self-sufficient on their back-country dairy
farm. John's father, Chauncey, obtained the little cash he
needed by driving a wagon load of butter forty miles
through the woods to the nearest market town. As to
culture, little reading matter besides the traditional Bible, a hymnal, and an occasional newspaper graced the
Burroughs household. Years later, when John became the
most celebrated nature writer of the time, none of his ten
brothers and sisters felt moved to read his books.

With needs few and the soil rich, the family enjoyed long
periods of ease. After the usual farm chores, young John
had the freedom to hunt or fish, to range at will through
the rolling Catskills. "Ah, I am there now!" he remembered in old age, transporting himself back to the maple-
sugaring days of early spring. "I see the woods flooded
with sunlight, I smell the dry leaves, and the mould under
them just quickened by the warmth; ... I see the brimming
pans and buckets, always on the sunny side of the trees,
and hear the musical dropping of the sap...." Elsewhere he
remembers a life centered on the cathedral-like barn: "My
memory is fragrant with the breath of cattle."

"The freshness of the farm boy's outlook" and "a sense of
fundamental calm," notes contemporary author Edwin
Way Teale, pervade Burroughs' nature writings. Readers

born in the heady Gilded Age responded to Burroughs' reflections precisely because they evoked the natural richness and innocence of a way of life quickly passing from the American scene. But Burroughs was no mere country bumpkin blessed with a flair for idyllic descriptions. The accuracy of his observations on wildlife rival those of Audubon, at times outstrip Thoreau's. And his work ranges far beyond nature writing. Approximately two-thirds of his nearly thirty books deal with travel, science, theology , philosophy, and literary criticism. Although much of his more speculative work may not carry great impact for today's readers, his probing analyses of Emerson, Thoreau, and Whitman remain essential for modern scholars approaching these three literary giants of the last century.

Burroughs' own scholarship began in a one-room schoolhouse near Roxbury, New York. There he wrestled

Bird lover Henry Ford sent Burroughs a Model T. The nature writer proceeded to drive "the blind, desperate" contraption into the side of his barn. Ford Archives, Henry Ford Museum, Dearborn, Michigan

with Jay Gould, the future financier, while absorbing the rudiments of a country education. His father's butter sales, however, provided little extra money for the luxury of advanced learning. John was able to manage only about six months of further study at nearby Hedding Literary Institute and Cooperstown Seminary. By then in his late teens and in need of supporting himself, he moved on to teaching jobs, first in New Jersey, then in New York and Illinois.

Though his future was unsure, he married Ursula North, and with the romantic self-importance of youth informed his new wife: "If I live, I shall be an author." He set his course by contributing literary essays to the *Saturday Press*, a New York weekly with a bohemian slant. So closely did Burroughs' developing style resemble Emerson's that the public mistook one of his unsigned articles in the *Atlantic Monthly* as the work of the famous New England philosopher. Burroughs students still debate whether Emerson or the poet Walt Whitman had the greater influence on the maturing writer. Whatever the eventual findings of the scholars, both men were Burroughs' lifelong philosophical mentors, contributing much to his transcendental view that physical nature reflects man's inner spirits.

But neither man had the dramatic impact of John James Audubon. In 1863, while idling in the library at the West Point Military Academy, Burroughs discovered a large illustrated book. With the first glance at Audubon's *Birds*, he "took fire at once. It was like bringing together fire and powder." The volume provided the young man with a focus that would expand to other wildlife encountered on his woodland ramblings. "I was almost wild," he said of a birding expedition into the Adirondacks a few months later.

In the midst of his new enthusiasm, however, Burroughs needed a better paying job than teaching; he also wanted to meet Walt Whitman, an avant-garde poet with a small but zealous following. Combining the two goals, Burroughs set off for Washington, D.C., where Whitman was nursing the wounded brought in from Civil War battlefields. The two were soon hiking through the woods surrounding the nation's capital, and on these excursions Whitman's expansive view of the world infected young Burroughs, now working as a Treasury guard. Burroughs' first book—the first of a lifetime of writings about the poet—was *Notes on Walt Whitman* (1867). Meanwhile, during working hours Burroughs sat guarding a vault at the Treasury Department and completing the manuscript of his first book on nature, *Wake-Robin* (1871), whose title was suggested by Whitman. But the influence was not all one way. Burroughs sharpened his companion's eye for nature, and he influenced much of Whitman's imagery ... the hermit thrush symbol, for instance, in "When Lilacs Last in the Dooryard Bloom'd," Whitman's famous poem inspired by the death of Abraham Lincoln.

Despite the literary excitement of his camaraderie with Whitman, the Treasury guard recognized that "my blood has the flavor of the soil in it; it is rural to the last drop." After nine years, homesickness for his native ground overwhelmed him. Returning to New York, he built Riverby, a substantial stone house on the banks of the Hudson River. He would live in the area for the rest of his long life. In order to support his family, for a while he worked as a bank examiner. Then, as one book followed another, his finances improved, and he was able to divide his time between writing and tending his vineyard and favorite celery patch.

"I am bound to praise the simple life," he said, "because I have lived it and found it good." The tender reflections on his idyllic childhood in the Catskills, and his loosely-structured essays pointing out the wonders of forest rambles became ever more popular as the possibility of the "simple life" faded for a society plunging into nationwide industrialism. Yet Burroughs' hard-won pastoral reality had at least one nettlesome complication. His wife, Ursula, looked on her husband's books as "unremunerative dawdling," as Perry D. Westbrook puts it. Oddly enough, she had a warm place in her heart for disheveled Walt Whitman, who during the Washington days strolled in late for Sunday breakfasts to gobble up her pancakes. But she disliked her husband's unrefined country friends, who tracked leaves into the house when they came to visit. Besides, the country life, whatever charms it held for her husband, fell far short of her aspirations. Once a year she'd pack up and move to more civilized Poughkeepsie, ostensibly to avoid the blizzards raging ten miles up the Hudson. For his part, to keep from getting underfoot while she was at Riverby, husband John often took refuge in Slabsides, a cabin he built in a swampy place a mile from his home. Their married life was a standoff.

If John Burroughs' cup contained little at Riverby, it more than overflowed with public adulation at Slabsides. Vassar girls, newspapermen, portrait painters, and curious bicyclists streamed to the rough cabin hideaway looking for the last of a vanishing species: the simple American folk hero grown wise from contact with the earth. Aging John Burroughs would greet them in worn farm clothes and might invite them for a walk to the spring for a drink. In him they found the embodiment of the white-bearded, amiable, and patriarchal image they were seeking.

Fame produced fame. Literati lavished endorsements on the vineyardist. William Dean Howells referred to *Wake-Robin*: "It is a sort of summer vacation to turn its pages." A few years later none other than Henry James accurately called the author of *Winter Sunshine* (1875) "a sort of reduced, but also more humorous, more available, and more sociable Thoreau." The railroad magnate E. H.

Harriman offered Burroughs an expense-paid tour of Alaska if he would be the historian of his expedition. From humble but shrewd Yankee stock, "John o' Birds" often accepted such invitations. After all, he reasoned, rich people had the right to spend their money as they pleased. Henry Ford, who surrounded his mansion near Detroit with five hundred bird houses, found himself so charmed by the New Yorker's ornithological passages that he bought the old Burroughs family farm and presented it to the writer as a gift. Delighted by another Burroughs book, the automobile tycoon had a Model T crated up and shipped to Riverby. By then in his seventies, Burroughs was still game to master "the blind, desperate" contraption. But in an oft-repeated American cliche of the period, he drove the shiny automobile into the side of his barn.

Honors crowned his recognition. The distinguished American Academy of Arts and Letters elected the Seer of Slabsides to its membership. Yale and Colgate awarded him honorary degrees. The White House responded to new Burroughs volumes with notes of appreciation. President and Mrs. Roosevelt found themselves joining the national pilgrimage to the cabin by the celery field. Soon T. R. and Burroughs were frequent companions, the President calling the author "Oom John," in reference to his avuncular qualities. Not to be outdone, Burroughs returned the compliment by dubbing Roosevelt "His Transparency." On one occasion, T. R. invited Burroughs on a railroad trip to Yellowstone National Park, and chuckled to himself when crowds rushed forward at some stops to cheer John Burroughs rather than the President of the United States.

As to activism, "John o' Birds" might have spared the occasional scourgings he administered himself by saying, "I was never a fighter; I fear that at times I may have been a shirker." Though he rarely took public stances on the conservation issues developing during this progressive era, he lent his support to such wildlife organizations as the American Game Association, and in 1913 he campaigned openly for passage of the McLain Bird Protection Bill.

Yet the most valuable contributions of this usually passive man were far broader, though less direct. They lay in the public's near frantic enthusiasm for his nature writings, a renown that prepared the nation for change from exploitation to stewardship—a change not yet complete. And his popularity covered the whole spectrum of society to a degree not since duplicated. One after another over a period of fifty years—from *Wake-Robin* in 1871 to *Under the Maples* in 1921—his volumes celebrating country pleasures appeared in the bookstores. More importantly, school texts included Burroughs' essays, thus instilling in the young sympathetic attitudes toward the natural world.

His influence on the rich and the support his fame gave to conservation's leaders is even more difficult to measure. As far as is recorded, he worked no miraculous conversions, neither on railroad tycoons, automobile producers, nor tire manufacturers. But praising Burroughs became fashionable among the wealthy. In a somewhat bewildered tone, Harvey Firestone admitted that through rubbing shoulders with Burroughs he had glimpses of "a different world." Whatever else might be said, such industrialists at least became less antagonistic toward the growing impulse for preserving the nature that John Burroughs tenderly revealed. At times they saw the wisdom in what Burroughs once wrote Firestone: "We live in an age of iron and have all we can do to keep the iron from entering our souls"—and they dug into their pockets to support fledgling conservation causes.

Teddy Roosevelt was doing more than being gracious when he invited the celebrated celery farmer on the railroad trip to Yellowstone. Such Presidential programs as the creation and expansion of national forests were under

"I am bound to praise the simple life, because I have lived it and found it good. Ford Archives, Henry Ford Museum, Dearborn, Michigan

almost constant fire from exploiters. Furthermore, preservationists took Roosevelt to task for his hunting fervor. Burroughs helped the President's image with both groups. The nature writer not only carried a certain amount of clout with opponents of conservation by virtue of his public stature, he himself was a reformed hunter, who confessed, "I do not outrage the woods; I do not hunt down a bird." Roosevelt had created a public stir by stating that he would find a mountain lion trophy in the nation's first national park. But the public's outrage at the planned violation rapidly cooled when newspapermen reported that the unarmed President had settled for chasing a mouse while John Burroughs watched approvingly. This and other Burroughs appearances with T. R. helped

strengthen the President's political hand. As historian
Perry D. Westbrook notes, Burroughs "quite unknowingly
had become a political force, and not a small one, in the
cause of conservation."

However, the Seer of Slabsides was not at all unknow-
ing in a larger sense. For years he tried through his writings to resolve the dualities in Western civilization: of
good and evil, of matter and spirit, of nature and science.
Throughout much of the intellectual struggle he maintained a sense of optimism, but in his later years he looked
into the future and saw that "wisdom cannot come by
railroad, or automobile, or aeroplane, or be hurried up by
telegraph or telephone." Man had deceived himself with
"howling locomotives ... pouring out their huge volumes of
fetid carbon." Through strong words that indicated disil-
lusionment with progress, at the age of seventy-five he
warned readers of the *Atlantic Monthly*: "A riotous, waste-
ful, and destructive spirit has been turned loose on this
continent, and ... a nature fertile and bountiful ... has been
outraged...." Industrialized civilization had become "an
engine running without a headlight."

All his life John Burroughs drew sustenance from famil-
iar faces and from the countryside of his boyhood. For
years he struggled to maintain the old family homestead,
just over the Catskills from Riverby. Each year he faith-
fully visited the graves of relatives. As Burroughs approached the age of eighty-four and saw his friends dying,
his old haunts changing, sadness crept into his life. Still,
New York's rolling hills remained the source of strength
and vision. He died returning on a train from a winter in
California, asking with his last words, "How far are we
from home?" Some lines he wrote twenty years earlier
might serve as his epitaph: "Here I sit," he mused, "night
after night, year after year in my little Study perched
upon a broad slope of the Hudson, my light visible from
afar...."

George Bird Grinnell. Editor, hunter, founder of the first Audubon Society, the refined Grinnell quietly primed Teddy Roosevelt for conservation reforms. The Smithsonian Institution

Chapter 6

George Bird Grinnell:
Western Frontiersman,
Eastern Editor

While Frederick Law Olmsted was snapping politicians away from his grand designs for Central Park and in Washington, D.C., and John Burroughs was guarding a Treasury vault, soldiers gazing over the ramparts of Fort McPherson beheld a strange sight out on the Nebraska flats. Coming toward them at the head of a dusty plume was not a military supply train nor a band of rambunctious Sioux but wagons loaded with twelve students from Yale University.

Led by the august paleontologist Professor Othniel C. Marsh, the little party, one of the earliest expeditions of its kind, would spend the summer of 1870 hunting fossils for Yale's Peabody Museum. Marsh was on the verge of picking from the West's ancient sea beds substantial evidence for Darwin's theory of evolution, about to begin years of feuding with other bone hunters over fossil treasures. The students, however, looked to the summer ahead as a lark, an extended recess in the Wild West.

They were in for some jolts. As a sample of what the months ahead would bring, the soldiers told them how

67

earlier that very day Indians had ambushed some white hunters near the fort. The students gazed upon long-haired and buckskinned "Buffalo Bill" Cody, the post's chief scout, who had led the counterattack. In the wilderness of Nebraska, the young scholars sensed their inadequacies. Few of them had ever slept without sheets, ridden a horse, or fired a gun—let alone learned how to dismount on signal and throw their rifles over the saddle to face the enemy. The soldiers of the 5th Cavalry who formed their escort dubbed them "pilgrims."

As they rode out into the little known expanses of Montana and Wyoming, they became hardened to the 100° heat, the thirst, and bad bacon. For their part, the soldiers enjoyed the break in routine, good humoredly helping to gather Pliocene femurs and tibias. After the first shock, the young Easterners learned to ignore the smoke signals that followed their heavily armed column. Miffed at the invasion, the Indians set the prairie on fire; the Yale men lit backfires. When the warriors crept in at night, to howl like wolves from the nearby hills, the undergraduates responded with school songs.

Eleven of the twelve volunteers returned East to finish at Yale, pursue prosperous if unglamorous careers, and years later perhaps reminisce to their grandchildren about "Buffalo Bill" and their bizarre summer. But after nearly two years in his father's New York brokerage firm, George Bird Grinnell still couldn't get the excitement out of his system. In 1872 he was back in the West, this time to hunt buffalo with the friendly Pawnee tribe. Grinnell would return nearly every summer for the next forty years, to send back crates of scientific specimens over the Northern Pacific Railroad, but mostly to savor the colorful frontier life that future generations would know only in their dreams.

Luckily, work at the Peabody Museum kept him from accepting General George Armstrong Custer's invitation to join the expedition that ended with Sioux war cries on the Little Bighorn. But the man who had complained during early forays that he wasn't able to catch a renegade in his rifle sights saw the West in changing perspectives as he matured. In later years, he lived with the now languishing tribes "as friend and brother," note Margaret Mead and Ruth Bunzel in *The Golden Age of American Anthropology*. Sharing the concerns of Carl Schurz, Grinnell was one of the few influential whites of the time to fight for the welfare of native Americans. In addition, such books as *Blackfoot Lodge Tales* (1892), *The Cheyenne Indians* (1923), and *The Fighting Cheyennes* (1915) established him as an authority on Western Indian lore.

This well-placed reputation and his self-effacing personality obscured Grinnell's broader contributions, as did the conservation efforts of Theodore Roosevelt, spurred on by Gifford Pinchot, his ambitious lieutenant. President Roosevelt heralded his own natural-resource programs in razzle-dazzle terms that left the public, and many historians, believing that conservation—not unlike Athena leaping from the head of Zeus—had sprung full-grown from the Roosevelt administration. The analogy would be closer to the truth if George Bird Grinnell were substituted for the fathering Greek god.

In 1875 Grinnell joined Captain William Ludlow's column of troops as a naturalist on an expedition into Yellowstone National Park. The nation's sole park remained only partially explored; Ludlow's job was to survey the area and give Congress an account of the "wonders" it had somewhat casually decreed an inviolate domain three years earlier. Despite its remoteness, Ludlow and Grinnell found the park infested with commercial hunters. With their repeating rifles, they were skimming off nature's abundance, each year leaving tens of thousands of buffalo carcasses rotting in the sun while their hides sped East over the transcontinental railroad. As the naturalist of the expedition, Grinnell used his portion of Ludlow's report "to call attention to the terrible destruction. It is certain that the large game will ere long be exterminated." With these words, the first official protest to be found in government documents, twenty-six-year-old Grinnell began his career as a conservationist.

It was not coincidence that the young Easterner echoed the concerns of the artist John James Audubon, who decades before had wrung his hands over similar scenes of Western slaughter. In order to escape crowded New York City, in 1857 Grinnell's prosperous father moved his family to "Audubon Park," the Hudson River estate that the ornithologist had left to his heirs. There, in what was still a wooded part of Manhattan, Grinnell grew up almost a part of the Audubon family. With Jack Audubon, a grandson of the artist, he scrambled to the top of the barn. Perched on the ridgepole with the famous painter's old musket, the two boys blasted away, rather ineffectively, at clouds of passenger pigeons. With other local children, Grinnell attended a little school conducted by Audubon's widow in her bedroom. To the stockbroker's son she was "Grandma." Her influence ran so deep that when he later started the first Audubon Society, "he named it as much for her as for her husband," states Grinnell scholar John F. Reiger.

George Bird Grinnell wondered at the magnificent portraits of birds, at the antlers and powder horns that graced the Audubon household. Further, though Audubon had died some years earlier, his sons continued their father's work of painting and collecting. Grinnell watched John Woodhouse Audubon open crates of specimens shipped to him from all over the continent. The boy climbed into the loft of the barn, where he found stacks of Audubon's red-bound ornithological biographies. There he sat, reading about the naturalist's explorations up the Missouri and Yellowstone rivers. And he read of "the terrible destruction of life, as it were for nothing, ... as the tongues only were brought in, and the flesh of these fine animals was left to rot on the spots where they fell." Grinnell would retrace Audubon's footsteps in the West, but his reaction to what he saw would be more than a bitter but ignored lament. On the part of a wealthy and politically influential Easterner, it grew into a sophisticated campaign, an "elaboration," as Reiger calls it, of Audubon's unheeded alarms.

This might not have come about had it not been for the diagnosis of a neurologist. Exhausted from his labors at the Peabody Museum, in 1880 the young scientist complained to a doctor of persistent headaches and insomnia. As Grinnell reports in his unpublished *Memoirs*, "the specialist concluded that I must either change my work or be prepared to move into a lunatic asylum or the grave." Fortunately, an opportunity to his liking appeared close at hand. For some time Grinnell had contributed articles on hunting and natural history to *Forest and Stream*, one of the early periodicals devoted to outdoor sports. When its stockholders forced founder and editor Charles Hallock to resign because of his drinking bouts, thirty-one-year-old Grinnell took over the post.

He proved to be an outstanding manager. With his Yale Ph.D. in paleontology, he brought an unsurpassed scientific background to the newspaper. More importantly, rough-and-tumble experiences on the frontier balanced his refined Eastern qualities. In the thick of conservation battles, no Western exploiter could point to the editor of *Forest and Stream*—a man who had ranched with "Buffalo Bill," who knew the excitement and danger of outwitting renegade Sioux—as an effete city dweller who didn't understand the problems of the West. And to cap his success, Grinnell's innate business sense soon had the publication making, as he put it, "plenty of money."

Up until the latter years of the nineteenth century, for

rural Americans hunting was more a necessity than a sport. By the time of substantial urbanization, when citizens turned to field and stream for pleasure, they found their game, thought inexhaustible according to common wisdom, nearly gone. The loss was especially obvious in the rapidly industrializing and densely populated East. The new editor continued the policy of foresighted Hallock, using *Forest and Stream* as a rallying point for disgruntled sportsmen. Reminding readers of the well-managed preserves in European countries that produced game on a sustained-yield basis—in contrast to the dramatic slaughter Grinnell had witnessed with his own eyes—the newspaper lobbied for law enforcement and innovative reforms. Specifically, Grinnell proposed a system of game wardens, state-regulated bag limits, and conservation programs financed through hunting fees. The paleontologist's campaign—the front-page editorials in *Forest and Stream*, the pamphlets distributed free-of-charge to Congressmen and ordinary citizens alike—drew the nation's major magazines, and with them the public, into the early wildlife preservation struggles that culminated in massive game-law reforms passed early in the next century.

Since then, conservationists have learned that their goals, if even partially achieved in their lifetimes, come only after multiple and sometimes seemingly disastrous setbacks. George Bird Grinnell stands out in contrast. The student who nearly flunked out of Yale as a dreamy, prank-playing undergraduate revealed "an ability for ceaseless work, great physical and intellectual discipline," comments biographer Reiger. Prodding, flattering, always minimizing his own contributions, he guided every one of his major undertakings to eventual success. And they reflected his own varied background by being broad as well as deep. Grinnell recognized that game laws, no matter how effective, were useless if wildlife had no place to live. During one of the nation's most heady periods of industrialization, he saw nature as a whole; to counter the busyness of the Gilded Age, he set out to preserve great tracts of wilderness intact. The result was the emergence of the national park system and the concept it embodies today.

At the time, America had only one national park, Yellowstone, which owed its existence as an official "pleasuring ground for the people" not by virtue of its wilderness of peaks and forests but because of geological happenstance. The geysers and bubbling mudfields had provided sufficient drama to attract, if only briefly, the attention of a nodding Congress. Nearly two thousand miles away from Eastern population centers, rarely visited except by eager hide hunters, it existed in the minds of any who thought

Grinnell needed something concrete to generate deep public sentiment. He found it in the buffalo, an enduring American symbol. One result of his campaigning was the landmark legislation passed by Congress in 1894, designed to protect the animals in Yellowstone National Park. Yellowstone National Park

about it at all as a kind of national sideshow.

Tourists, what few there were, hammered away at the creamy geyserite and hauled it off in their wagons for curios. One superintendent staked mining claims within the park, then spent much of his time back in Washington lobbying for development. Even the most inexperienced hunter didn't have to worry about his lack of skills, advertised the Yellowstone Valley Hunting Club in Eastern newspapers. The outfitters furnished not only arms and ammunition but guaranteed trophies for its greenhorn clientele. Meanwhile, poachers were doing a brisk business as the price of a buffalo head soared to $500 during the final years of exploitation. Occasionally the U.S. Cavalry might pounce on a lawbreaker, but often the case was laughed out of a distant and unconcerned court. Finally, one irritated Congressman suggested that the government shouldn't be in the entertainment business. According to him, the park, like all public lands, should be sold off for development.

Sitting in the New York office of *Forest and Stream*, George Bird Grinnell knew and loved Yellowstone. Its boundaries were already established; the problem as he perceived it was that few people cared about what was taking place within them. His job was to arouse the public and change its perceptions of the languishing reserve. His job was to define for the public what a national park should be.

For years a small but influential band of Grinnell's friends had scurried about Washington, lobbying for the sanctity of Yellowstone. But the basic trouble still lay with mass indifference, and the editor used his increasingly popular *Forest and Stream* as a public forum. Through its pages he fostered a shift in national attitudes, which was to form the broad basis for future conservation gains. Up until then, the history of America had been largely one of a Westward-moving free-for-all, each man, whether railroad magnate or penniless homesteader, wresting from the land what he could, according to individual power and wits. In contrast, Grinnell suggested that some land should be held inviolate for the benefit of all. The idea began to take hold, as the public realized that the prevailing laissez-faire system was essentially undemocratic, designed to reward the shenanigans of a few aggressive entrepreneurs at the expense of the commonweal. As to the Yellowstone park, the hide hunters, miners, and uncontrolled loggers, lectured the editor, were making off with the public's property, robbing all Americans of their disappearing heritage.

Once Grinnell established a link between public land and public welfare, his campaign made headway; but he needed a concrete symbol to generate deep public sentiment in ideal and vague theory. He found this symbol in the buffalo.

By the late nineteenth century, the country already was regretting the passage of the frontier—its freedom and vastness typified by the once limitless shaggy beasts. In little more than a generation, buffalo numbers had plummeted from an estimated sixty million to a few hundred frightened and ruthlessly pursued creatures—a fact appreciated by a readily sentimental public. In "The Last of the Buffalo," one of the most moving yet accurate accounts of the animal's demise, Grinnell cautioned that Yellowstone harbored the last wild herd. He had pegged the future of the park to an enduring American symbol.

The arrest of an habitual poacher clinched his case. In March 1894, a soldier and the chief scout at the park, Felix Burgess, cut across the trail of Edgar Howell, following it through the snow to six severed buffalo heads. Shots rang out nearby, and peering over a hill, the two men spied Howell flaying the skins from five fresh kills. Armed only with a revolver, the scout crept over the snow toward Howell, known in the area for his fiery temper, and arrested the cursing poacher, whose hands were soaked in buffalo blood.

Very probably this little drama played out in the far West would have gone unnoticed in the East if Emerson Hough, a reporter for *Forest and Stream*, had not been visiting the park. Hough telegraphed the story to New York, and it appeared that same month with all the vivid details—the villain, selfishly destroying the country's last wild buffalo herd, at last brought to justice.

Public reaction was enormous. Hundreds of thouands of Easterners signed petitions to Congress—a Congress caught off balance because for years it had turned aside legislation sponsored by Grinnell's friends to protect Yellowstone. Shamed by the mass outcry, the same body now scrambled to pass the "Act to Protect the Birds and Animals in Yellowstone National Park."

Today, millions of people think of national parks in idyllic terms, as last refuges from sonic boom, brown air, and freeways that make life in much of urban America a nerve-wracking, disorienting experience. Yet Yellowstone's new jail perhaps best symbolized the change that took place in 1894. The Yellowstone Act closed gaping loopholes in existing statutes and for the first time spelled out preservation in detailed legal terms. Federal marshals now hauled in anyone found possessing geyserite, timber, or dead animals. Judgment came swiftly. The lawbreakers appeared before a resident federal commissioner, appointed not by local politicians, but in Washington. The park's jail stood as a firm reminder of the new protective attitude, backed by stiff fines and sentences of up to two years.

Drawing on his own Western experiences and his perceptions of the country's needs, Grinnell established a precedent for all future national parks. Starting with the concerns of George Catlin, Audubon, and Thoreau, he solidified conservation ideals and theory into the philosophy of the National Park Service, created in 1916. Yet the politics of lobbying offended his patrician sensibilities, and though he was the prime mover behind the concept of preservation, the editor shifted the credit to others.

Historians tend to view the emergence of the national parks and national forests, both developing around the turn of the century, as two separate, though related movements. It is true that broad-based public sentiment for preservation buoyed the cause of federal park lands, as the dramatic response to Edgar Howell's arrest illustrates. On the other hand, early forest advocates typically were a more select group—and more practical in their motives. They aimed their campaigns at influential politicians and businessmen, insisting that the country could only have continued prosperity with properly managed water and timber resources.

The prolonged public debate generated by *Forest and Stream* over Yellowstone also called attention to the future of all resources. For years Grinnell argued with fellow businessmen for sound lumbering practices in New York's Adirondack Park (established in 1885), a reserve the size of Connecticut. The newspaper also directed the mass awareness created by the Yellowstone issue toward the rapidly coalescing movement for a national forest system.

It was not by chance that when Congress granted President Harrison the authority in 1891, he created the Yellowstone National Park Timberland Reserve—the country's first national forest—from lands adjacent to Yellowstone Park. Grinnell's insistence helped determine this decision. And in the marriage of park and forest lay the future of conservation. While some activists—either as park or forest advocates—hurled brickbats at one another, Grinnell had the flexibility to see the necessity of a dual approach—preservation of some lands and scientific management of others. It was a concept that Grinnell passed on to Teddy Roosevelt and through him set the nation on its present two-fold conservation program.

While the name of forester Gifford Pinchot dominates the outstanding record of the Roosevelt Presidency, actually the credit for much of this success belongs to George Bird Grinnell. From a similar well-to-do New York background, Grinnell established a warm friendship with T. R. beginning in 1885, some fifteen years before the future President met the aggressive Pinchot. Grinnell recognized Roosevelt as a man of growing political influence. The two hobnobbed in the editorial offices of *Forest and Stream*, recalling their ranching days in the West. On the basis of this common experience, Grinnell encouraged T. R. to submit material to the newspaper and fed his enormous ego, while channeling Roosevelt's bounding views of man and nature into gentler perspectives.

When T. R. favored a railroad through Yellowstone Park, the editor bided his time, slowly and patiently working a conversion. When in 1887 Roosevelt gathered fellow patricians into the Boone and Crockett Club, Grinnell soon took over the reins of this trophy-hunting organization, steering it and its exclusive founders to take up his own causes. Quite naturally, as governor of New York, Roosevelt turned to Grinnell, his fellow editor in a series of Club books, as his closest adviser in resource management. In short, by the time Teddy became President, quietly groomed by Grinnell, he was ready for Pinchot.

The relationship between Roosevelt and Grinnell illustrates an important but frequently overlooked aspect of conservation's early days—the role of wealthy Easterners. Grinnell's father managed the financial portfolio of railroad magnate Commodore Cornelius Vanderbilt. Through his connections, the young paleontologist Grinnell rode free and in first-class luxury into his Western adventures. The Grinnell family owned over one-third of the stock of *Forest and Stream*, a propitious circumstance for Grinnell's takeover of the newspaper. And lastly— beside his prestigious education, nearly impossible in his day without a wealthy background—Grinnell circulated among the enlightened patrician establishment of the Northeast. Stirred by the new cause of conservation, the group pitched in to give fence-sitting Congressmen and cabinet members "the treatment" at lavish dinners. Clearly, the tactics were elitist, but given the political realities, they represent an effective and necessary maneuvering for conservation.

As adventurer and editor, George Bird Grinnell served as a bridge between East and West, between preservationists and utilitarians, between the aspirations of the privileged and those of ordinary citizens. Born in the year of the California Gold Rush, he went West with a different vision of riches, one that sustained him throughout his long life. Plagued in later years by a debilitating heart condition, Grinnell outlived his closest friends, the Indian chiefs and Army scouts of the frontier. He died at the age of eighty-eight, lonely and nearly forgotten.

Theodore Roosevelt. "Let us rather run the risk of wearing out than rusting out." He led the charge for conservation.

Theodore Roosevelt Collection, Harvard College Library

Chapter 7

Theodore Roosevelt: Leading the Charge for Conservation

A month before Christmas, 1902, Morris Michtom showed his wife a cartoon in a New York newspaper. It caricatured a stalwart President Theodore Roosevelt sparing the life of a bewildered bear cub. Mrs. Michtom made several replicas of the bear and displayed them in the window of their Brooklyn candy store. In a few years the stuffed animal was accompanying thousands of children to bed, a symbol of the righteous—some would argue the word should be "self-righteous"—leader of the nation.

Far more persistent than any emblem since dreamed up by straining politicos, the Teddy Bear and the legend behind it represent Theodore Roosevelt's appeal to the ordinary citizen. At the height of T. R.'s popularity, a visiting Englishman observed that "Roosevelt is not an American, you know. He is America." Attempting to explain the President's giddy support, another man—known to be sane in other respects—blurted out his reaction to a Roosevelt speech: "Roosevelt bit me and I went mad."

Born in 1858 to one of New York City's patrician families, young Teedie, as his parents called him, attended

Harvard, where he first considered the sciences, then decided on a life in politics, in order "to do something to help the cause of better government." His rise to become the youngest President of the United States followed a course not exceptional in itself: state legislator, U.S. Civil Service Commissioner, Chief of the New York Police Commission, Assistant Secretary of the Navy, Army officer, Governor of New York, and Vice-President. But Teddy Roosevelt brought luster to each rung of the political ladder. He saw himself as guardian of virtues that were according America the position of the world's leading nation, and he dashed about with a vitality that made virtue seem exciting rather than stuffy.

His famous charge on horseback up San Juan Hill during the Spanish-American War was no more brilliant or brave than the unsung exploits of men in hundreds of other battles in the country's military history. However, to the reporters who always dogged him, eager for the lively copy he generated, the robust New Yorker—his pistol drawn, shouting encouragement to his troops, polka-dotted kerchief flapping rakishly from his sombrero—seemed the paradigm of a leader with "the fighting edge," who could guide America in its world supremacy. "Let my men through!" he demanded to a hesitant officer crouched among soldiers of another company. After the battle, Roosevelt announced, "We have had a bully fight." And his Rough Riders, many of them Western gamblers and saddle-worn cowboys who could tell a faker from the real McCoy, cheered him. To them, and to much of the nation reading about its new war hero, he was the embodiment of manly virtue. Some years later when he led the country in its first national campaign for conservation on the Presidential level, he did it with the same forceful energy, with the same sense of crusading righteousness, as when he dodged through the bullets up San Juan Hill.

"Look," moaned one Republican boss, "that damned cowboy is president of the United States.
Theodore Roosevelt Collection, Harvard College Library

On the other hand, a dramatic lifestyle presents a large target for detractors. Roosevelt's short stature, spectacles, New York accent, and sometimes outlandish dress drew satiric chuckles. Added to these objects of ridicule, both political parties of the time were riddled with corruption, typified by the skullduggery of the Democrat's Tammany Hall organization and by the Republican bossism of financiers Jay Gould, James J. Hill, and J. P. Morgan. Roosevelt entered politics during an era when young Turks were mounting strenuous attacks against the self-seeking leaders of his Republican Party. By pressing for sweeping reforms, they guaranteed a constant struggle for anyone attempting to hold the GOP together.

T. R.'s heart was with the reformers. Using his famous trustbusting "Big Stick," he translated idealism into changes for the public good: restraining the steel and railroad monopolies that were choking their competition and gouging consumers. He accompanied these actions with words that warmed the heart of the common man: "I do intend, so far as in me lies, to see that the rich man is held to the same accountability as the poor man." However, the captains of industry held the party's purse strings, forcing Roosevelt at one point to accept J. P. Morgan's campaign check for $150,000. Blustering Roosevelt, for all his rhetoric, knew when to tread lightly in order to stay in the political arena.

If Roosevelt's enforced dance of compromise on the home front left him open to charges of hypocrisy, in his foreign policy he rarely dissembled—though this policy caused liberals, who were often pacifists, to grind their teeth at their sometime hero. For all its granted drawbacks, Roosevelt praised Western society's civilization as the ultimate good. Having said that, he shouldered the white man's burden to prepare the "backward" peoples of the Philippines, Puerto Rico, and Cuba for democracy—at the point of a gun if necessary. As a corollary of this world view, he recognized potential conflicts with other industrialized and expanding nations. To remind Germany, Japan, and Great Britain that might was on the side of right, he sent the nation's Great White Fleet of warships steaming around the world.

Whatever the political storms his boisterous policies at home and abroad fomented, one point needs to be kept in mind: the enormous popularity of these policies with the general public. "His flair and his integrity," writes biographer David Burton, "combined to give Roosevelt a variety of enemies, but they also provided him with a great many friends and admirers." Roosevelt's political stands matched the mood of a United States eager for reform within and expansion abroad.

His popularity often allowed the President to defy Congress and the traditional leaders within his own party, enabling him to hand conservationists, for decades standing on the fringes of political power, their first solid gains—perhaps the greatest gains they have ever made in one sweep. Seeing conservation as essential to his broad plans for domestic change, Roosevelt promoted it with the thundering rhetoric of the progressive idiom:

> We do not intend that our natural resources shall be exploited by the few against the interests of the many, nor do we intend to turn them over to any man who will wastefully use them by destruction, and leave to those who come after us a heritage damaged by just so much. Our aim is to preserve our natural resources for the public as a whole, for the average man and the average woman who make up the body of the American people.

There is irony in this bold position. Despite reformist tendencies, T. R. remained wary of what he deemed fanaticism. At one point he dubbed those who were ferreting out government improprieties as "muck-rakers," and at another he lumped Carl Schurz with the "loud-mouthed" proponents of reform. No doubt his penchant for orderly change stemmed from his patrician background. Then again, he became President after an anarchist shot William McKinley at Buffalo's Pan-American Exposition of 1901. He himself would know the horror of suddenly looking into an assassin's gun and of suffering a wound, if only a slight one, during his unsuccessful Presidential campaign of 1912. When it came to conservation, however, T. R. saw himself as the leader of a holy cause, and he pursued his goals with much the same fervor he occasionally ridiculed in the proponents of other reforms.

He had always loved the outdoors. His father, a founder of the American Museum of Natural History, instilled fascination for nature in his son. Nine-year-old Teedie worked in his bedroom assembling bird nests and seashells into his own Roosevelt Museum of Natural History. The boy became an avid bird lover, an amateur naturalist, who took time out from politics to travel the world, sending back specimens for the Smithsonian and the U.S. Biological Survey. A bright and active youngster, he faced a future marred by asthma, but he overcame the debility by boxing, wrestling, and long exercise in the outdoors, thus establishing "The Strenuous Life," as he later termed it in a famous speech, as his ideal.

As a rancher in North Dakota, he hunted buffalo, caught thieves, subdued bullies, and once stood off a menacing band of Indians. These were adventures to write home about, the excitements of a young city man savoring the Wild West. More significantly, in the West he witnessed "at first hand," says James Trefethen, "the ripening of the bitter fruits of unwise land use." A lover of danger and the hunt, he founded the Boone and Crockett Club, an organization of wealthy Easterners devoted to preserving habitat for big game. But most important to his conservation policies was his association with a man ready with a program that would turn into national projects the President's longings to preserve nature.

Rarely in the history of the country has there been a relationship as close, as symbiotic—and as effective for conservation—as that between T. R. and Gifford Pinchot. Some seven years younger than the President, Pinchot also came from a patrician and influential family; he was also a reformer, a lover of the strenuous physical and moral life, a champion of the underdog. Serving as the "unofficial crown prince" of the Roosevelt administration, he walked, talked, galloped, and swam with the President on boyish outings—deftly fielding the Chief Executive's badly swatted tennis balls, all the while maintaining the relationship of protege to mentor, but reinforcing the President's values, offering suggestions, ultimately giving shape to many of his conservation policies.

For all the self-serving that one might read into it, the friendship was genuine, characterized by mutual admiration. Roosevelt reflected on Pinchot's "fearlessness, his complete disinterestedness, his single-minded devotion to the interests of the plain people," and concluded that "Among the many, many public officials who under my administration rendered literally invaluable service to the people of the United States, he, on the whole, stood first."

In later years there would be sharp differences that caused pain between the two men, but puritanical Pinchot glowed through the heady Presidential days with his hero, who, much to the younger man's satisfaction, rarely drank, didn't smoke, and limited his profanity to an occasional "By Godfrey!" As noted earlier, some people made light of such habits. To emphasize T. R.'s extreme propriety in language—in contrast to his bullishness in other matters—Henry Pringle recounts a time during roundup when "two hardened cowboys nearly fell from their saddles" when rancher "Roosevelt called in his high voice to one of the men: 'Hasten forward quickly there!' " Years after Roosevelt gave up ranching, the command survived, repeated as a mock battle cry across the bars and ranges of the Bad Lands. But whatever guffaws Roosevelt suffered from cowpunchers and, later, from political satirists, in the judgment of Pinchot and most of the nation, the mannerisms reflected a goodness that went all the way through the man: "He said and he believed that the public good comes first, and he practiced his belief." And that's what counted most of all, for Pinchot and for conservation.

A missionary's drive powered both men. However, though Pinchot applauded T. R.'s general reforms, he wasn't about to see the President's energies diverted from his own foremost goal. A remarkable example of single-mindedness, Pinchot all his wealthy life had schooled himself to promote a rational forest policy and, once established, to become its federal administrator. After an education at Yale and then at the National Forestry School in Nancy, France, young Pinchot returned to this country to hang out his shingle in New York City as the nation's first native-born forester. Because to most Americans the country's woodlands still seemed unlimited, and hence in no need of care, business was poor—Pinchot gave away his consulting services in the hope of proving the need for them. His break came when Frederick Law Olmsted suggested him as the manager of Biltmore Forest, the North Carolina estate of financier George W. Vanderbilt. With his keen eye for publicity, the young forester advertised his Biltmore successes with a display at the Chicago World's Fair.

In the meantime, urged by Pinchot, Roosevelt, and the American Forestry Association, President Benjamin Harrison in 1891 had quietly established 13 million acres of Western forest reserves, the beginning of the present national forest system. Five years later when the Secretary of Interior asked for guidance in administering this vast tract, Pinchot joined the National Forest Commission, its youngest but most experienced member. Then, when the directorship of the Department of Agriculture's Forest Division fell vacant, Pinchot presented himelf, a natural for the job. He soon turned the obscure group of statisticians into a campaigning agency of change—just when Roosevelt was emerging as a national reform leader.

Even before Theodore Roosevelt, suddenly promoted by an assassin's bullet from Vice-President to Chief Executive, could move his stuffed buffalo heads into the White House, his old friend Pinchot was camped on his doorstep, waiting with a detailed and badly needed plan for the federal timberlands. Pinchot's program, the new President realized, would translate his morality into concrete results; by controlling rampant timber corporations, it would also dovetail with his projected campaigns against monopolies. Further, T. R. reveled in Pinchot's style of assertive righteousness. Together they schemed to end the evils of natural resource waste. Roosevelt, chortled Pinchot, was for the program, "horse, foot, and dragoons." Yet, as always in government, the two schemers had to deal with political realities.

"Look," moaned one Republican boss, "that damned cowboy is President of the United States!" Traditional leaders, financially supported by the freewheeling timber industry, shifted in their seats as the new President preached in his first State of the Union message that "The preservation of our forests is an imperative business necessity"—words Pinchot had penned into the speech. In essence, they proposed what Interior Secretary Carl Schurz had unsuccessfully urged on Congress two decades before, a plan since advocated by a growing number of conservationists: scientific management that would result in sustained-yield forestry on federal lands. This goal would be achieved by expansion of the forest reserve system and by the creation of a national forest service to manage it.

Yet Roosevelt moved with caution. He was, after all, President by accident, with all the political uncertainties his position entailed. Furthermore, for him to carry out Pinchot's ideas, the forest reserves would have to be transferred from the Department of Interior to Pinchot's Department of Agriculture. The move would generate opposition that the new President, feeling his way and eyeing the next election, wished to avoid. Pinchot would have to bide his time, but meanwhile the "unofficial crown prince" scurried about behind the scenes to prepare the way, "laying pipe," as he put it, for the expected change.

In 1904 the largest wave of support ever recorded for a Presidential candidate swept colorful T. R. back into office. A year later Congress bowed to his popularity by upgrading Pinchot's Forestry Division to the U.S. Forest Service and transferring the reserves to the new agency's control. Now, with the machinery for conservation firmly in place, T. R. and Pinchot set a new goal: to add millions of acres to the system.

However satisfied conservationists were at this point, the youthful Forest Service, with its tough and unprecedented regulations, raised howls of discontent from people

The debut of the Teddy Bear. Soon thousands of children were dragging the stuffed toy to bed. It represented Roosevelt's appeal to the ordinary citizen.

Theodore Roosevelt Collection, Harvard College Library

accustomed to a free hand in exploitation. To add to the growing confusion, T. R. made one of his few obvious and still rather puzzling political mistakes—he announced that he would not run for reelection. The news weakened his leverage with a Congress becoming difficult to move. In the meantime, the two conservationists in the White House enjoyed a spree of setting aside national forests from public lands. One Western newspaper lamented that soon "There would be little ground left to bury folks on." Alarmed and increasingly hostile Congressmen began their own schemes to undo the runaway T. R.-Pinchot team.

They did it in the usual Congressional way—by tightening the purse strings on the Forest Service. They also passed legislation taking away the President's power to create forests by decree. Roosevelt wisely didn't wish to worsen the situation by using the veto, but he had another card to play. He and Pinchot pulled out their maps of the public domain, and in the ten days given a President to sign legislation, they burned the midnight oil, carving out twenty-one new forests with enthusiastic swipes of their pens—"midnight forests" grumbled the opposition. All in all, during his career Roosevelt set aside some 148 million acres of national forest—a huge total, one well over four times the size of his native New York.

As a forward-looking scientist and unblushing patriot, Gifford Pinchot represented the utilitarian wing of conservation. To him, and to the majority of early activists, conservation meant the use of resources in ways that would guarantee the republic's future prosperity. While granting the necessity and good sense of the approach, other people concerned about nature were pained by its narrowness. Men such as John Muir saw nature as worthwhile in its own right, possessing scientific and spiritual values beyond economics, which cried for absolute preservation. Thus the preservationists, as they have been labeled, often found themselves in opposition to the nation's chief forester.

As much as he was under the influence of Gifford Pinchot, Teddy Roosevelt was not a slave to his lieutenant's outlook. He had a broader vision of the natural world. The man who lectured Congress about the "imperative business necessity" of conservation could also gaze in wonder over the Grand Canyon and say, "Leave it as it is. You can not improve on it. The ages have been at work on it, and man can only mar it." As a result, T. R. set the country on a dual course of wise use and preservation.

Having introduced conservation through the front door of politics by stressing the benefits of good business practices—an approach that Congressmen and governors, always attuned to money matters, could readily understand—the President swept past a puzzled Pinchot to establish a record in preserving nature that rivals his comprehensive endeavors in the causes of practical forestry, land reclamation, and water development. Responding to the need for wildlife protection, he promoted hunting regulation and created America's first federal wildlife refuge on Florida's Pelican Island. He so relished the new idea that he proclaimed some fifty additional reserves that now dot the map from Alaska to Puerto Rico. To stem the looting of archaeological sites on public lands, he supported passage of the Antiquities Act of 1906; then under its provisions he created sixteen national monuments totaling 1.4 million acres. And while trying to keep Pinchot busy with his new Forest Service, he further gladdened the preservationists by approving five national parks—more multiple millions of acres set aside as national treasures.

"We are face to face with our destiny," Roosevelt thundered to the country at a time when destiny seemed a prize to be grasped by the strong, "and we must meet it with a high and resolute courage. For us is the life of action, of strenuous performance of duty; let us rather run the risk of wearing out than rusting out." It was an age when power, abruptly applied, rather than complex negotiations, carried the day and seemed to ensure the future.

Historians debate heatedly over the wisdom of many of T. R.'s brusque policies. But as far as conservation is concerned, Teddy Roosevelt emerged at precisely the right time—when the abuses to the natural heritage had gone on long enough to appear criminal to many Americans, yet when sufficient public land still remained to be saved by a strong-willed President. Teddy Roosevelt thus was able to accomplish what had eluded Carl Schurz: he placed conservation in the realm of official government policy. However, environmental victories are never inviolate. As activists soon realized, the federal bureaucracy's stewardship of nature could be a mixed blessing.

William T. Hornaday. "A man with clipped beard and flashing eyes," as one historian described Hornaday. Another observer sighed, "He delights in a row." New York Zoological Society

Chapter 8

William T. Hornaday:
Warrior for Wildlife

"Just what is the nature of the next raw deal that the Furies have in store for the harassed game of this nation, only the devil knows," railed William T. Hornaday in a typically acid outburst. "Perhaps it will be the wholesale slaughtering of game en masse with poison gas. Perhaps for masses of ducks and geese at rest it will be a sportsmanlike form of the Lewis machine gun. Quien sabe?"

Patient, polite, and steady prodding by reasonable men and women have characterized decades of environmental progress, but not all conservationists reflect the gentleness of a John Burroughs or the liberal refinement of a George Bird Grinnell. As activists have slowly come to realize, under some circumstances a militant approach is the only one that works. Militancy reached its full expression during the years following Rachel Carson's pesticide revelations in the early 1960s. But its forerunner was a man who had been dead and largely ignored for thirty years, and a man not wholly admirable.

With William Temple Hornaday one learns to accept the good with the bad. He divided the world into two categories: friends and enemies. Friends were those who agreed with him absolutely. All others — including those who questioned even the fine points of his programs — were prey to be hunted down, cornered, and verbally cut to pieces with the ruthlessness of one who perceives himself as the hero of a sacred war. This self-righteous stance appealed to those who wished to see causes in simplistic terms. Yet conservation issues, as numerous as they were, could not absorb all of Hornaday's bounding energies. At different times he thundered against aliens, Jews, Germans, Bolsheviks, and those who consumed alcoholic beverages. Conservation's leaders blushed at his over-zealous and often unjust attacks. They breathed easily only after his death in 1937, whereupon they allowed him to slip into an obscurity that fails to credit his substantial contributions, some of them cornerstones to conservation and natural history.

Hornaday made an eighty-three-year career of bragging. Born in 1854 amid humble circumstances on an Indiana farm, he traveled at an early age by wagon to the family's new homestead on an Iowa prairie. To hear him recount his life, it was as if Providence had chosen to lead the clodhopping farmboy down the "corridor of time" to create "masterpieces" of stuffed birds and buffalo, then to go on to become the director of the famous Bronx Zoo, whose collection of animals was not only "the largest in the world" but also a kind of "earthy paradise."

Entering Iowa State College, he soon became "crazy," as he put it, to learn how to mount animals. But the course offerings were limited at the provincial school. "Knowledge *is* power," he later admonished readers by way of explaining his decision to seek professional training in taxidermy at Ward's Museum, in Rochester, New York.

There Professor Henry Augustus Ward made good use of his new student's developing talents and frothy enthusiasm. In 1874 the professor launched the former farmboy on a series of world-wide collecting tours. Hornaday ignored the annoyances of disease, glum native helpers, and headhunting tribes. Often alone, still in his early twenties, the ebullient youth plunged into the jungles of South America and Asia on "a glorious orgy" of shooting elephants, pythons, and tigers. He emerged several years later with crate on crate of "zoological riches," as he described them. They indeed formed one of the most comprehensive collections of the day. Raised on the fictional success stories of Horatio Alger, the public thrilled as it read through ten editons of *Two Years in the Jungle* (1885), Hornaday's enthusiastic report of one portion of his real-life adventures.

It was the beginning of a long career marked by self-generated fame and practical accomplishments in several fields. Often the two went hand in hand. Hornaday's budding renown won him the position of chief taxidermist at the National Museum in Washington, D.C. The realities he faced contrasted with his youthful vision. Although by the end of the nineteenth century the sciences were taking a prominent place in an increasingly technological society, a museum-related studies languished in ignorance and hidebound tradition. Despite the efforts of Professor Ward's school, at the time perhaps only twenty men in the entire nation could mount specimens with skill approaching artistry. In constrast to the airy and informative institutions of today, museums were warehouses crammed helter-skelter with dusty artifacts. The few zoos that existed kept their arbitrary selections of despondent animals in small iron cages.

Ambitious Hornaday set out to rejuvenate the whole field, to make museums and zoos lifelike, useful, and accessible to the general public. Looking upon taxidermy as an educative art, he created three-dimensional displays of animals in natural settings, giving a "verisimilitude of free wild life." Reflecting on Hornaday's contributions, a colleague praised the innovations as "perhaps the first of the great habitat exhibits" that now grace America's museums.

His work in starting a department of living animals at the National Museum so impressed members of the Smithsonian Institution that they asked Hornaday to oversee planning a zoological park. Congress appropriated nearly $300,000 for the new enterprise, but as the blueprints worked their way through the bureaucratic mill, others altered Hornaday's concepts. In 1890 he resigned in a huff.

For the next six years Hornaday sold real estate in Buffalo, New York, but he couldn't get museums out of his blood. From Buffalo came a badly needed text, *Taxidermy and Zoological Collecting* (1891). A few years later the New York Zoological Society offered him the prospect of creating a zoo from the ground up, and he took the job. This time he had a free hand in "the greatest effort of my life — at imperial New York," the "wonder city of the world." He went on to rhapsodize: "The size of the New York Opportunity of 1896 was sufficient to inspire one anew, one more chance to bring the lives and personalities of thousands of interesting wild animals within reach of millions of people! And that was the Big Object." Turning his views of grandeur into realities, Hornaday developed the Bronx Zoo into a monument of integrated planning.

He laid out buildings and grounds for the maximum education and comfort of the public — which in turn had the pleasure of viewing a spectacular variety of healthy wildlife in natural surroundings. As the director observed without a hint of humility, "The New York Zoological Park is an object lesson of which many American cities may well take heed." For once, Hornaday underestimated his achievement. The vision that he worked to improve until his retirement in 1926 set a standard not only for similar institutions in the United States but for many around the world.

Granted his stamp on the developing science of "museology," as Hornaday liked to call it, his accomplishments in conservation were far greater. The country's first forester, Gifford Pinchot, dominated the movement at the turn of the century with his efforts to create a vast system of national forests. Forceful and enterprising Pinchot, however, had a blind spot, one shared by many other conservation activists of the time. He dreamed of government-managed forests producing timber ad infinitum, the backbone of the country's economic prosperity. But for all the board feet of timber that crowded Pinchot's vision, he couldn't see the wildlife that lived in his woodlands. For him the birds, bear, deer, and lions that had made forests their homes for thousands of years hardly existed.

Thus even as the national forests were taking shape, wildlife populations sank to low ebbs. Still believing in the myth of abundance, Americans hunted for the last remnants of the buffalo, wolf, grizzly bear, elk, and several species of bird life. At the same time, the government was slowly turning federal lands over to private ownership for exploitation. Citizen organizations had begun setting aside wildlife preserves in the East, but their efforts necessarily were on a small scale. Urged by President Roosevelt, the government established a number of critical habitat refuges in the far West, but they fell far short of the need. Through over-hunting and habitat loss, the nation was about to lose a viable wildlife population.

As often happens in such a state of affairs, a reaction set in at the height of the crisis. Farmers once shot wild animals as pillagers of their crops. Moved by Hornaday's many books and educated by programs of the federal Biological Survey, some of them changed their minds. They now saw hawks and foxes as unwitting helpers in their battles against mice and insects. Hunters in-

creasingly recognized that their sport would soon end unless they cut down on their bag limits and provided breed-
ing grounds to insure a steady supply of flying and running targets. They were joined by the arms and ammunition manufacturers, who saw an abrupt end to profits with
the disappearance of game. But most forceful in the reaction was the general public. Sensitized by such writers as
John Muir, John Burroughs, and Ernest Thompson Seton,
citizens clamored against the demise of their wildlife heritage. As their spokesmen, such organizations as the National Association of Audubon Societies gave political
muscle to the movement to halt wildlife slaughter and to
create refuges.

Contrary to what he liked to think, William T. Hornaday did not single-handedly inspire the enlightened
policies coalescing in the first decades of this century,
though he did indeed become the "most active and, at
times, most acrimonious of American wildlife conservationists," as the *New York Times* wryly put it. If the first
purpose of the New York Zoological Society was scientific
collecting and study, "the protection of our native
animals" ran a close second. In hiring Hornaday as
director of its zoo, the Society sparked into action a campaigner who made the Bronx Zoo a world showplace. At
the same time he threw himself, over the remaining forty
years of his life, into conservation with a zeal that produced much heat and light — and often an obscuring
smoke.

Hornaday became a rallying point. Because of his in-
temperate nature and his penchant for drama and over-
statement, a ready public followed this colorful figure as
he spearheaded change. Historian of the conservation
movement James B. Trefethen, sums up the reasons for
the museum director's success: "A man of elegant appear-
ance, with clipped beard and flashing eyes, Hornaday was
a forceful speaker and persuasive writer, the ideal

crusader type. In his makeup there was no room for compromise, and he regarded any concession, even to logical
argument, as a sign of weakness." Piqued to action, many
citizens at this time felt there had been too many disastrous concessions — concessions responsible for the
downward wildlife spiral. Hornaday's flashing eyes and
forceful preachings embodied their determination. Trefethen describes one Hornaday fusillade at a wildlife bill
that used World War I as an excuse to liberalize bag limits:

> Hornaday moved in for the kill. This was the sort of
> rough-and-tumble verbal battle in which he was at
> his best. Rising to oratorical heights, he ended a pre
> pared attack on the bill with the words: "Sportsmen,
> rally round the flag! You know what market hunting
> did to game in the old days....

His flashing rhetoric consistently delighted reporters.
Trefethen attests that Hornaday "received more newspaper publicity than any other conservationist of his
time."

Yet public support and stirring speeches aren't always
enough. The Zoological Society depended on private fortunes for much of its support, and the Zoo's director made
good use of his contacts with the money concentrated in
the "wonder city of the world." To finance his campaigns,
in 1910 Hornaday created the Permanent Wild Life Protection Fund — an organization with one active member,
William T. Hornaday. With their generous checks, the
wealthy — who often harbored sentimental if mostly passive concerns for nature — could enlist in the ranks of "the
Army of Defense." The result, in Hornaday's words, was
that "money in good, round sums instantly began to flow."
At the end of the financial tide of just one year, the fund
overflowed with $51,980. All of it, as stated in the bylaws,
was to be spent at the discretion of one man: William T.
Hornaday. He was the envy of other conservationists
struggling to keep their activist organizations afloat with

nickle-and-dime contributions.

Hornaday knew how to keep the money flowing. His biennial statement eulogized supporters as saving America from becoming "as barren of wild mammals as the Sahara Desert!" To top off the flattery, the report featured full-page photographs of the major donors, praised as holding the "firing line" against the "enemies of wild life." And there were political advantages to Hornaday's fundraising. Congressmen not swayed by Hornaday's revivalist urgings received a compelling message with their complimentary copies of the statement — where the likes of powerful industrialist Andrew Carnegie glowered at them from its pages. Soon not only did bird-loving Henry Ford jump in with his check for $5,000; he also ordered one of his chief advertising men to forget about selling model T's and head for Washington to lobby for Hornaday-supported legislation. All the while, the Zoo director kept beating the drums for popular conservation support with informative, if at times frenetic, books: *The Extermination of the American Bison* (1889), *Our Vanishing Wildlife* (1913), and *Thirty Years War for Wild Life: Gains and Losses in the Thankless Task* (1931). The latter featured reproductions of awards, certificates, and medals lauding the savior of America's wild creatures, William T. Hornaday.

Due largely to Hornaday's efforts, the federal government launched a crash program to save the American bison. The success of the Wichita Wildlife Refuge in Oklahoma led to the creation of other preserves urged by Hornaday. By 1910, commercial hunting was about to push Alaska's fur seal into oblivion, when William T. Hornaday pounced upon the Department of Commerce with such violence that its Secretary begged the Zoological Society to call off its director. Hornaday, of course, only paused long enough to sink his teeth in a little deeper. A few months later the United States signed a treaty with

Hornaday inspired a crash program to save the American bison. Hornaday (at left) is sending a bison to the Wichita Wildlife Refuge in Oklahoma. The success of the refuge led to the creation of other preserves." New York Zoological Society

England, Russia, and Japan outlawing seal slaughter. Such Hornaday coups encouraged less bold activists to step from the wings and advocate other wildlife causes in desperate need of support.

Yet surprisingly, the fire-and-brimstone Hornaday concentrated most of his life energies not on championing the larger mammals — the bears and lions that approximated his own personality — but on bird species about to follow the passenger pigeon into extinction. In his often one-track mind, the villains of the crisis were hunters, "the Benedict Arnolds of conservation." He thundered to a public, as eager as a lynch mob for retribution, that an army of 7,500,000 — larger than the combined military forces of the entire world, he somehow calculated — marched out each year to blast away at helpless creatures. Himself a hunter with an impeccable code of sportsmanship, he branded others "game hogs." In his estimate, the greedy and ignorant class of hunter belonged to the "ten percent of the human race [consisting] of people who will lie, steal, throw rubbish in parks, and destroy wildlife whenever and wherever they can do so without being stopped by a policeman and a club." Having said this, he appointed himself chief constable and set about passing laws to control the lawless element.

His efforts coincided with the passage of state and federal regulations which, in the first two decades of this century, established the main outlines of today's wildlife laws. Among them are the Lacey Act, the Federal Tariff Act of 1913, and the McLain Bird Protection Bill, also known as the Migratory Bird Act. Such legislation scientifically designates open seasons, sets bag limits, outlaws the sale of game, and protects certain species from all hunting. Again, contrary to what he liked to believe, Hornaday was not solely responsible for the new laws or for public attitudes that demanded their passage. But he does deserve much credit for successful lobbying and for the tight legal language of the regulations.

For all his accomplishments, did Hornaday do more harm than good? Often his rage blinded him to good sense. As a writer for *The Commonweal* put it: "To the end his chief foes were the manufacturers of high-powered munitions, the bird-eating cat, and similar embodiments of evil unadulterate." He glowed as a sentimental public applauded his tirades against hunters. There is little doubt that unrestrained shooting took a deadly toll — and that the depredations of the domestic cat didn't help — but especially in his later years Hornaday glossed over the far more critical factor of habitat loss. His hatred of human enemies spilled over into the animal world. Predators — the golden eagle, coyotes, hawks, and owls — were Saracens to be eliminated with religious fervor. With what strikes many today as a sad lack of foresight, he said that the gray wolf "should always be killed. No danger of his extermination." Though many people at the time shared his division of the animal kingdom into "good" and "bad" species, this mistake is less excusable in zoologist Hornaday.

Besides his own Permanent Wild Life Protection Fund, William T. Hornaday founded or helped support many organizations: The Boone and Crockett Club, the American Bison Society, and the Camp Fire Club. Yet his overbearing personality alienated many members, and his uncompromising positions caused internal furors that split an emerging conservation movement in need of unity. Along with other staunch wildlife supporters, George Bird Grinnell, editor of *Forest and Stream,* eventually threw up his hands after years of trying to work with Hornaday. "He delights in a row,"moaned Grinnell.

On the other hand, *Science* magazine reminded readers at his death that "behind the hundreds of admirers who attended his final services stand the mute inhabitants of our forests and uplands, who found in him a stout-hearted and able defender." Some times call for a cantankerous personality such as Hornaday's to raise the more disagreeable questions — and to insist that they be addressed — an extremist who can stir up the public. Whatever may be said of the campaigner's excesses, he produced results when reforms were badly needed. Probably anything less than the stormy Hornaday would not have been enough.

Benton MacKaye, the thinker behind the creation of the
Appalachian Trail. Harvey Broome, courtesy of *The Living Wilderness*

Chapter 9

Benton MacKaye:
The Reinvasion by Nature

Like a king expanding his domain, in 1905 Gifford Pinchot sent small teams around the country to report back on
potential lands for his new Forest Service. The leader of
one of these explorations, young Benton MacKaye (the
name rhymes with sky), just that year had received a
master's degree in forestry from Harvard University.
Knapsacks strapped to backs, MacKaye's three-man ex-
peditionary force tramped through New Hampshire's
White Mountains. After a summer of investigating New
England's backyard hinterland, the men reported to
Washington that the White Mountain range played a
major role in protecting New Hampshire's water resources
and thus deserved inclusion in Pinchot's national forest
system.

Their finding may strike us as obvious today, but at the
turn of the century the complexities of ecosystems were
little studied and even less understood. Further, the report represented a wedge for establishing national forests
in the East. Though he didn't realize it at the time, Mac-
Kaye was coming to the aid of the Chaplain of the U.S.

Senate, a spokesman for thousands of Easterners.

In the same year as MacKaye's unheralded study, Reverend Edward Everett Hale reminisced, "I have slept under pine trees which were high, tall, beautiful pine trees when North America was discovered." He continued sadly, "I went up through the same region two years ago with a friend, and found my pine trees all gone and sumac and blackberry bushes in their places. It makes a man cry to see it."

Reverend Hale was remembering the New England he had wandered through as a boy, its forests invaded by loggers, its pristine wildness nearly gone by 1905, a loss felt throughout the heavily populated Eastern United States. A newspaper in Wheeling, West Virginia, lamented over the surrounding mountains, charred by fires that inevitably followed the axemen: "The havoc is calculated to fill a lover of the woods with dismay... nothing but a dreary wreck." The predictions of George Perkins Marsh had become reality; it seemed that industrialization would dismantle nearly all of nature in the East.

Early conservationists, often an elite band of two factions, advocating either forest or wildlife reform, had laid the groundwork for change. But despite the sense of loss in New England and West Virginia, the ordinary citizen of the crowded Eastern seaboard found it difficult to feel a personal stake in fights to establish national forests among the peaks of the Rockies or to save egrets in Florida's gloomy swamps. Over the years, a third group slowly emerged to fill the psychological gap and add a new dimension to the conservation movement.

Americans have always been an outdoor people. Having conquered and severely disrupted nature, they next developed a different enthusiasm for it. They looked to nearby hills and broad river valleys for entertainment, exercise, scientific study, and spiritual sustenance. By the 1850s summit houses dotted the rounded mountaintops of the Northeast. Honeymooners and holidayers bounced over crude roads to the "tiptop" hotels or later rode up in style on a cog railway to wonder at the panoramas of nature below them.

Other people walked. They spread out over the countryside, eager for fresh air and weekend respite from their work in dingy factory towns. Some of them were seeking more ethereal renewal in the woods, where Emerson's nature-centered and popular transcendental philosophy promised a spiritual mirror of themselves. Whatever the motives behind it, the vogue spawned hiking societies. The oldest of these, the Appalachian Mountain Club, with headquarters in Boston, was founded in 1876, to be followed by the Green Mountain Club and the Dartmouth Outing Club. Easterners also took their enthusiasm with them when they moved West. In 1892, activist and explorer John Muir gathered several men into a San Francisco law office to incorporate the Sierra Club. Its motto reflected the new impulse spreading across the nation: "to explore, enjoy, and preserve" the country's wild lands.

The hiking movement in fact was a rediscovery of the American hinterland, one far gentler than the first wave of settlement and exploitation. Volunteers spent weekends and summer holidays axing out trails through the underbrush, constructing shelters, and delivering scientific lectures on their adventures in the new-found countryside. The enthusiasm also opened the public's eyes to a relationship with nature characterized by generations of ignorance and abuse. "We discover a thing by losing it," Benton MacKaye would later observe. What the hikers, amateur scientists, and spiritual seekers soon realized as they escaped New York City and Boston to shoulder their packs up and down the trails they had built — trails that often passed through expanses blighted by logging, forest fires, and spreading suburbs — was that they were quickly losing the woodlands and wildlife they were just beginning to appreciate.

Thus they saw that to enjoy also meant to preserve. Yet while activists in the nation's capital pored over maps of the West to set aside huge blocks of public real estate as federal forests, parks, and wildlife refuges, this approach would not work in the populous East. There the government owned little unoccupied land, a bleak situation that resulted in a bold move. In the East the land would have to be bought back by the government — an obvious but extraordinary proposal for the time, one that raised strenuous objections. Some Congressmen huffed that they wouldn't spend one penny from the federal coffers for mere scenery. But the public, largely inspired by the hikers and supported by such diverse organizations as the Daughters of the American Revolution, garden clubs, and local chambers of commerce, raised such an outcry for saving America's beauty that in 1911 a jolted Congress passed legislation sponsored by Representative John Wingate Weeks of Massachusetts.

One of the most significant acts for preserving countryside in the East, the Weeks Forest Protection Law satisfied a legal technicality by purporting to carry out the government's mandate for watershed protection, the very impulse behind Benton MacKaye's survey of the White Mountains. Beyond that, the law's provisions laid the basis for a much wider accomplishment: the system of preserved lands that Easterners now enjoy. Ironically, a saddening factor favored land acquisition. Because abuses had left much of the East almost worthless for commercial development, the land came cheap. In Michael Frome's words, "Farming was almost impossible because of stream and soil erosion, and the mountains had been thoroughly cut and burned over and lay in waste and ruin." Organizing "save a tree" campaigns, public-spirited citizens bought what the government couldn't purchase under the guidelines of the Weeks Law.

Despite their effectiveness in linking preservation with patriotism through their skill in inspiring schoolchildren to contribute their pennies, even in enlisting help from the National Association of Manufacturers, for the most part hiking clubs remained local organizations striving to protect nearby natural treasures. To sustain momentum with Congress and to gain publicity from national magazines and maintain public interest, any movement needs wide appeal and a specific national goal. This was provided by an unusual, one might say eccentric, Yankee, a practical dreamer and spiritual descendant of Thoreau — the same Benton MacKaye who began his long and varied career as one of Gifford Pinchot's foresters.

Musing over a map of the new preserves, MacKaye noted their location along the crest of the East's spine, the rolling Appalachian Mountains, within relatively easy access of city residents. Local hikers had established trails over some portions. Why not, he asked himself, connect the sections already built and extend them through new territory to create the nation's first hiking trail on a truly grand scale? It would be a "wilderness trail," as Tom Floyd of the Potomac Appalachian Trail Club now describes it, where urban dwellers "could renew their link to the wild spaces."

The public was ripe for the idea when MacKaye published "An Appalachian Trail: A Project in Regional Planning" in the October 1921 issue of the *Journal of the American Institute of Architects*. Within a year, Boy Scouts finished the first official section, over New York's Bear Mountain. By 1937 the world's longest designated hiking trail was complete. Enjoyed by millions of people since then, the trail begins on Mt. Katahdin, in Maine, winds through fourteen states, and ends 2,031 miles to the south on Georgia's Springer Mountain. Established in 1925, and centrally based in Washington, D.C., the Appalachian Trail Conference coordinates maintenance and

Hiking societies added a new dimension to the conservation movement. Benton MacKaye (in the foreground with a knapsack) helped give them wide appeal and a national goal.
Harvey Broome, courtesy of *The Living Wilderness*

preservation of the federal, state, and private lands through which it passes. Outdoor enthusiasts, wryly comments Lewis Mumford, have accomplished "by purely voluntary cooperation and love what the empire of the Incas had done in the Andes by compulsory organization."

The Appalachian Trail, then, represents a culmination of conservation awareness in the East, and it remains a focus for oudoor pleasures as well as a rallying point. Over the years, droves of desk-bound volunteers from Eastern cities have gladly broken the urban pace with backpacking holidays and stints on maintenance crews. And these same men and women have felt personally affronted whenever subdivisions and spreading freeways threatened their outdoor bailiwick. They have written thousands of letters to Congressmen and turned out en masse at public meetings to protect the forests of the Appalachian Trail. Thus, as David Brower of Friends of the Earth puts it, the hiking movement has "built battalions of people who care. Without those people, there might have been no solitude at all."

But what about the second half of MacKaye's 1921 proposal, "A Project in Regional Planning?" It would add, belatedly, a fourth dimension to conservation. George Perkins Marsh, F. L. Olmsted, Carl Schurz, and Teddy Roosevelt had urged society to recognize the need to bring its demands in line with the limited resources of the planet. By the 1920s and 1930s an ecological crisis seemed imminent to a second generation of planners. Such men as Aldo Leopold, Lewis Mumford, and Benton MacKaye not only proposed nationwide programs of social change but banded into organizations to carry this out. Still, as Mumford stated it, twentieth-century America remained unwilling to face "the problem of living on the land it had already settled." As MacKaye described the needed shift of perspective: "Our early settlers first planted civilization by inroads of population through the forest; we today, in order to restore civilization, must develop forest inroads...." MacKaye's Appalachian Trail, then, was only one element in a scheme to launch a "counterinvasion" against freewheeling industrialization. His goal was nothing less than to save America.

"Bah," protested "The Father of the Appalachian Trail" to the promptings of one interviewer a few years before MacKaye's death in 1975, "my personal life isn't important. I am interested in ideas." The wily Yankee didn't like to discuss the background that shaped his thinking far more than he was willing to admit.

His father, Steele MacKaye, enjoyed the reputation of being one of the country's leading actors and playwrights.

A schoolmate of novelist Henry James and the painter Winslow Homer, he began his bohemian career at the age of fourteen by running away from his wealthy parents to study art in Paris. His frenetically romantic career, highlighted by the compulsion to gamble — and lose — huge sums of money on grandiose plans, titillated Victorian society. Philosopher William James remembered Steele MacKaye as "effervescing with incoordinated romantic ideas of every description." The actor, still pursuing his elusive dreams, died of nervous exhaustion in Timpas, Colorado.

Son Benton determined to avoid such pitfalls. His life proved a modified version of his father's — he controlled the eccentricities that accompanied the elder MacKaye's originality. Paul T. Bryant summarizes the influence: "Young Benton early reacted against the mercurial impracticality of his idealistic father, but he absorbed his father's vision of improving society. The result for Benton was an Emersonian idealism grounded in a Thoreauvian appreciation of practical ways and means."

Born in 1879 in Stamford, Connecticut, Benton spent his first decade tailing his actor father from city to city. But the MacKayes ended the rigors of the theater's peripatetic life by making Shirley Center, Massachusetts — located only twenty miles from Walden Pond and Thoreau's former bean patch — a home base for the family. It was a thoroughly rural New England town, just being discovered as a refuge by artists and intellectuals. Imagining himself a latter-day Humboldt, young MacKaye, like Olmsted in his boyhood, spent free time exploring the fields and mountains surrounding his home. And as was also true of Olmsted, the synthesis of community and rural life in the New England village — the quiet harmony of farm, country store, and town hall — became MacKaye's ideal for the nation.

Concentrating on his own ideas, Benton MacKaye

avoided his father's continuing financial turmoil by ignoring money matters. From 1905 until his retirement in 1945, he worked variously and sporadically for the Forest Service, Department of Labor, Indian Service, Tennessee Valley Authority, and the Rural Electrification Administration. As did Robert Marshall, he strove to open bureaucratic eyes with innovative approaches to related social and environmental problems arising from industrialization. At times — as when the Forest Service consented to the country's first wilderness area in 1924; or later, when President Franklin Roosevelt implemented plans to rehabilitate both the people and the lands of Appalachia through the TVA — the government seemed to be listening to such thinkers as MacKaye. However, despite an initial flurry of hope, government agencies seemed unable to make the imaginative leaps necessary to come to grips with new problems. In MacKaye's view, federal programs reacted to, rather than anticipated, crises. Despite government efforts, cities deteriorated, the automobile proliferated, and precious cropland continued to blow away in the Dust Bowl.

MacKaye took the course of many prophets rejected in their own time. Periodically rebuffed and discouraged during his stints with the government, he withdrew to rural Shirley Center. There, surrounded by a helter-skelter of notebooks and clippings in his shabby Victorian home heated by a potbellied stove, he thought and wrote, ever hopeful and engrossed as he refined his plans to shape America's future. As to everyday needs, he drew on his savings, and when these ran low, he lived, according to fellow planner and friend Lewis Mumford, "like the Biblical prophet, off what the ravens brought."

It would be a mistake, however, to characterize Mac-Kaye solely as a twentieth-century, self-reliant, New England hermit. True, his eccentricities amused friends, who noted that he kept a Mood Chart — and that he washed his dishes precisely at 2:30 p.m., so that the day's bleakest task would correspond with the low ebb of his emotional cycle. The extreme fear of dogs in a man who could outgrin a bear in the wilds caused additional chuckles. A fellow activist remembers: "He would meet our well-behaved pet with such a purposefully booming affectionate greeting (Gude Dawg! Gude Dawg!) that she would slink away to hide."

The other side of his personality was a "warm and generous spirit," marked by readiness for banter and the love of good food and drink shared with companions. Out on backpacking trips, MacKaye led the singing — and dancing — around the camp fire. The little band of planners with which he associated could break out of its serious thinking with unpredictable ebullience. An official of the TVA recalls that "we once danced 'Little Old Log Cabin in the Lane' on the passenger platform of the Southern Railway station in Knoxville while waiting to see Benton off on one of his infrequent trips to Washington." Certainly, much of the group's energy came from frustration; but the joie de vivre also arose from its sense of being involved with planning for a future just possibly made brighter through its efforts.

A German, Oswald Spengler, had caused a shiver to run through Western civilization with his *Der Untergang des Abendlandes (The Decline of the West)*. World War I was finishing its paroxysms, and many intellectuals, having little faith that the conflict had ended all wars, could really believe the book's main thesis — that like years passing through their seasons, all civilizations go through a sequence of spring, summer, autumn, and winter. According to the book, the Western world was in its winter, its death throes. Spengler pointed particularly to one symptom of the slow demise: overgrown, unmanageable cities. He noted the history of ancient Rome and Carthage and the decay of modern metropolises. The comparison seemed to confirm his gloomy conclusion.

Basically, MacKaye agreed with Spengler's analysis, as far as it went. MacKaye, however, held out hope. If a society could understand the reasons for enervation, it could then act on this knowledge to short-circuit the cycle and begin the process of rebirth. The causes perceived neither by Rome or Carthage — nor by present-day New York or London — stemmed from environmental abuse, accelerated in the twentieth century by modern technology.

As with environmentalists before and since, Benton MacKaye saw technology as neither good nor bad in itself. The problems arose from its misuse and overuse — "How at once to do and not to overdo?" as he succinctly put it. Michael Frome states the approach: "Such Thoreauvian concepts imply no antagonism to progressive civilization, but rather its defense — defense from destruction in the jungles of formless, shapeless sprawl. . . ."

Thus one might look on MacKaye as a traditionalist rather than a radical. He wanted to defend the traditional American values of the pastoral dream — open space, social and environmental diversity, the abundance of resources resulting in prosperity and freedom of choice. In contrast, by the turn of the century the nation had struck out on a radical adventure, shifting from a rural to an urban society dominated by the automobile — a change with little concern for where the new direction would lead.

The New Englander foresaw the "wilderness of civilization" and the "slum of commerce." In reacton to the government's largely closed-eyes attitude toward the coming crises, in 1923 MacKaye joined the Regional Planning Association, an informal "group of insurgents." Living in or near New York City, these innovative "architects and planners, builders and rebuilders," as they called themselves, pondered how the nation might substitute "harmonious balance" for the recent "blind creation" of urban

America. Stimulated by his fellow thinkers, in fifty years of writing articles and books — particularly *The New Exploration* (1928) and *From Geography to Geotechnics* (1968) — Benton MacKaye outlined how the developing country could reverse the trend toward disaster. It could, if it chose, remodel "an unshapen and cacophonous environment into a humanized and well-ordered one."

Yankee simplicity and practicality typified MacKaye's thinking. In essence, it called for keeping wildness and technology separate so that society could enjoy the advantages of both. A founder of The Wilderness Society, its president for five years (1945-1950), and a member of its governing council for seventeen, MacKaye maintained that wild lands form a nation's basic resource, both economic and spiritual. Thus, he drew up maps designating additional mountain ranges and river systems to be preserved. These would protect the timber and watershed treasures on which city life depends. As inviolate preserves, they would form buffers between urban areas, limiting the unmanageable spread of cities one into another, while offering outdoor recreation to nearby population.

As to the cities themselves, the New Englander remembered the harmonious microcosm of Shirley Center and asserted, when few were listening, that when cities grow beyond a certain point, they defeat their purpose. They lose the sense of community essential for smooth functioning and individual happiness. Partly to limit their spread, partly to enhance their environment by a "reinvasion" of nature, he saw the ideal city as a wheel. A greenbelt formed its outer rim, beyond which it could not expand, while roads radiating from its hub preserved natural, park-like spaces along their right-of-ways.

Roads, in fact, were chief villains. The proliferation of the "gasoline locomotive," with the attendant spread of "motor slums" into the countryside was "a curse," and it set MacKaye's teeth on edge. He praised the example of Radburn, New Jersey, "a new kind of city — a town deliberately built for the motor age" by MacKaye's associates, one which took its cue from Olmsted's Riverside, Illinois, built decades before. Typically, main roads passed through cities, creating environments of noise, congestion, pollution, and danger. Radburn preserved tranquility by confining through traffic to through avenues; dead-end streets in residential sections discouraged unwanted traffic. MacKaye, however, was not a horse-and-buggy primitivist; he simply wanted to keep the machine

Benton MacKaye (at right) with other founders of the Wilderness Society. From left: Bernard Frank, Harvey Broome, and Robert Marshall. Mable Abercrombie Mansfield, courtesy of *The Living Wilderness*

in its place. As he saw it, the automobile was built for speed, and he appreciated the advantage. He advocated motorways outside population centers, designed with limited access, overpasses, and centralized facilities for motorists — in other words, freeways.

"This is not utopia," insisted the crusty, impatient Yankee, "merely intelligence, effectively applied." However, MacKaye had his blind spots. His visions of organic, sensible growth all but ignored the realities of population increase — from 50,000,000 to over 200,000,000 in his own lifetime. That fact alone would have made any plan, no matter how intelligent, difficult to carry out. He didn't foresee that massive use of the automobile would make the word "freeway" nearly synonymous with urban blight. And lastly, his designs didn't take into account the psychology and politics of a nation that traditionally placed the short-term economic advantage of the individual before the long-term welfare of all.

Yet as far back as the 1920s, "The Father of the Appalachian Trail" was suggesting solutions to problems that now plague America. Though not carried out as he envisioned, his proposals have resulted in some major gains. One of the first to propose a wilderness bill, he lived to see the national wilderness system become a reality decades later, in 1964. Activists have expanded his idea for the Appalachian Trail into the National Trails System Act, passed in 1968. Insisting with Thoreau that man is "rooted squarely in the earth," he urged massive preservation, suggesting for instance that ecological study areas representative of the continent's natural diversity be set aside for the future — a proposal yet to be carried out.

As to MacKaye's farsighted approaches to today's gnawing problems, the Washington *Post* comments: "Throughout his life, Benton MacKaye's thoughts have run ahead of his time. Had the post-war explosion of cities been guided by his principles, we would have a finer, more habitable country; we would have been spared the cost and ugliness of urban sprawl; and we should have a less burdensome task of rebuilding our cities."

Robert Marshall, best-selling author, political radical—and one of the most effective lobbyists for wilderness protection during the 1930s. "He could always pull you out of the squirrel cage," said a friend. Sigurd F. Olson, courtesy of *The Living Wilderness*

Chapter 10

Robert Marshall:
Last of the Radical Bureaucrats

The woodsman undressed, cranked up his record player, then leaped into bed. He lay there listening to Schubert's *Unfinished Symphony,* while watching the northern lights dance in the arctic night outside his cabin window. Before drifting off to sleep, the millionaire thought about his Eskimo and sourdough friends and reminded himself that he had again returned to "the happiest civilization of which I have knowledge." Years later hikers in the lower forty-eight remembered that their famous companion preferred riding to trail heads on the running board of a car — better to awaken his senses to the coming experiences. A romantic indeed, some might conclude, one of those exuberant and wealthy few who can afford to indulge occasional whims for rustic adventure.

On the trail, however, Robert Marshall quickly proved otherwise. A typical day for him was forty miles over rugged terrain with a full pack, and he was known to do seventy miles cross-country — no pace for a dilettante. He was indeed a millionaire, a man of culture with a Ph.D. in plant physiology who could quote as easily from the Latin poets as from Bertrand Russell or build a boat with an axe to cross an arctic river. He was a best-selling writer, a radical, and for all that one of the government's most effective bureaucrats, "one of the most colorful figures" in conservation, according to historian Roderick Nash. Marshall had the good sense and humanity to learn the name of each sooty-faced man on a fire line, and he loved to dance as much as he loved the wilderness.

Shortly after his death, an unusual accolade to a bureaucrat appeared in the *New Republic*. "Gap in the Front Lines" testified to his ability to move others: "He was an unwearied, unsentimental, common-sense radical who never supported any movement without participating in it wholeheartedly and responsibly. He was the one guy who could always pull you out of the squirrel-cage and make you feel again the excitement, importance and opportunity in what you were trying to do." Little wonder that Eskimos, Washington socialites, and fellow bureaucrats — whether or not they agreed with his politics — enjoyed Marshall's company.

The movement that Robert Marshall crystallized had a long but disconnected history. In 1864, Frederick Law Olmsted and other Californians persuaded the government to set aside the Yosemite valley as a scenic preserve. Prodded thereafter by various citizen groups, Congress added units over the years and in 1916 brought them together under the National Park Service. In the 1920s a hesitant Forest Service began a policy of creating primitive areas, when a young ranger, Aldo Leopold, convinced the agency to forbid exploitation on a half million acres of New Mexico's Gila National Forest.

The concept of keeping part of America as wilderness was slowly taking hold, but by the 1930s it still lacked a spokesman to consolidate the often vague notions of preservation into national policy. Aimed at moving citizens both inside and outside government, Robert Marshall's articles in the *Nation,* the *New York Times,* and *Nature Magazine* stressed that wilderness "is melting away like the last snowbank on some south-facing mountainside during a hot afternoon in June." Uniquely talented and well-connected, Marshall became the pivot on which the country turned toward a firm wilderness commitment. The legislation implementing his ideas, however, came twenty-five years after his death, and since history often is slow to sort out individuals responsible for change, he has yet to receive full credit for the accomplishment.

"As a boy," reflected the founder of the Wilderness Society, "I spent many hours in the heart of New York City, dreaming of Lewis and Clark and their glorious exploration into an unbroken wilderness which embraced three-quarters of a continent. Occasionally my reveries ended in terrible depression, and I would imagine that I had been born a century too late for genuine excitement." Pioneers straining to hack and hoe a livelihood from the wilds rarely thought of their awesome surroundings in such wistful terms. But the city boy's dreaming, an intensified version of America's yearning for a lost past, formed the mainspring for Marshall's activist future. And when a biographer finally emerges to analyze this wilderness zealot, he doubtlessly will explore the rich background that resulted in a life of messianic and joyous drive.

The son of a Jewish immigrant, Robert Marshall's father remembered family stories of repression and hardship in European ghettos. As did other immigrants' sons, he strove to make the most of the opportunities America offered. A legal genius who completed Columbia University's two-year law course in half the usual time, Louis Marshall became a wealthy and internationally famous lawyer. But though he spoke half a dozen languages and frequently appeared before the Supreme Court, he never forgot his humble origins. To him, as was the case with immigrant Carl Schurz, America represented for humanity a liberal dream not yet fulfilled, and he spent much of his life arguing for the civil and religious liberties still denied to many Jews, Blacks, Roman Catholics, and American Indians.

As part of his vision of America as a land of potential justice and plenty, he also shared George Perkins Marsh's concerns about the country's hasty dismantling of its natural heritage for the benefit of a few. Putting his legal skills and prestige to work for conservation, he supported bird protection reforms; and during New York's constitutional convention of 1914 he led the fight, against lumbermen, to retain the "forever wild" guarantee for the immense reserve of Adirondack State Park. For twenty years he served on the board of trustees of the New York State College of Forestry. Friends summed up his career by praising his victories for civil rights and "his championship of the American forests and of all America's natural resources."

A lover of what he defended, the lawyer built a vacation home in the heart of the Adirondacks. His son grew up, then, not only among the refinements of wealth and the reformist commitments that shaped his outlook but also with opportunities to indulge his wilderness reveries. Still yearning for the days of Lewis and Clark, the boy backpacked through the mountains around the Marshall summer retreat. It came as no surprise to his family that he decided to become a forester. This choice of profession combined the sense of wonder and incipient strivings for reform reflected in lines he wrote at the age of eight, after a trip to Lake Champlain:

> Where once the Indians used to dwell,
> From the steamboat comes a smoky smell.

Robert Marshall's professional life can be formulated in one paragraph. After receiving a Bachelor of Science de-

*Young Marshall in 1925 with Ward Shepard (at right) in
Montana's Mission Mountains. A typical day for Marshall was
40 miles over rugged terrain with a full pack.* The Living Wilderness

gree in 1924 from the College of Forestry at Syracuse, he
went on for advanced degrees from Harvard and from
Johns Hopkins University. With the exception of four
years as Director of Forestry in the Office of Indian Affairs, he spent his entire career with the U.S. Forest Service. Various positions involving field work, laboratory
research, and administration took him to the state of
Washington and to the Northern Rocky Mountain Experiment Station in Missoula, Montana. In 1937, head of the

Forest Service Ferdinand Silcox appointed him Chief of the Division of Recreation and Lands, a post created especially for Marshall.

Such an outline might summarize the careers of many bureaucrats who leave behind little more than undistinguished legacies of dutifully performed functions. It gives little idea of Marshall's influence both inside and outside government — of the strenuous efforts responsible for major shfts in public policy, of the political climate in which these changes took place, or of the essentially artistic personality of the individual who engineered them.

As a millionaire, Robert Marshall did not have to work, but having made a commitment that involved his entire outlook, he threw himself into work with a drive, daring, and creativity that most men with families to support and bills to pay would not have risked. His exploits as a hiker, his father's reputation as one of the nation's foremost constitutional lawyers, and his scientific credentials as a research scholar, combined with his renown as a best-selling author, allowed him to move as a *wunderkind* among hidebound government bureaucrats.

But many bureaucrats weren't as conservative as might be supposed. The Depression was on, with millions of people out of work and listless in the world's richest country. Obviously, some traditional policies had gone wrong, and the New Deal administration of President Roosevelt made Marshall's socialist approach to natural resources seem far less radical than they would have appeared in more prosperous times.

Then, too, though the profit-hungry timber industry continued to wreak havoc on privately-owned forests, it hadn't as yet begun to eye the public domain. With notable exceptions, the Forest Service, responsible for most federally administered timberlands, protected them with the progressive zeal inspired by Gifford Pinchot when he founded the agency in 1905. In addition, the traditional rivalry between the preservation-oriented Department of Interior and the use-oriented Department of Agriculture flared again under Interior Secretary Harold Ickes. It played directly into the hands of a small but earnest and politically sophisticated band of wilderness advocates led by Marshall. Temperamental Ickes pointed to abuses under Agriculture's domain and demanded that the national forests be transferred to his own department, brought "home" under the protective wing of Interior. His repeated campaigns, launched with the fervor and acerbity of a religious fanatic battling the heretics, were unsuccessful, but they jolted Secretary of Agriculture Henry A. Wallace into action. Publicly railed at by Ickes from without and gently prodded by liberals Silcox and Marshall from within, beseiged Wallace strained to make his Forest Sevice the model of conservation. Among other changes, he consented to wilderness expansion in order to placate both factions.

As for Marshall's techniques, friends recalled his diplomatically tempered chutzpah at work in an atmosphere ready for change: "Bob had the nerve to get all kinds of people together — Congressmen, prima-donna braintrusters, professional civil servants, promoters of this or that — hand them a dubious drink, and then insist that they debate the public ownership of resources."

He backed up his lobbying efforts with an array of alarming statistics, all pointing to one central fact: twenty percent of the nation's forests enjoyed conscientious stewardship under the U.S. Forest Service, but the other eighty percent remained in private and careless hands. Driven by the necessities of the capitalistic system, timber companies were competing to see who could cut the fastest on the major portion of the country's forest resource — with profits, rather than the future, in mind. As George Perkins Marsh had predicted, profligacy was beginning to show: timber shortages, floods, erosion — the loss of

America's once scenic and bountiful woodlands.

In short, despite their efforts since the latter years of the nineteenth century, conservationists had failed. "The proof," warned Marshall, "is the condition of our forests: unbelievably worse than before the conservation movement started." His assessment was not the hyperbolic tirade of an alarmist. Supporting his judgments were the writings of such professional foresters as Gifford Pinchot and George P. Ahern. In 1929, the latter had published a documented account of current abuses, bleakly entitled *Deforested America*.

Basically, Marshall offered a twofold solution. Since private enterprise was not working for the nation's good, he wrote in *The People's Forests* (1933), timber lands should be nationalized, placed under control of the federal government to insure rational, long-term use. This course, Marshall reassured Americans, was not radical: "Most of the older countries have public control of private forests, from the well-nigh complete control of Sweden, Japan, and Switzerland, to the partial control of France and Germany. In most countries, public control of forests needed for protecting mountain and river systems is taken for granted." Despite the precedents, the suggestion was branded "communistic," and it failed to take hold, though it did result in some nominal changes in forest regulation.

Closest to Marshall's heart was the preservation of wild America, and in this effort he enjoyed phenomenal success. From his vantage point as a high Forest Sevice official, he prepared inventories of roadless areas, and by skillfully playing on interagency rivalries, singlehandedly added the huge total of 5,437,000 acres to the government's preserve system — 5,437,000 acres to be kept as pristine as when the first white man laid eyes on them.

Still, a shadow of instability hung over the coup. The new reserves, set aside by administrative decree, could just as easily be opened again to exploitation by the pen of a future head of the Forest Service not sympathetic to wilderness. The solution lay in protecting the gains under the aegis of the far more permanent sanction of Congressional action. To accomplish this feat — and to add further units to the wilderness system — Marshall, for all his talents, clearly needed the broad-based political backing that could come only from a national organization. Yet at the time, remembered one of his hiking cronies, "there was no strong body of wilderness sentiment in existence." Marshall, it seemed, was standing alone.

The appropiate organization came into being almost by happenstance. In 1934, Marshall joined Benton MacKaye and Harvey Broome for a jaunt into Tennessee's Great Smoky Mountains. There they witnessed the negative side of the New Deal. While many of Roosevelt's public-works projects served useful ends, others did irreversible damage by extending unneeded roads into wilderness areas. The upshot of the hikers' grousing was The Wilderness Society, founded in 1935 to save the remaining remnants of wild America from all technological invasions.

The Society began with eight dedicated and politically active members. Besides Marshall, who provided the financial backing, they included lawyer Broome; MacKaye, the planner of the Appalachian Trail; wilderness celebrant Aldo Leopold; and Robert Sterling Yard, an editor with a long career of conservation publicity work, going back to the early days of the National Park Service. The organization, one of the most effective lobbying groups of its kind, has served its purpose well, today boasting tens of thousands of wilderness supporters. Without their combined efforts, which culminated in passage of the Wilderness Act of 1964, the nation would not have the splendid and still expanding wilderness system envisioned by Marshall nearly fifty years ago.

Behind Marshall's successes in the political arena lay one central ability. Through his personality and writing, he was able to communicate his own deep love of wild lands. Author Paul Schaefer recalls his first chance meeting with the bureaucrat on an Adirondack peak: "As we spoke he seemed to be chafing at the bit. A strong, cool wind whipped his hair. He exuded a restless, dynamic strength of purpose — strength which had been nurtured in the remote Arctic wilderness." Marshall's books and articles projected the same simple power. They spoke about the need of wilderness preservation, but they emphasized the author's own explorations, adventures infused with personal thrills and spiritual enrichment. "He seemed," testifies one admirer, "to personify the limitless sweep of mountains, the ancient rocks, the unbroken forests...." In brief, Marshall reawakened a fundamental, if at times dormant, love of nature.

Realist that he was, Marshall did not gloss over the complexities of preserving wilderness in a society that glorified the machine. He asked, in a time when such questionings had not yet become fashionable, whether adding more technological gadgets to the gross national product each year was bringing the fulfillment that should be the end of a truly humane society. In fact, while giving the scientific and economic benefits of preservation their due, he used the psychological necessity of wilderness as the pivot on which his arguments turned.

Echoing psychoanalyst Sigmund Freud, he pointed to the "horrible banality" of an over-civilized society, which repressed rather than encouraged diversity and creativity. In contrast, he suggested that wilderness not only made badly needed physical demands on a sedentary society but it also provided a retreat to the freedom of the primitive. "It is," he described the benefits, "the last stand for that glorious adventure into the physically unknown that was commonplace in the lives of our ancestors, and has always constituted a major factor in the happiness of many exploratory souls. It is also the perfect esthetic experience because it appeals to all of the senses."

Thus Marshall combined conservation with social theory, for in his mind untrammeled nature served the public good. He advocated not only great swaths of wildness preserved for the exhilaration of the backpacker but summer camps for ghetto children and rustic facilities for the less hardy among the general public. This stance placed him in line with America's pastoral counter-vision espoused by such diverse thinkers as Thomas Jefferson, Thoreau, and John Muir — and continued today by such environmental leaders as David Brower and Edward Abbey.

For all that, Marshall didn't swamp his readers in social theory. Instead, he enlivened his writing with anecdotes, humor, and curious facts. He once made an analysis of logger's parlance. Basing a study of their idiom on ten conversations, he once reported that "of this record it transpired that an average of 136 words, unmentionable at church socials, were enunciated every quarter hour by the hearty hewers of wood."

He drew on his wide-ranging knowledge to entertain and inform with such pieces as "Lucretius on Forest Fires" and "Precipitation and Presidents." The latter made a statistical, and only partly tongue-in-cheek, case for predicting the outcomes of Presidential elections on the basis of annual rainfall. But his imaginative style went far beyond statistics and formal argument to drive a point home. Once challenged to state the specific number of wilderness areas the country should have, he countered, "How many Brahms' symphonies do we need?"

The wilderness ideal that Marshall held up — as well as his effectiveness in stating it — can best be seen in *Arctic Village* (1933). As an adult still haunted by the exploits of Lewis and Clark, he made several trips to map the unknown territory of the Koyukuk River drainage near Wiseman, Alaska, a tiny village just above the Arctic

Circle. There he found a self-sustaining hunting and mining society of seventy-seven whites, forty-four Eskimos, and six Indians spread over an area as large as the combined states of Massachusetts and New Jersey. His book included more than the revels of standing on peaks to survey arctic vistas never before seen by any human, native or white. With a thoroughness reminiscent of the classical sociological study *Middletown*, he analyzed the economic, communal, and sexual activities of the hardy wilderness dwellers. Despite the demands of their harsh surroundings, they knew almost no crime, racial strife, or poverty. Instead, "people in the Koyukuk realize that they are living together in an isolated world, sharing its work, its dangers, its joys, and its responsibilities. They recollect countless personal associations of the most intimate character imaginable. Such factors seem to furnish them with an urge to act decently which in most cases is sufficient to obviate any necessity for the more usual compulsions of law."

After reading *Arctic Village*, even H. L. Mencken couldn't contain his amazement. "How peacefully they live together, how easily they escape most of the evils that go with the outside, and how content they are to remain in their remote isolation," he marveled. Reviewers in the *New York Times*, the *Nation*, and the *Saturday Review* praised the world of *Arctic Village* with similar enthusiasm. The book quickly climbed to the best-seller list. Caught in the malaise of the Depression, the public was questioning the validity of its highly urbanized, crime-ridden, and often lackluster culture. And Marshall, while not suggesting that people strike out for the arctic wilds as a solution to their ills, had proved his point. He had shown alternatives, values that might be found and fostered through experiences in the wilderness areas he was fighting to preserve.

When Robert Marshall died in 1939 at the age of

thirty-eight, friends said that his sudden heart attack resulted from his strenuous pace. In spite of the successes of his short life, it should be remembered that many people viewed him as a maverick within government, one who, as Nash says, "broke sharply with existing government policy and marked [himself] as a radical, especially among foresters." He was among the last innovative conservationists in the federal bureaucracy who had hope that the government could be flexible and idealistic enough to make changes for the public good.

Though his tactics worked in his own time, his belief in a flexible and idealistic government proved wrong. After World War II, growing corporations came to dominate America's economic system, gaining decision-making powers in the federal agencies designed to regulate them. Wilderness advocate Michael Frome reflects on the present Forest Service, now dominated by the timber industry: "Innovative thinking like that of such figures as Robert Marshall is not encouraged." Rachel Carson and Ralph Nader soon discovered that activists, since the days of Robert Marshall, have had to take up embattled and frequently bitter adversary positions outside government, depending on massive public outcries to move a reluctant bureaucracy toward environmental reforms.

Franklin Delano Roosevelt in 1936, pressing key to close the gates of Norris Dam, a unit of T.V.A. Was F.D.R. promoting conservation or runaway technology?   UPI

Chapter 11

Franklin Delano Roosevelt:
The Debt Falls Due

An eleven-gun fusillade made the holiday crowd flinch as Theodore Roosevelt's caravan chugged into view out of the high desert canyons. Overweight and still bubbling about his African trophy-hunting expedition the previous year, the former chief executive had traveled to the Arizona Territory in March 1911 to dedicate a dam named in his honor.

It was an impressive first fruit of his presidential days. Created during T.R.'s administration, the U.S. Reclamation Service labored eight years to complete the structure that rose 284 feet, a masonry apparition out of the chasm of a tamed river. At the time, it was the highest dam in the world. As the water shot out of the spillways and seethed through the twisting canyons of the Gila River toward plains nearly a hundred miles away, farmers near Phoenix were counting their future profits while blessing a beneficent government.

In the following years the scene was repeated throughout the West, as similar projects made deserts bloom, increasing the prosperity of an already prosperous nation.

Celebrating another dammed river, David O. Woodbury wrote in *The Colorado Conquest:* "It has turned a broad wasteland of sand and sage into a garden: it is lighting and watering a new civilization." However, America took T.R.'s well-intentioned plans for prodding profits from nature to extremes. Ditched, dammed, logged, and plowed with abandon from coast to coast, the land eventually kicked back — as George Perkins Marsh, decades before in *Man and Nature,* had predicted it would. The nation would learn that spurring nature could help demolish, as well as help build, a civilization.

Twenty-two years after Theodore Roosevelt's dedication of the Arizona dam, his fifth cousin laid a hand on the family's Dutch Bible to become President of a despairing nation. A quarter of the work force — thirteen million people — had no jobs. Factories stood idle; every bank in the country had closed. In Europe, Hitler and Mussolini were rallying their people from economic sloughs with fascism, while in America listless and hungry men shuffled through the streets. Some observers feared the nation was tottering toward revolution.

Economic theorists still debate the causes of the Great Depression. Though these causes were international and complex, there is little doubt that prolonged abuse of nature contributed heavily to the near collapse of the world's most technologically advanced nation. Stewart Udall, Secretary of the Interior under Presidents Kennedy and Johnson, uses stronger language to describe the process: "The economic bankruptcy that gnawed at our country's vitals after 1929 was closely related to a bankruptcy of land stewardship. The buzzards of the raiders had, at last, come home to roost, and for each bank failure there were land failures by the hundreds. In a sense, the Great Depression was a bill collector sent by nature."

"It seemed every field in western Kansas began to move," testifies Vance Johnson chronicling the Dust Bowl of the 1930s. Across America's wheat lands, once prosperous farmers stood in awe as their rich prairie soil blew away. Children lost their way home from school in the dust. The clouds rose to thousands of feet, then drifted eastward to create palls over Baltimore and New York. Meanwhile in the West, ranchers formed their cowboys into firing squads. In one mass slaughter near Fort Worth, they shot 61,000 emaciated cattle in less than six weeks.

"Land failure," continues Udall, "meant the failure of people." Foreclosures drove thousands of families off their farms, and with characteristic pioneer hope they went West. Arriving with mattresses tied to the tops of their gasping model T's, droves of Okies and Arkies, however, found little welcome or employment in California. Millions of acres across the country lay stripped of trees, flooding and eroding from generations of misuse, producing a rural poverty that deepened the economic lethargy of the cities. The new president had inherited near chaos.

From a long line of Knickerbocker aristocrats, Franklin Delano Roosevelt's father busied himself building steamship, coal, and railroad empires. His wife augmented the Roosevelt wealth with the Delano's shipping fortune. On their Hyde Park estate overlooking the Hudson River, James and Sara lived in Victorian gentility. Born in 1882, their son grew up bright and full of energy, accepting his birthright as a matter of course. He spurred his Welsh pony around the estate or sailed his father's yacht with the self-assured elegance of a prince. His parents took him abroad so often that he acquired a foreign accent. He went to exclusive Eastern schools, Groton, then Harvard.

"It would have seemed preposterous," puzzles Roosevelt biographer Frank Freidel, "to believe that this stripling, almost too high-toned for Groton, would in another generation become a new Bryan, a professed champion of the common man." Yet in conservation alone — not to mention examples readily found in other fields throughout history — George Bird Grinnell, Gifford Pinchot, and Robert Marshall all used their wealth to promote the common good through liberal causes. Families of Roosevelt's class gave at least lip service to democratic ideals, ideals that occasionally a tradition-breaking upstart took seriously.

At the age of nine, Franklin wrote an essay on Egypt for his Swiss governess: "The working people had nothing.... The kings made them work so hard and gave them so little that by wingo! they nearly starved and by jinks! they had hardly any clothes so they died in quadrillions." With the sophistication of four more years, he mused on his own heritage: "Some of the famous Dutch families in New York have today nothing left but their name.... One reason of the virility of the Roosevelts is this very democratic spirit. They have never felt that because they were born in a good position they could put their hands in their pockets and succeed. They have felt, rather, that ... there was no excuse for them if they did not do their duty by the community...." With the benefit of hindsight, it appears that Franklin already was on the road to the New Deal.

Eyebrows shot up in Knickerbocker drawing rooms when, at the age of twenty-nine, the scion left his job with a toney Wall Street law firm and announced his candidacy for the New York senate. For Democrat Roosevelt, running for office in his heavily Republican county seemed a futile undertaking. Yet in unpatrician style, he rented a red Maxwell, and with flags flying from the fenders, he bumped over country roads to pump the hands of cornhusking farmers. As it turned out, his opponents squabbled among themselves, throwing the election to the young attorney. Such luck and risk-taking typified his family, whose ancestors had sailed the China seas to turn escapes from pirates into fortunes. In Albany, Roosevelt irreverently bucked his own party's machine, the infamous Tammany Hall, by championing progressive reforms. Then in 1913, Woodrow Wilson rewarded the New Yorker's support in the Presidential election by appointing him assistant secretary of the Navy.

Throughout World War I, he performed his duties with such characteristic efficiency — and attention to his growing public image — that the Democratic convention of 1920 nominated him for Vice-President. Despite a landslide for Republican Warren G. Harding, tall and suave Roosevelt had gained invaluable nationwide exposure. The polio that crippled him for the rest of his life struck in 1921, but it didn't rob him of the high spirits and genuine warmth that later helped restore America's confidence during the bleak Depression years.

Remaining politically active during his convalescence, in 1928 he ran for Governor of New York — again against an unfavorable tide. Added to this disadvantage, voters looked with skepticism at a man who for all his abilities campaigned in leg braces. Presidential candidate Al Smith shot back at his friend's detractors, "A Governor does not have to be an acrobat." As a political worker noted, Roosevelt's "broad jaw and upthrust chin, the piercing, flashing eyes," drew attention away from his infirmity. Smith lost, but Roosevelt won by a comfortable margin. Democrats began thinking of him as a possibility for the presidential race of 1932.

The Governor of the Empire State pleased farmers with his work for rural tax reform and consumers generally with his efforts to cut the cost of public utilities. The rest of the country, stunned by the Depression, took note of New York. While Herbert Hoover sat hidebound in the White House, Governor Roosevelt was rallying his administrative machinery to provide relief for his state. A mild progressive until then, he was learning the value of innovation. In the 1932 presidential campaign, he easily toppled the incumbent.

F.D.R.'s slow shift from Hyde Park patrician to New

Dealer owes much to the influence of cousin Theodore Roosevelt. Franklin, twenty-four years his junior, grew up watching robust "Uncle Ted," as he sometimes called him, become one of America's most popular Presidents. As a young visitor to the White House, Franklin was kept entertained by T.R.'s rollicking table talk. He later courted T.R.'s niece Eleanor — an idealist and progressive influence in her own right — given away at their wedding by the President himself. Significantly, the cousins' careers followed similar patterns. In his Navy office, F.D.R. sat behind the same desk once used by his boisterous cousin. Although T.R. was a Republican and the two Roosevelt presidencies, separated twenty-four years, faced different sets of problems, the cousins often shared a common rhetoric. F.D.R.'s words — "I am fighting as I always have fought, for the rights of the little man as well as the big man — for the weak as well as the strong, for those who are helpless as well as for those who can help themselves" — might have come from the mouth of colorful Uncle Ted. They typified the progressive thrust of both administrations.

As for conservation, from their youths both loved the outdoors. T.R.'s main contribution lay in preserving what was left of wild America by creating government reserves. The job of the second President Roosevelt was to restore the abused land, to expand and add more sophisticated details to his cousin's unfulfilled plans for federal resource management.

While still in his twenties, Franklin assumed responsibility for Hyde Park. He recognized that years of overproduction had sapped the strength from the old farmstead. As a remedy, he planted its depleted soils in trees — Norway pine, poplar, hemlock — "in the hope that my great grandchildren will be able to try raising corn again — just one century from now." Patrician F.D.R. understood stewardship — understood the significance of

Wealthy F.D.R. restored the depleted soil of his own Hyde Park estate. Then as President he toured farms in the Dust Bowl. In this photograph he talks to homesteader Steve Brown, near Jamestown, North Dakota. Franklin D. Roosevelt Library Collection

an America overgrazed, overfarmed, and carelessly logged. When crippled, he drove an especially equipped car through his forested estate to check on progress in the groves. The trees meant not only spiritual solace to him, they "symbolized," says Arthur M. Schlesinger, Jr., "his desire to renew the land." For the new President, well-managed, thriving Hyde Park represented a Utopia in miniature; his ecological dream was to reshape worn-out America in its image.

With the country in disarray, Roosevelt had plenty of opportunity for reshaping. As was true of his famous cousin, F.D.R. matched crises with daring. He gathered a cadre of bright, often young, specialists about him, eager to try out their new ideas. In the first hundred days of his administration, the President met the Depression with bold changes, massive federal programs designed to put people back to work and start the rusted wheels of the economy turning. In contrast to Herbert Hoover's aloofness, Roosevelt proceeded with flair, humor, and self-confidence. "Reporters," says Schlesinger, "took from his press conferences images of urbane mastery, with the President sitting easily behind his desk, his great head thrown back, his smile flashing or his laugh booming out in the pleasure of thrust and riposte."

Looking back today on Roosevelt's innovations, some liberals accuse him of doing just enough in the way of reform to preserve the capitalistic system with all its supposed evils. At the other extreme, conservatives condemn him for starting the nation down the road to a debilitating socialism. Whatever the case, F.D.R.'s schemes brought results. And whether they reached out to pluck the jobless from bread lines to put them to work building roads, or whether they sent out teams of social workers to correct children's nutritional deficiencies, they set a precedent for government planning that would affect the life of every American.

His comprehensive ideas held true for conservation policies, which ranged from game-law reform to pollution control, from soil conservation to expansion of national parks, forests, and wildlife refuges. Roosevelt's immediate goal was to provide jobs while restoring the land. The President also took the long view: the nation could avoid such unnecessary bankruptcy as the Dust Bowl through permanent programs of resource care.

His administration's most striking example of an integrated approach is the Tennessee Valley Authority, a mammoth project focused on seven southern states. Forest fires, floods, tuberculosis plagued the region. Years of unchecked lumbering and farming had left the people in the drainage basin of the Tennessee River with the lowest incomes, the most ramshackle housing, the poorest diets — and the least hope — of any area in the nation.

A series of dams on the Tennessee provided jobs and eventually abundant electricity to the undeveloped area. The dams curbed flooding, and locks opened the river to navigation. In a further boost to agriculture, TVA developed a fertilizer plant at Muscle Shoals. The TVA administration not only sponsored development of recreational sites and reforestation of bare hillsides, it helped combat malaria and provide library services. Further, in order to revitalize the political processes, planning was undertaken with the cooperation of local governments. TVA restored the land while giving prosperity a chance to take hold again according to Roosevelt's ideals of a rural, Jeffersonian democracy.

Another program brought immediate relief to cities as well as to the countryside. Enrolling unemployed youths from blighted urban areas, the Civilian Conservation Corps (CCC) sent these young men into hundreds of forest camps. They fought fires, planted trees, built much of the trail system now in use on our national parks and forests, and improved watersheds — helping to pay off the overdue debt to nature. While learning construction trades, the CCC men received $30 a month, but much of their benefit was intangible. They were strangers to the wilderness, to ice on drinking water in the mornings, and to forests that stretched endlessly drainage after drainage. Some couldn't take the program's rigors. Rattled by quiet nights interrupted by hooting owls and wailing coyotes, they escaped back to the jangle of subways and the comforting noises of the streets. For most, however, the experience was a revelation. One testified, "I weighed about 160 pounds when I went there, and when I left I was about 190. It made a man of me all right." Another, full of nostalgia, promised himself, "Some day when these trees I planted grow large I want to go back and look at them."

Other agencies enlisted professionals for Roosevelt's multifaceted approach to land restoration. The Soil Conservation Service, concerned with controlling erosion, sent out teams to instruct growers on the techniques of crop rotation, terracing, and contour plowing. The Agricultural Adjustment Administration, responsible for striking a balance between agricultural production and market demand, also stipulated that farmers benefiting from its programs practice soil conservation. A "permanent long-range planning commission," the National Resources Board, received a broad Presidential mandate to

F.D.R. with notables at C.C.C. camp in Shenandoah Valley, Virginia. Left to right: General Malone, Louis Howe, Harold Ickes, Robert Fechner, F.D.R., Henry Wallace, and Rex Tugwell. Some boys ran away. Franklin D. Roosevelt Library Collection

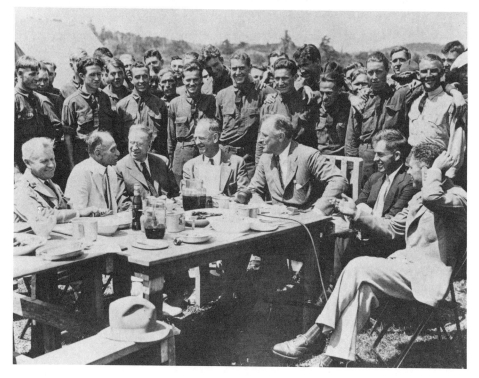

peer fifty years into the future and "put the physical development of the country on a planned basis."

None of these herculean jobs was accomplished without the usual bumps and grinds of politics, storms from Congress, interagency jealousies, and disagreements among the planners themselves. Occasionally, there were dramatic feuds. At the turn of the century, the Department of Interior had transferred the national forests to the Department of Agriculture. As a result, Interior now and then coveted its former woodlands. Harold Ickes, one of Roosevelt's most enthusiastic cabinet members, developed grand designs for his agency. He wanted to turn Interior into an all-encompassing Department of Conservation — a superagency that would include the national forests in its new fold.

Over in Agriculture, Secretary Henry Wallace naturally resisted, with the intrigues of a jealous Renaissance prince, the campaign for transfer that Ickes promoted. When aging Gifford Pinchot, first head of the Forest Service, jumped into the fray in Wallace's behalf, Ickes dealt the old forester a blow by calling him "the Lot's-wife of the conservation movement." Responding in kind, Pinchot drew on current events to label Ickes "the American Hitler."

The combatants broke their lances on this issue for years, while Roosevelt stood placidly on the sidelines. He had a keen administrative sense. The running battle kept the two agencies busy proving their worth, as they strained to outstrip each other in conservation work. While internecine feuds and wrangles with Congress burst out periodically, streams across America began to run clear again, and crops were growing where sand dunes had once buried farmers' fences.

Nevertheless, some conservationists had misgivings. They saw engineers waving on bulldozers to reshape entire watersheds, CCC boys blasting unneeded roads into the wilderness, and formerly unemployed artists painting tableaux on new buildings in the national parks. Was such busyness really conservation — or was it conservation run amuck?

As the doubters saw it, government agencies develop a destructive momentum. Their prestige is based on the number of dams, visitor centers, and parking lots they build. Aldo Leopold reflected on the intricate interactions of the biosphere in contrast to the federal programs begun in Roosevelt's day. He argued in *A Sand County Almanac* (1949) that "we are remodeling the Alhambra with a steam-shovel, and we are proud of our yardage." In essence, the question is one of humility, of learning respect for the land's complexity. For all the good it can accomplish, technological civilization seems unable to resist "land doctoring," as Leopold called it, that leads to "derangements" in nature.

Bearing out Leopold's fears, well-intentioned government programs have created unforeseen results that now nag the nation. Air pollution, crime, and motorized crowding plague our national parks. Electricity from dams on the Colorado River may have sparked the economy of Los Angeles, but it has also encouraged the city to sprawl into what many people today regard a smog-shrouded urban monster. The Tennessee Valley Authority, for all the relief it provided decades ago, is now one of the nation's largest users of strip-mined coal. And it has dutifully followed the urgings of industry and government to construct nuclear generating plants.

Roosevelt's vision of a healthy land gave conservation a strategic boost at a critical time. However, concerned with the immediate problems of unemployment and land restoration, he did not understand the full implications of his plans. As was true of the dreams of his cousin, the programs he generated have led to excesses promoted by an entrenched bureaucracy, often industry-backed. Because of these abuses, most conservation progress since F.D.R.'s administration has resulted from pressure outside, rather than within, the federal government.

Howard Zahniser, a man of goodwill and humor, became executive secretary of The Wilderness Society. "We are not fighting progress. We are making it," he told opponents of wilderness preservation. The Living Wilderness

Chapter 12

Howard Zahniser:
Genial Man Behind the
Wilderness Act

"Why should not we, who have renounced the king's authority," asked Thoreau rather dreamily, "have our national preserves in which the bear and the panther may not be 'civilized off the face of the earth' — our own forests not to hold the king's game merely, but for inspiration and our own true recreation?" Naturalists kept this notion alive, but it was slow to bear fruit in reality. The early national parks were a partial answer to Thoreau's plea to "keep the New World *new*," but for years they remained few in number, badly administered, and for the most part ignored by the public.

The public ignored other wild places under federal control, unmarked islands so inaccessible or economically unattractive that the rush for exploitation only lapped around them. They represented the last remnants of what the country might save as untrampled heritage. Bent on more than dreaming, in 1924 a young ranger named Aldo Leopold risked his government career to implement Thoreau's vision. When he persuaded the U.S. Forest Service to set aside one-half million acres in New Mexico's Gila National Forest as an inviolate reserve, the timber-cutting agency had created, though somewhat reluctantly, the country's first wilderness area. From then on, in theory at least, the Gila Wilderness would be left to evolve, not according to man's use-oriented plans, but according to nature's ageless designs.

The Gila was only one wilderness, only a beginning. By the 1930s, Robert Marshall was articulating the concept of a national wilderness system, making it an issue of public debate. Throughout the Depression, urbane, socialist Marshall politicked Washington's elite and cajoled the Forest Service into designating addition units to be protected along Gila lines. To further his aims, he helped create The Wilderness Society, to which he passed on not only his ebullient spirit but a substantial endowment from his private fortune. And with his fatal heart attack in 1939, some said he gave his very life to the cause of wilderness.

On the verge of success, Marshall rallied his followers to "mobilize all our resources, all of our energies, all of our devotion to the wilderness" for the final push. World War II and Marshall's untimely death postponed the victory. Furthermore, the year after the worldwide conflict ended, the Forest Service experienced a change of heart. Pressured by the timber lobby, it began disassembling the units of wilderness that Leopold and Marshall had hoped would become the seedbed for a series of reserves stretching across the country. Clearly, if America were to save even tokens of its once pristine land, someone would have to take up Marshall's standard — and, facing the new postwar enthusiasm for economic growth, he would have to begin well behind where his optimistic predecessors had left off.

The task fell to an unlikely candidate. Howard Zahniser had little of Marshall's chutzpah, and certainly none of his wealth. He lacked the compelling quirkiness of a Benton MacKaye, the storminess of a Hornaday, the political connections that eased the way for Teddy Roosevelt. A former high-school English teacher, his delights centered on a private collection of nature books, on writing bits of humorous verse for the entertainment of friends. Bespectacled, round-faced, tending to be pudgy, he didn't even look the part of such forerunners as Muir and Marshall, men who had captured the public imagination with a combination of intellectual toughness and physical exploits. Once thrust into the complex political struggles for passage of wilderness legislation, however, Zahniser soon developed his own vital, if humble, style. His son Ed Zahniser recalls, "Even toward the end of the eight-year legislative battle to pass a wilderness bill, when success was in sight, he saw himself as a mere cog in an inexorably turning wheel. He would joke that whoever had designed the wheel — *Zahniser* means 'gear maker' in German — might have made a better choice of materials."

"Nature was his God," observes a colleague. The gentle evangelism that marked Zahniser's conservation career had roots in his upbringing. His father was a minister, his mother a minister's daughter. Their son's natural exuberance, curbed in the religious household, found expression outside the home. The future leader of The Wilderness Society grew up in the docile beauty of Pennsylvania's Allegheny River Valley — a beauty first made specific through the guidance of a local schoolteacher.

But young Zahniser's eyes were bad, and the family had no money for optometrists. Howard saw only blurs when the teacher pointed to birds. In his teens he finally received a pair of eyeglasses, and his reaction is telling. "Putting them on for the first time, he jumped fences and ran through fields," says his son, "marveling at how much there was to see and how distinctly beautiful it was." Howard Zahniser would marvel for the rest of his life.

At Greenville College, in Illinois, the minister's son reveled in literature courses — at the expense of fulfilling the standard requirements. "I crammed four years of college into five," he chided. Despite his literary self-indulgence, Zahniser worked hard, graduated, became a reporter for the *Pittsburgh Press,* and later a teacher in Greenville's high school.

Beginning in 1930, government employment provided him a satisfying niche for fifteen years. In this respect he followed Rachel Carson, another Pennsylvanian. Also like Carson, he did editorial and broadcasting work for the Fish and Wildlife Service. And following a pattern similar to that of the future author of *Silent Spring,* he found further outlets for his writing in free-lance projects. From 1935 to 1959 Zahniser turned out essays and a regular book-review column, "Nature in Print," for *Nature Magazine.* True to the gentle Zahniser style, he avoided negative and cutting reviews; instead Zahniser emphasized new volumes that would prove useful and enjoyable for his readers. In the meantime, while Carson's books were revealing the wonders of the world's oceans to mass audiences, the clergyman's son was doing his own wondering, cutting "his wilderness teeth," to use his son's phrase, on backpacking trips into New York's Adirondacks and Tennessee's Great Smokies. On these vacation forays Zahniser became friends with wilderness advocates Paul Schaefer and Harvey Broome, and through them he absorbed the ideas of Marshall and Benton MacKaye. Like Carson, he was unintentionally preparing to become embroiled in conservation at mid-life.

The death of Robert Sterling Yard in 1945 left The Wilderness Society's two major positions vacant: executive secretary and editor of the *Living Wilderness.* By then Zahniser had developed his own visceral "relationships to the primeval." Compelled by the wilderness crisis and fired by Marshall's vision, he quit government employment to become the Society's paid professional staff of one.

In the 1940s the ambitions of The Wilderness Society had the charming but fey aspects of windmill tilting. The Society's two thousand members stood enthusiastically behind a primary goal — to pass legislation enacting the national wilderness system envisioned by its founders in the previous decade. To do so, the Society would have to ride over the roadblocks thrown up by mining and timber industries, among the country's most politically adept and financially well-heeled lobbying groups. Secondly, the little band would have to alert a nation — one traditionally careless of preservation and now drowsy with postwar prosperity — to its diminishing natural heritage. As David Brower sums up the perennial dilemma: "Conservationists have little to compete with. Their ultimate weapon is the hard job of exploiting everyone's native love of a beautiful land. The love is there, but a thousand conflicting demands get in the way." As to the goal of The Wilderness Society, "It was political madness, some political scientists observed, to try to take on so many opponents at once." Yet the Society's hopeful leader, approaching middle age, had exchanged government security for a shaky financial future. His new salary was only half his former modest government pay, and his wife, Alice, was expecting their fourth child. Zahniser had stripped himself for battle.

However, wilderness advocates were about to enjoy some unexpected advantages. Despite its new identification of happiness with a soaring gross national product, the public was again to prove the old axiom that people most appreciate a thing when they are about to lose it. Social historian Roderick Nash comments on the psychological reaction to wilderness in the mid-twentieth century: conservationists' "efforts would have been fruitless without the responsive chords they struck throughout American society. Public appreciation of wilderness increased steadily as the nation's pioneer past receded."

A national furor over a park prepared Howard Zahniser for his ultimate accomplishment. To satisfy scientists rejoicing over a treasure trove of fossil bones, in 1915 President Wilson declared eighty acres on the Colorado-Utah border a national momument. For years it lay there baking under the Western sun, rarely visited except by a few happy paleontologists. In 1938 Franklin D. Roosevelt expanded the protected area. Few entrepreneurs objected. Dinosaur National Monument's 200,000 sprawling acres consisted of jumbled, seemingly useless desert landscape. But by the late 1940s, the Bureau of Reclamation was eyeing Dinosaur as a dam site — as well as Glacier and Grand Canyon National Parks for similar water projects. Meanwhile, taking advantage of its new affluence and mobility, the public was driving around the country, in record numbers visiting national parks. The Dinosaur Monument issue now brought the public up short. Were park lands, touted as belonging to all the people, truly inviolate? Apparently not. Encouraged by conservationists, the public shook itself from years of lethargy to make Dinosaur's harsh real estate the conservation battle of the century — a *cause célèbre* for park integrity.

Famed novelist and Sierra Club member Wallace Stegner edited a book, *This Is Dinosaur,* featuring stunning photographs of the preserve's stark beauty. Thousands of people who never would have considered a trip West to gaze at crumbling bones felt appreciation and anger after viewing a color film on Dinosaur's fragile wonders. Millions read illustrated broadsides, distributed by dam opponents, asking them point-blank: "Will You DAM the Scenic Wild Canyons of Our National Park System?" Quickly developing his talents as conservationists campaigned for Dinosaur, Howard Zahniser of the Washington, D.C.-based Wilderness Society assisted his West Coast counterpart in the fray, David Brower of the

Sierra Club. Beyond the issue of inviolability, they argued that the dam was a financial mistake, actually a water-wasting project — an ill-conceived scheme designed to benefit a privileged few at the cost of tax dollars and ruined wild lands. On the floor of the Senate, wilderness allies Richard Neuberger and Hubert Humphrey spoke out against a vast engineering plan that smelled of the pork barrel.

The man who had cut his wilderness teeth roaming the Adirondacks was now cutting his activist teeth on the complexities of politics. Finally, after years of interminable hearings and several failures, in 1956 Congress passed a law forbidding dams in national parks and monuments. The prolonged debate had united conservationists for the first time in years; it had shown them that Americans would rally to support wild places. Counting on the momentum, Zahniser drew up plans for a national wilderness system. Characteristically, while struggling over the wording, he joked that he'd "much prefer to state all this in iambic rhyming couplets." Friends Hubert Humphrey and Representative John P. Saylor introduced the bill — unrhymed but in Zahniser's exemplary prose — in the Eighty-Fourth Congress. Its uncertain progress proved less dramatic than the sharp debate over Dinosaur, but the eight-year struggle eventually resulted in a far larger gift to the nation, one given in large measure by Howard Zahniser.

Once captured by Marshall's vision and his eyes opened to see that it was very late for wilderness, Zahniser proved just how far the talents of a seemingly ordinary man can be developed in carrying out goals on a national scale. Lacking Marshall's originality, he possessed important qualities that foreshadowed a new kind of conservationist that was to build on the accomplishments of more dashing mentors. Most important, he could write with inspiration. When he lectured that we are projecting "into the eternity

Zahniser planning his route on a pack trip in the Idaho back country. When Zahniser woke the next day, this horse and 14 others had broken loose, leaving the party stranded 20 miles from civilization, according to an account in an old edition of Life *magazine.* James Marshall, courtesy of *The Living Wilderness*

of the future some of that precious unspoiled ecological inheritance that has come to us out of the eternity of the past," Zahniser was linking citizens with a cause beyond their ordinary, mortal lives.

Concerning practical affairs, he could handle the details of a volunteer organization which was facing the upheavals of phenomenal membership growth, while loosening the purse strings of wealthy supporters. The man who enjoyed nothing more than to read the *Divine Comedy* or *Walden* aloud with friends campaigned in kindly, low-keyed avuncular manner. In the face of granitic opposition, Zahniser drew people into the movement by persuasion. Paul Oehser, a retired official of the Smithsonian Institution, sums up the method: "Zahnie was famous for getting along with people. He had a way with him. Even his adversaries grew to respect and love him. He was never caustic or vindictive." Typically, when invited to justify his wilderness views to the assembled Society of American Foresters — a group opposed to preservation — he began his speech, "I do not come here to quarrel...." After the talk, the foresters peppered their guest with questions. By the end of the session, they couldn't help but respect the gentle man who had entered enemy territory full of goodwill and humor. Cheerful Zahnie became the "walking symbol of the Wilderness Bill."

Seeking a national consensus, preaching the transcendental view that "we are a part of the wildness of the universe," Zahniser hurried about lecturing and distributing conservation literature from large pockets sewn inside his suit coat. David Brower, now president of Friends of the Earth, remembers the struggle. For Zahniser "the hardest times were those when good friends tired because the battle was so long. Urging these friends back into action was the most anxious part of Howard Zahniser's work." But always regaining the energy he passed out to others, Zahniser refused to give in to what he blithely dismissed as "the ills of cynicism." His stamina was fueled by the fear that "we can no longer afford to lose wilderness." In many ways, buoyant Zahniser was exactly the man for the job. Like Marshall before him, he drove himself until he died in harness, still fighting for what he saw as an essential cause for the nation.

In all likelihood, anything less would not have been enough. Exploiters of natural resources reacted to the new environmental enthusiasm by launching an anti-wilderness campaign. As far as wilderness was concerned, the lands under question — much of them rocky peaks and high valleys — were not especially lucrative for mining or lumbering. Yet as with almost all the battles for preservation in America, the one for wilderness generated fears, some of them irrational. Accustomed to centuries of doing to the land what they wanted, some Americans looked upon the idea of leaving two or three percent of the nation untouched as heretical. Not wishing to seem unpatriotic by denying the spiritual worth of America's natural beauty, they were often forced into a curious logic. While declaring that "the American Forestry Association wholeheartedly believes in the enjoyment of wilderness" — such pleasure being, after all, an American pastime of long standing — the organization's chief executive feared recognition of timberlands as something other than reservoirs for the sawmills. Apparently, many foresters wanted to enjoy wilderness without preserving it.

Federal bureaucrats also felt threatened. This was to be expected of the Forest Service, which had developed a keen eye for turning trees into board feet for the marketplace. If some of its bailiwick — even a small portion — were withdrawn from exploitation, wouldn't that mean fewer rangers on its payroll, and hence fewer secretaries, pickup trucks, hard hats, paper clips, and forms in sextuplet — in short, the anathema of most bureaucrats, a smaller bureaucracy? It would. Even the traditional land-preserving agency, the National Park Service, suffered from trepidation, worried that curbs on future access roads, scenic drives, and tramways would mean a loss in bureaucratic status.

In response to the objections, Howard Zahniser wisely emphasized the basic issue — the preservation of "our oldest resource," as he called it. Newly quickened by the lateness of the hour, the public generated thousands of pages of hearing testimony and tens of thousands of letters to their representatives in Washington. Yet for eight years Congress vacillated, tugged by exploiters on the one hand and the clamors of their more ordinary constituents on the other. Nash provides an insight into the wrangling: sixty-six different times, the Wilderness Bill was rewritten and resubmitted into the legislative mill.

Meanwhile, weary Zahniser was crisscrossing the country, attending each federal hearing on the issue, perhaps as wearily repeating the words that for all their repetition represented a fresh vision for him: a national program establishing wilderness for "the first time in the history of the earth." It was a step that no civilization had taken before, a test, as he saw it, of our cultural development. Zahniser answered critics from the timber industry: "We are not fighting progress. We are making it." In the spring of 1964, Zahniser sensed victory, but he would not taste it. He died of a heart attack at the age of fifty-eight, only a few weeks before Congress, overwhelmed by what Nash calls "a remarkable volume of sentiment for preservation," at last bowed to the public weal and passed the Wilderness Act.

Granted the help of David Brower and millions of persistent citizens, the Wilderness Act of 1964 remains Howard Zahniser's monument. As might be expected from such a prolonged legislative storm, the bill emerged with some compromises. The act allowed mineral exploration on wilderness lands until 1984, and it did not entirely eliminate the motorboats and aircraft that hikers come to wilderness to escape. But in one sweep it did estabish nine million acres of untrammeled land, while creating a review process for possible inclusion of other *de facto* wilderness. Finally, it created the impetus for a second wilderness act, passed in 1974 and specifically aimed at setting aside badly needed preserves in the populous Eastern United States. As the provisions of the two acts are implemented, Howard Zahniser's legacy to the nation keeps on giving.

Rachel Carson. "Hogwash" and a "hoax" howled some critics, but Silent Spring *propelled the conservation movement into the heady clamor of the late 1960s and early 1970s.*

Erich Hartmann, courtesy of Rachel Carson Council, Inc.

Chapter 13

Rachel Carson: The Issue Becomes Life Itself

"Hogwash" and a "hoax," howled its critics, as *Silent Spring* soared onto the best-seller lists. Admirers countered by calling the book "a real contribution to our salvation." Whatever their sentiments, those embroiled in the controversy agreed that it "was one of those rare books that have the power to move the whole nation." Its immediate effect was to help revitalize a flagging environmental movement, but the book began by reminding readers of their slowly changing ecological heritage.

This process has gone on for eons: forests replace deserts, mountains heave up through forests, and oceans flood over peaks to be replaced again by deserts. In his brief existence, man has also been an agent of change. To wrest protein from animal life, Stone-Age Indians drove herds of buffalo over "jumps" or set fire to grasslands. Making room for cornfields, colonists on the Eastern seaboard flailed away at the gloomy forests with their awkward, straight-shafted axes, oblivious to the long-term effects on what we today call "the web of life." As George

Perkins Marsh pointed out, some societies went too far. They so wrenched the land for immediate gains that future generations suffered. Still, despite these abuses, human life has persisted.

Around World War II, however, new factors appeared in the equation of survival. Technological man started releasing new substances into the biosphere, lethal concoctions foreign to the ancient chemistry of the earth. In the short run, they may be beneficial, but once released, they can't be recalled, and they kill indiscriminately by altering the chemistry of the cells on which life is based. Referring to the abrupt introduction of such pollutants as strontium 90 and DDT, Rachel Carson presented the new crisis in *Silent Spring:*

> The rapidity of change and the speed with which new situations are created follow the impetuous and heedless pace of man rather than the deliberate pace of nature.... The chemicals to which life is asked to make its adjustments are no longer merely the calcium and silica and copper and all the rest of the minerals washed out of the rocks and carried in rivers to the sea; they are the synthetic creations of man's inventive mind, brewed in his laboratories, and having no counterparts in nature.

Utilitarian conservationists such as Teddy Roosevelt had looked upon stewardship of the earth as a means of insuring the country's economic future. Others such as Robert Marshall worried that man's spirit would wither as an increasingly artificial environment replaced his natural surroundings. Rachel Carson warned the public of a different dilemma. The issue now became not board feet of lumber or the curative power of wilderness, but the viability of life itself. The mainspring behind the book's popularity was the most basic of fears, the fear of death — a slow and grotesque death, as Carson described the process. Her warnings inspired what has been termed the new conservation. Its issues are far more visceral than those espoused by either Roosevelt or Marshall, for they touch every member of the public directly.

In 1874, Othmar Zeidler, a German graduate student, developed a new compound, dichlorodiphenyl-trichloro-ethane. Zeidler looked on his experiment as an exercise in chemical synthesis, a step toward his doctorate degree. He cared little about what use, if any, the formula might have. For decades it lay forgotten in a filing cabinet. Sixty-five years later, Dr. Paul Muller reinvented the substance while working for the Swiss chemical firm of J. R. Geigy. Far more commercially minded than Zeidler, Muller took the substance home, caught some houseflies, and put them in a glass box with his new powder. The next day all the flies were dead.

Further experiments seemed to show that DDT, as he called it, was just what the pesticide industry needed: a product that killed insect pests on contact but did not injure people. Geigy's representatives in the United States and Britain began marketing the chemical in 1942. By then World War II was raging over the land masses and around the oceans of the world — and with it the malaria, typhoid fever, and dysentery that have caused more deaths during armed conflicts than swords, arrows, bullets, or bombs. Fearing a typhus outbreak after the capture of Naples, the Allies tried dusting this Italian city with DDT. Body lice carrying the disease keeled over, as had Muller's flies. Authorities credited the miraculous substance with saving 250,000 human lives. "This was," says Kenneth Davis, "but the beginning of DDT's march to glory. Soldiers and sailors by the million carried small cans of DDT powder to protect themselves against bedbugs, lice, and mosquitoes. They came to love the stuff."

Back in civilian clothes, they loved it equally well. The war had meant scarcity and rationing. With the postwar economy booming, the luxury-starved public rushed out to buy the washing machines and automobiles now rolling off the production lines instead of jeeps and tanks. In like manner, its enthusiasm soared for the results of technology refined during the War — penicillin, atomic energy, and DDT, now becoming available to make civilian life easy. The old Myth of the Garden, of Superabundance, had received a blow when settlers encountered the bitter realities of the Western frontier. But the Dream lived on, transferred, as Stewart Udall terms it, into the Myth of Scientific Supremacy. Science and its handmaiden, technology, could put a car — no, two cars — in every garage. And with a similar childlike optimism, householders armed themselves with aerosol bombs to rid their kitchens of bothersome flies, their gardens of leaf-eating beetles. Science could fix anything.

DDT proved more than a convenience. United Nations teams traveled the world, eliminating malaria from areas where the illness had blighted human life for centuries. In the United States, the Department of Agriculture promoted the poison as the salvation from Dutch elm disease and other real or imagined insect scourges. Representatives of the chemical industry advertised the synthetic killer across the countryside, pointing to the high agricultural yields that were feeding the world's population. In 1948, Muller received a Nobel Prize for his discovery.

A few people took note of robins writhing on their lawns after government airplanes, loaded with DDT, had sprayed their neighborhoods against the menace of mosquitoes with DDT and related poisons. A few scientists speculated that insects might build up resistance to the new compounds. There even were scattered lawsuits. But individual complaints were lost in a wave of enthusiasm, as the chemical industry tallied its profits. Still, for some people the unanswered questions about the long-range effects of pesticides became more nagging as ever larger doses of the compounds were turned loose. Then, almost overnight, *Silent Spring* united the doubters to create nationwide opposition to unrestricted use of chemical pesticides.

Viewed from hindsight, Rachel Carson seems an unlikely person to generate a public quarrel. Shy, even withdrawn, she lacked the dramatic appeal of many past conservationists — the combative aplomb of a Carl Schurz or the boisterous mysticism of John Muir. Yet her patient attention to scientific detail and her calm in answering critics became the qualities that won over the public during the often vicious personal attacks against her.

An outline of her career reflects her simplicity and strength, the sometimes plodding devotion to family and profession. When success came, it came almost as an embarrassment. The daughter of a real estate agent, Rachel Carson grew up in rural Springdale, Pennsylvania. Like many young people with strong but unformulated visions of a writing career, she signed up as an English major in college. However, inspired by a required science course, she switched to biology in her sophomore year. "It never occurred to me," she observed looking back on her education, "that I could combine the two careers." In this she eventually succeeded, but not until after an ordinary climb on the academic and bureaucratic ladders.

Graduating magna cum laude in 1928 from Pennsylvania College for Women, Rachel Carson pursued a master's degree in zoology at Johns Hopkins University. Additional study followed at the Woods Hole Marine Biological Laboratory, on Cape Cod. From 1930 to 1936 she taught at Johns Hopkins and the University of Maryland, then moved to Washington, D.C., as an aquatic biologist with the Bureau of Fisheries.

In the Depression years she was lucky to get a job. Her father had died a year earlier, and she needed the steady income of government work to support her mother and

Early in her career, Rachel Carson worked as an aquatic biologist for the U.S. Bureau of Fisheries. In the photo above she is gathering specimens of tide life along the Florida Keys. Time magazine later accused the writer of "frightening her readers."
Rex Gary Schmidt, courtesy of U.S. Fish and Wildlife Service

other relatives. As for her writing, the *Baltimore Sun* paid for a series of articles about fisheries, and her position at the Bureau involved creating scripts for radio broadcasts about life in the ocean. So far, her professional life was personally satisfying but undistinguished.

Her chief at the Bureau urged her to submit one of her articles to the *Atlantic Monthly*. "Undersea" appeared in the September, 1937 issue. In one of those flukes that beginning writers dream about, an editor at Simon and Schuster spotted the essay. He invited Miss Carson to dinner in New York and suggested she expand the piece into a book. Released a month before the excitement of Pearl Harbor, *Under the Sea-Wind,* as would be true of her next two books, combined keen scientific insights with lyrical prose to give readers intimate portraits of the sea.

Yet despite the enthusiasm of its publisher, the book proved a financial failure. In the meantime, the Bureau of Fisheries combined with the Biological Survey to become the present Fish and Wildlife Service. Eventually Rachel Carson became chief editor of its publications. Fellow workers remember her as a taskmaster tempering high editorial standards with humor.

Essentially, from the publication of *Under the Sea-Wind* onward, the story of Carson's public career becomes the story of her books. In 1951, the Book-of-the-Month Club chose *The Sea Around Us* as an alternate selection. Capitalizing on public response, Oxford University Press reissued her first book, which joined *The Sea Around Us* on the best-seller list. Finally, RKO pictures rendered this volume into an overdramatized but Oscar-winning movie. Besides the honors, publishing royalties put the author on a comfortable financial footing for the first time in her life. She left her government job, built a summer cottage on the Maine coast, and looked forward to a quiet life of study and writing.

In 1955, Edwin Way Teale wrote Rachel Carson, "You have done it again!" He was referring to *The Edge of the Sea*. Again, professionals and laymen alike praised her for accurate and poetic revelations, which now concentrated on the rich ribbon of life found where oceans meet continents. Friends teased Rachel Carson about the danger of becoming a cult figure to her growing audience.

There was little chance of that for staid Rachel Carson. In her view of the world, her musings along Maine's Sheepscot Bay remained far more essential than awards or speaking engagements, and she might have gone on writing reflective but not disturbing books for her admirers. However, along with her growing popularity came a slow change in her commitment, and with it an often unpleasant public debate.

The Depression administration of Franklin Delano

Roosevelt had placed major emphasis on preserving natural resources. However, World War II absorbed much of the concern for the environment, and the movement continued to flag through the Cold-War era. Yet along with others who treasured the natural heritage, Rachel Carson questioned the country's pell-mell rush into a postwar development in which technology and growth seemed to be the nation's new gods. Throughout her years in the Fish and Wildlife Service, she had witnessed the loss of habitat as suburbs spread into the countryside, the predator programs that mindlessly poisoned coyotes and mountain lions. As an avid bird watcher, she noted the decline of hawk and eagle populations. President Eisenhower's appointment of Douglas McKay as Secretary of Interior typified the malaise accompanying prosperity. In the words of Frank Graham, Jr., "McKay's comprehension of conservation was best reflected by his characterization of conservationists as 'punks'; his program consisted chiefly of leasing away public lands and driving out dedicated wildlife specialists." Environmentalists called him "Give-it-Away" McKay.

Unlike the historian and vitriolic environmentalist of her day, Bernard DeVoto, Rachel Carson was not one to rush to the barricades. But when McKay fired the capable director of the Fish and Wildlife Service, she wrote an angry letter, which appeared in the *Washington Post*, then later in the *Reader's Digest*. Referring to those who fought for national parks and wildlife refuges, she said, "Apparently their hard-won progress is to be wiped out, as a politically minded Administration returns us to the dark ages of unrestrained exploitation and destruction." Those were harsh words from a person known for the gentle writing of *The Sea Around Us,* but they are an indication of what would grow into the major contribution of her life.

In 1958 an old friend from Massachusetts wrote her that local authorities claimed their DDT assault against mosquitoes "was entirely harmless." Yet she and her husband found dead birds scattered over their yard following the aerial spraying. The friend went on to vent her frustration over the fact that as the summer progressed, mosquitoes waxed more virulent, while harmless insects such as bees disappeared. In writing a response, Rachel Carson did some research on DDT and found that "the more I learned about the use of pesticides the more appalled I became." She saw "that everything which meant most to me as a naturalist was being threatened, and that nothing I could do would be more important" than to write a book investigating the synthetic poisons.

As was true of George Perkins Marsh, Rachel Carson began work on her most influential book in later years — she was 51, Marsh in his early 60s. The renowned ambassador, however, was condensing the observations of a lifetime into *Man and Nature* while working under pleasant conditions in balmy Italy. Carson, on the other hand, was striking out into new territory, so far little explored by anyone, including herself. And, though financially independent by the time, she was writing against a host of nearly crippling personal circumstances.

With the death of her mother soon after starting *Silent Spring,* Rachel Carson suffered the shock of losing "the strongest single influence of her life," according to Carson biographer Paul Brooks. Throughout work on this book she cared for a school-age grandnephew. Flu, a sinus infection, and an ulcer dogged her, meaning less time at her desk. All this was the more troublesome because of the natural pace of her writing. Marsh wrote in a white heat once his pen warmed to the task; Carson composed slowly, turning out 500 words on a good day. In the midst of working on the new manuscript — while also supporting passage of the Wilderness Bill and preparing a new edition of *The Sea Around Us* — she began radiation therapy for the cancer that killed her in 1964.

Most telling in the comparison between the two writers is their attitude toward the evidence supporting their books. In a word, both were painstaking researchers. She knew that *Silent Spring* would provoke economic interests, that opponents would scrutinize its pages for factual weaknesses. She spent four and a half years evaluating every scientific source.

The powerful sweep of *Man and Nature* showed how past civilizations misused the environment. Marsh illustrated forests degenerating into deserts, wheat fields into stony and abandoned valleys, "the forlorn monuments to human greed or improvidence." In 1862, nearly a hundred years later, *Silent Spring* followed a similar pattern. As with Marsh's volume, Carson's best-known book is long and necessarily detailed, though its organization is straightforward, its major points readily summarized.

From the outset, Rachel Carson acknowledged the benefits of chemical pesticides when properly used. The dangers came from their abuse by a society "largely ignorant of their potentials for harm." The DDT innocently sprayed on rose bushes by thousands of home gardeners washed away into rivers. Plants absorbed the chemical from the water; fish ate the plants. Birds and humans ate the fish. Only twenty years after its introduction, researchers were finding DDT not only in animals but in human mothers' milk and in the fatty tissues of the entire population. Further, she described the threat as insidious, because the compounds are "unseen and invisible." Their quiet damage — whether sending birds into the death throes of paroxysm or, she suspected, causing cancer and mutations in humans — can occur years after release of the poisons. Pesticides fit into an age-old pattern: what first appeared a boon would prove an instrument of man's destruction.

Further, not only was their use harmful and expensive, in many instances the chemicals didn't work. Destructive creatures such as a spider mite actually thrived following the sprayings designed to eliminate them. The chemicals killed their natural enemies with greater efficiency. In other cases, Darwin was confirmed: through the process of selection, only the stronger insects of a species survived the chemical assaults. They lived on to reproduce a progeny of super individuals. With ever more powerful doses of pesticides required to subdue them, their populations grew ever more resistant. Man had placed himself on a chemical treadmill: the faster he ran, the faster it spun. Carson urged sensible alternatives. She outlined biological controls that sterilized and trapped pests or pitted one insect species against another — all of them methods harmless to man.

Despite the disadvantages she cited, pesticide programs had expanded year by year. Money talked louder than science. According to an irate and rebellious English scientist, pesticide proponents promised "salvation at the end of a spray nozzle." The industry counted its profits. At the same time, it channeled part of the huge returns into universities. What seemed a charitable gesture became, under Carson's analysis, a tax-deductible scheme to keep potentially critical entomologists in line.

She also delved into the psychology of government bureaucracies. A few years before the publication of *Silent Spring,* President Eisenhower — not known for his attacks on the status quo — warned about the lack of concern of the military-industrial complex, of technologies and bureaucracies running roughshod over the nation's welfare. Following similar reasoning, Carson observed that in contrast to undramatic biological controls, "the chemical weed killers are a bright new toy. They work in a spectacular way; they give a giddy sense of power over nature to those who wield them, and as for the long-range effects — these are easily brushed aside as the baseless imaginings of pessimists."

Stung by those allegations, industry counterattacked

savagely. In Frank Graham's words, they "saw *Silent Spring* not as a scientific challenge, but as a public relations problem." Instead of tackling Carson's arguments head-on, their well-funded campaign against the book condemned it as an emotional and inaccurate tirade. An editorial in *Chemical and Engineering News* compared *Silent Spring* to "indiscriminate shrieking." Some opponents went on to attack its author personally, reminding readers that unmarried Carson was an "unfulfilled woman." They falsely claimed that this "devotee of some cult" associated with "mystics and food faddists." A review in *Time* magazine accused her of "frightening her readers." It labeled her warnings about contaminated water supplies as "nonsense."

The Myth of Superabundance had lulled the American public, but not entirely. The mushroom cloud that blossomed over Hiroshima in 1945 now hung over an uneasy planet as evidence of man's destructive capabilities. By the time *Silent Spring* appeared, Americans remembered sitting down three years earlier to Thanksgiving dinners without cranberries; the Food and Drug Administration had ordered the fruit off grocery shelves because of contamination by the pesticide aminotriazol. And only weeks before the book arrived in stores, they read newspaper accounts of babies born with eerie birth defects — victims of the tranquilizer thalidomide prescribed to their mothers during pregnancy. The chemical dream had its darker side.

As runaway sales indicated, *Silent Spring* brought the uneasiness of years to a flash point. The *Saturday Review* ran a picture of Rachel Carson on the cover of its September 29 issue with the caption, "*Silent Spring* marks the beginning of a national debate." The Book-of-the-Month Club offered the volume as its October selection. *CBS Reports* featured the book on two programs. In the next two years it sold over 1,000,000 copies.

The public was indeed frightened. Reporters peppered President Kennedy with questions about his stand on DDT. He directed his Science Advisory Committee to give the issue a thorough airing. The growing intensity of concern spawned other government investigations. For the first time, they probed the long-term effects of the pesticides that government and industry had promoted for years. A good deal of bureaucratic backtracking went on, for as one official characterized the atmosphere of the questionings, "where the shot hit, the feathers fly." To his credit, Secretary of Interior Stewart Udall, soon to be a pallbearer at Carson's funeral, broke ranks from shuffling politicians and issued directives severely limiting pesticide use on public lands under his control.

Throughout the national debate Carson retained her typical calm. As she hoped, the investigations largely confirmed her allegations. As scientific evidence mounted in her favor, there came a change. Along with other former critics, *Time* switched its position. The magazine now praised Carson "for her part in wakening her countrymen to the possible perils from pesticides and other chemicals." More importantly, Congress introduced a series of pesticide regulations that gave impetus to other conservation reforms such as the Wilderness Act.

On her death, *American Forests* ungrammatically but accurately concluded that "Rachel Carson's impact on worldwide conservation was more profound than any other individual of her time." She provided lagging conservationists with the momentum that propelled the movement into the heady clamor of the late 1960s and early 1970s. Inspired by Carson, Aldo Leopold, Robert Marshall, and other leaders, the new conservation is now characterized by grass-roots activism — by an awareness of the interrelatedness of man and nature, and by a chilling sense that decisions of the next few years will determine the future of the planet.

Yet "today the pesticide treadmill spins more wildly than ever," writes biologist Robert van den Bosch in *The Pesticide Conspiracy,* which was published in 1978. "We use twice as much insecticide as in 1962, there are more insect species of pest status than ever before, insect control costs have skyrocketed, and insecticide impact on the environment is the worst in history." Elsewhere, developing nations have turned to endrin, aldrin, 2,4,5-T, and a host of other compounds with mysterious names and supposedly wondrous properties, as shortcuts to prosperity. Musing on the future, Frank Graham remarks that the new conservation is so recent that its history "has yet to be written. It should be a splendid (and hair raising) adventure story, and the outcome will be in doubt to the very end."

In his youth, Barry Commoner roamed the slums of Brooklyn with the toughs in a block gang. It was one kind of preparation for the jungles of academe. University of Wisconsin, Stevens Point, Student Newspaper

Chapter 14

Barry Commoner:
Science and Social Duty

A green-striped environmental poster decorates his office door at Washington University. It loudly demands ECOLOGY NOW! from the microbiologist's visitors. Government reports, reference books, and manuscripts in progress overflow the desk and filing cabinets. With, as one observer describes it, "thick greying hair standing straight up from his head like a crew-cut gone to seed," the Professor of Environmental Sciences looms tall in the small room, forceful behind his black-rimmed glasses. He justifies the apparent chaos around him: "The main thing is that something is interrelated. It's like nature and ecosystems — intrinsic complexity."

In 1970, *Time* magazine featured an acrylic portrait of Barry Commoner on its cover and hailed the professor turned public advocate as the "Paul Revere of Ecology." Its lead article praised Commoner as a new brand of scientist, "concerned, authoritative and worldly, an iconoclast who refuses to remain sheltered in the ivory laboratory." Long before activism became fashionable, Barry Commoner was preaching to assemblies in church basements and union halls, warning about the dangers of nuclear fallout. He continues to draw on his prize-winning research "to shake them up," as he quipped to a *New York Times* reporter dogging the scientist on his way to a United Automobile Workers meeting. By "them" Commoner means the entire nation. And if disturbing people is the goal of his witty, sometimes abrasive, lectures, best-selling books, and scores of popular and professional articles, he has succeeded.

Activists expect to dodge a certain amount of fire by the industries, government agencies, and politicians whose policies they question. However, with his high profile, Commoner has made himself a large target for his own colleagues as well. Noting his ubiquity, some fellow scientists gripe that he represents the diligent researcher turned showman. Others strike closer home, attacking the research that forms the basis of any scientist's professional standing. A thrust by Paul Ehrlich, author of *The Population Bomb* and a shaker in his own right, indicates the emotional intensity of the running battle between the two scientists that has gone on for years. From the pages of *Science,* Ehrlich slices out that Commoner's "one-sided treatment of the complexities of the environmental crisis are typical of a dangerous trend of politically active scientists who appeal to the public for support when they receive little or none within their professions."

The first charge, of playing to the cameras, Commoner dismisses as "one of the hazards of doing your social duty as a scientist." That responsibility, Commoner insists, while shaking his finger at hesitant associates, includes not simply work in the laboratory but public airing of the results. Far-reaching decisions on nuclear power, pesticides, and population control, he believes, should be made through a broad democratic process, not by coteries of specialists. As to the second, referring to Ehrlich and others, who attack him, Commoner snaps a shot back over one shoulder at their "inhumane, abhorrent political schemes put forward in the guise of science" — then plunges into his next book, which will receive inevitable applause from *Time* and the *New Yorker*.

Are such fulminations the legacy of gentle Rachel Carson? Devotees of *Silent Spring* tended to see the world divided into enlightened defenders standing shoulder-to-shoulder against nature's villainous wreckers. Things have not turned out so simply. To a far greater degree than most people expected, ecology has proved to be a comprehensive science, touching as it does on aesthetics as well as the national budget, on the debate over nuclear power as well as the length of lines at the local gas station. As with other fields, this complex science also involves personality clashes and the distribution of envied research dollars. Barry Commoner's career illustrates how the study of nature can pit one scientist against his equally well-intentioned colleagues. Victory in such prolonged tussles can give the winner "an enormous kick," as science writer Anne Chisholm calls it. On a different level, the prospect of personal satisfaction also provides energy for the mill that, one hopes, will eventually grind out significant ecological truths.

Isidore Commoner was a Russian immigrant who worked as a tailor until he went blind. His son Barry grew up street-wise in the midst of poverty, roaming the slums of Brooklyn with the toughs of a block gang. It was one kind of preparation for the subtler jungles of academe.

Among Commoner's favorite reading is *Call It Sleep,* a 1934 novel by Henry Roth. The book portrays a sensitive boy growing up in the rough-and-tumble of Brooklyn tenement life. The professor's admiration for the novel points to another side of youthful Barry's personality. Within the walls of James Madison High School, he was so shy that teachers assigned him to a special class in speech correction. A course in biology sparked his eagerness to learn. Soon the former gang member was roaming the steel-and-concrete landscape looking for bits of nature to study. An uncle gave him a microscope and the young Barry spent hours in Prospect Park, returning home with samples of "goop" that danced to life under the lens.

At nearby Columbia University, he supported his studies in zoology by, among other odd jobs, doing research on medieval coins for an economics professor. He also developed enthusiasm for such liberal causes as that of the Spanish Loyalists. In 1937, at the age of twenty, the Brooklyn boy graduated with honors, the first in a succession of awards that have marked his scientific career. In one sentence the writer of the *Time* feature sums up the student's accelerating interests: "Bright and ambitious, he went to Harvard, closeted himself in a laboratory for three years, and left with a Ph.D. in biology."

By then World War II was on. Ironically, Navy Lieutenant Commoner spent much of his time promoting DDT, the new delight of pathologists. Working with engineers, he helped contrive a rig for fighter planes, which sailed off, equipped with their array of tanks and nozzles, to spray troops in the South Pacific. The experience sowed some early doubts in him about technology, reflects Commoner. "What they told us was only that DDT was a substance with a wholly unprecedented ability to kill insects of all sorts." However, "we learned from a few unpleasant experiences in a jungle in Panama that DDT makes snakes very excited. We learned another lesson when we sprayed an island shoreline in New Jersey and brought millions of flies to that unhappy place — to enjoy the huge mounds of fish that we killed." After the war, Commoner married psychologist Gloria Gordon, then took a job as an associate editor of *Science Illustrated*. In 1947, restless for the challenges of the laboratory, he left New York City for a position as associate professor of plant physiology at St. Louis' Washington University.

Commoner quickly became an asset to the University, an institution boasting a Gothic clock tower rising over the trees of a prosperous suburb. The students liked this lively, witty professor with a Brooklyn accent, who might begin the traditionally dull course in basic biology by throwing a challenge out to those from Ohio: "How is the swimming in Lake Erie?" He then filled a semester by expanding on the biological principles that affect the life of one of the nation's most assaulted ecosystems.

University administrators politely applaud good teaching, but what they really want from the faculty laboring in their libraries and laboratories is research that earns a reputation for the institution and, more importantly, attracts grant money. Commoner didn't disappoint them. Early in his career, he established himself as a brilliant researcher. His genetic studies of the tobacco mosaic virus shed new light on such viral diseases as hepatitis and poliomyelitis. Widening circles of investigation led to insights on cancer, petrochemicals, and the reproductive mechanisms of cells. For his work on the tobacco virus, in 1953 the American Association for the Advancement of Science honored him with the prestigious Newcomb Cleveland Prize, awarded to the most outstanding young scientist of the year. Soon after, Washington University showed its appreciation by promoting its up-and-coming researcher, still in his thirties, to full professor. Twelve years later, eyeing a host of subsequent honors, it rewarded Commoner with the chairmanship of its botany department.

Meanwhile, ecology was making a convert of the former street-gang member. His own researches with radioactive materials helped arouse his curiosity about the effects of fallout from the A-bomb testing of the 1950s. With other citizens, he founded the St. Louis Committee for Nuclear Information. As one of its projects, the volunteer group collected babies' teeth from across the country. Analysis revealed the presence of radioactive strontium 90. "I was making speeches in every church and hall in St. Louis," remembers Commoner, "describing the facts of atmospheric testing." Government agencies, he charged, were ignoring or suppressing the realities of fallout dangers.

At first, it was not a popular crusade. Supporters of Senator Joseph McCarthy heckled the professor, branding his efforts as un-American. But the evidence, pressed by a handful of activists across the nation — the forerunners of the ecological movement of the 1960s — was undeniable, once brought into the open. The debate led to widespread concerns resulting in the nuclear test-ban treaty of 1963. For Commoner, it marked a shift from a closeted scientist to a scientist with a public conscience. All in all, it provided good training for the biologist's future activism.

As they have become elaborated in his mind, Commoner's scientific views concern nothing less than the complex interaction of the entire biosphere. They range from the chemistry of individual cells to the functioning of ecosystems. They have encompassed such disciplines as physics and economics, microbiology and sociology, a spread that has been the nemesis of many an earnest ecologist who has dared strike out beyond his own specialty. Nevertheless, Commoner's broad outlook can be summarized into what he calls "my three laws of ecology. I invented these," he says inaccurately: "first, everything is connected to everything else; second, everything has to go somewhere; and third, there's no such thing as a free lunch."

In today's age of ecological awareness, few scientists or laymen would disagree with the statements; as dictums they seem obvious and innocent enough. It is, rather, when ecologists begin applying them to the realities of everyday affairs — when for instance the energy crisis is brought down to the dilemma of who gets less gas in his tank — that the feuding begins. Neither the dangers of crossing boundaries of his own specialty into other fields nor those of prescribing often bitter pills as antidotes to environmental ills have fazed Commoner. As a popularizer and gadfly, he has stirred the public through lectures and a continuous stream of articles in *Harper's, Ramparts,* and the *New Yorker*. However, the main outlines of his thinking — and an indication of the antagonisms his ideas often generate — can be seen in his books.

Science and Survival (1966) was not designed to ingratiate its author with fellow scientists or with government agencies that often support them. Using as its main villain the atmospheric contamination from atomic fallout, the book also touches on additional "pertinent examples of folly," as the *London Times* called them — pollution of the earth by detergents, insecticides, and carbon dioxide. "Sooner or later," the author warned, "we must pay for every intrusion on the natural environment." And we would have to pay, accused Commoner, because industry, government, and the writer's fellow scientists were irresponsibly pushing ahead with their pet projects while disregarding the long-term consequences to the public.

To the surprise of many readers, Commoner showed his daring by including in his dragnet the narrowness exemplified by the theory of Francis Crick and James D. Watson. A few years earlier this pair had stirred biologists to new excitement with their DNA and heredity revelations. So great was the enthusiasm of the scientific community that in 1962 the two investigators received a Nobel Prize for their work. Yet holist Commoner, taking an admittedly minority view, debunked the research as a false and Faustian fascination with unveiling "the secret of life."

In contrast, he urged a change in perspective similar to the one that had involved him with the St. Louis Center for Nuclear Information. Instead of aiming for dramatic discoveries, often conceived in self-interest and abetted by secrecy, he believed "the issues created by the advance of science can only be resolved by moral judgment and political choice." Commoner wanted to make moralists of his colleagues. Like *Silent Spring, Science and Survival* was an attack on a broad front, intended to arouse public distrust of the author's own profession. Reflecting on Commoner's long list of his colleagues' projects that disregarded the earth's welfare, a writer for the *New Yorker* pondered, "one can only wonder how many more mistakes are being made."

"Ecological irresponsibility can pay — for the entrepreneur, but not for society as a whole," continued Commoner in a similar vein. Beyond the attack on his own profession, *The Closing Circle* (1971) struck two related nerves with its observations on technology and population. *Newsweek* called the book "the calmest, most convincing call to alarm in years." And the reaction from Commoner's detractors was all the more pained and immediate as sales placed *The Closing Circle* on the best-seller list.

The book pointed to World War II as the critical watershed period for the earth. Since then, industrialized societies have undertaken a major shift from natural to synthetic products. To a large degree, the heralded spinoffs from war technology have replaced biodegradable cotton, wood, and manure with synthetic fibers, plastics, and nitrogen fertilizers — all products that place heavy strains on ecosystems. The shift is leading the world into an ecological dead end. "We have broken out of the circle of life," converting the earth's "endless cycles into manmade, linear events." Glibly swept up in "progress," people often don't recognize the consequences. We have, the book estimated, twenty to fifty years before the damage becomes irreversible. It was a disturbing but certainly not an unorthodox judgment.

But Commoner pressed on with this line of thought, leading his readers toward a controversial conclusion about population growth. From 1946 to 1966 pollution in the United States increased about 200 to 2,000 percent. The population, slightly more affluent over the twenty-year period, increased 42 percent. Hence, the critical factor in the ecological crisis is the new technology — not increased population. Commoner asserts that the earth has the resources to support perhaps twice as many people as it now does. He dismisses, many experts say simplistically, population control as a key to ecological sanity. In doing so, he cites research indicating that in some countries a standard of living raised by an income increase of only a few hundred dollars a year per family automatically results in fewer children. According to his thinking, the poor need economic help, not family planning.

It is this point that causes the bitterness between demographers Paul Ehrlich and Garrett Hardin on the one side, who have pegged their careers to promoting zero population growth, and Commoner on the other. The debate continues, one scientist observes, each faction spending "valuable time figuring out ways to embarrass the other."

Appropriately, the most recent Commoner books probe another troubling aspect of modern life, the worsening energy crisis. Reviewing the laws of thermodynamics, *The Poverty of Power* (1976) proposes that the problem is not one of shortages but of profligacy. Burning coal or oil in centralized power plants to heat homes by electricity, for example, wastes 97% of the energy. The nation has created its own malaise by shortsightedness. By the same token, it has the opportunity — if it has the flexibility to seize it — of solving its energy ills without wrecking the environment. All the buildings in the country could be heated and cooled by solar power — a benign, limitless, and cheap source of power. The question is whether or not the people who run government and industry will permit these sane solutions to become realities.

So far, Commoner maintains the moguls have gone in the opposite direction. He reviews the economic fallacies and safety hazards of nuclear power — the diminishing supplies of uranium and the bizarre dangers of plutonium, the most toxic substance known to man. The decision of government and industry to go for broke with nuclear power is a modern-day pact with the devil.

Many critics applaud Commoner's thorough analyses of the problems but balk at his extrapolations into economics, which urge an unspecified form of socialism as a replacement for capitalism. "Read it for the science, pass up the economics," suggests Professor Peter Passell of Commoner's alma mater, Columbia University. Less delicately, a *Forbes* article entitled "Latter Day Wizard of Oz"

Microbiologist turned activist, Commoner emphatically maintains that his "social duty as a scientist" includes not simply work in the laboratory but public airing of the results.
Frank Armstrong, courtesy of Washington University, St. Louis, Missouri

depicts the author of *The Poverty of Power* as "a second-rate scientist and a no-rate economist."

Commoner's writing has become more strident as the energy crisis has worsened. In *The Politics of Energy* (1979), he levels his pen at the Carter administration and its energy "shenanigans." On the surface, the President's policies advocate conservation. In substance, however, the National Energy Plan calls "for an increased dependence on nuclear power and a greater production of coal products. The proposal, in fact, advocates a far heavier drain on our nonrenewable energy resources," according to a summary of the book by Robert Dahlin, an editor of *Publishers Weekly*. Barry Commoner presses his argument by claiming that former Carter energy czar James Schlesinger suppressed information on the one hand and juggled figures on the other. It is Commoner's loudest indictment of how officialdom, motivated by politics rather than concern for the nation's welfare, is hoodwinking the public.

The microbiologist turned activist gives increasing emphasis to solar power as the most flexible and practical method of extricating the country from the energy pitfall. "You know that solar energy is not a panacea. You don't say, 'Here's a gadget' and all is solved. I want to show that the application of solar energy is as varied as the geography of the country. You do it one way in one place, another way somewhere else." Yet he adds in an ominous vein, "A solar transition would have very serious consequences for oil and utility companies."

Will such financial interests block the shift to nonpolluting solar technology? Professor Commoner is not a gloom-and-doom environmentalist. Despite what he sees as the prevailing "shenanigans," he remains optimistic that substantive change can take place. He cautions that "the big danger is for people to throw up their hands. Because then it will be possible for the oil people to have their way with us."

Barry Commoner's forte, notes reviewer Passell, is his "remarkable ability to translate the conclusions of a half-dozen disciplines for those with little knowledge or interest in science." A virtue added to his talent as synthesizer and popularizer is his writing style. "The reader," praises journalist Philip Herrera, "rides as easily on Commoner's prose as on one of his favorite electric trains."

That sense of ease is deceptive, a refined by-product of the biologist's energy. In 1966 he began directing Washington University's Center for the Biology of Natural Systems, an environmental research group which he has since moved to Queens College in New York City. In 1979, together with author Studs Terkel, Grey Panther leader Maggie Kuhn, Georgia legislator Julian Bond, and other activists, he organized the Citizens Party, then soon became its candidate for the 1980 Presidential race. Billing his campaign as "populist" and "progressive," Commoner stumped the nation, determined to take the major decisions about solar power, military spending, human rights, and nuclear power away from huge corporations and return them to the citizenry — thus offering resurrected ideals and, for once it seemed, a real choice in the voting booth.

After, as realists predicted, Commoner lost the election, he bounced back with "It's clear that the country is hungry for real political discussion, which it didn't get from the major candidates." Hungry or not, the nation continues to feel ever sharper pains from the prevailing expand-and-expire approach to nonrenewable resources. And through books, articles, and lectures Commoner continues in his attempt to bring the country to its good senses. When he's not touring the lecture circuit — one year he gave over thirty major speeches, in addition to keeping up with his writing and research — he spends the day working at his office. Back when he lived in St. Louis, he used to walk the mile and a half home. His wife once presented him with a

bicycle to speed the trip. As a sign of his constantly whirl-
ing mental energy Commoner insisted on the stroll, calling it "a great time to use your head."

Ralph Nader. When the immigrant's son warned the American public about unsafe automobiles, General Motors hired gumshoes to investigate his private life. Says Nader, "I don't consider myself abnormal. I consider the auto industry abnormal." Public Citizen, Inc.

Chapter 15

Ralph Nader:
Slayer of Corvairs

Eyes twinkling, the brunette approached him as he idled through magazines in a drugstore, then suggested they go to her place for a discussion of foreign affairs. On another occasion, alleged the witness, a winsome blonde sidled up as he mused over the cookie display in a Safeway store. Would he like to help her, as she put it, move some furniture?

Aware of popping newspaper cameras, members of the Senate subcommittee looked on with appropriate shock as the young man with a hurt look in his big brown eyes reeled off the catalog of offenses. He had spotted gumshoes lurking in his hotel lobby in Des Moines; claiming they wanted to hire him, strangers descended on his acquaintances and asked about their friend's drinking habits, his sex life, his politics. Telephone calls aroused him in the night, demanding, "Why don't you go back to Connecticut, buddyboy."

A few months earlier, Ralph Nader had published *Unsafe At Any Speed* (1965), a book in America's muckraking tradition denouncing the automobile industry and

195

specifically condemning a General Motors' model, the Corvair. In an effort to discredit the best seller, GM sicked agents on its obscure author. Guards collared the spies, snooping even into the halls of Congress. Now contrite under the scowls of Senators Abraham Ribicoff and Robert F. Kennedy, GM's president James M. Roche apologized. But the damage had been done — to GM and to the public image of all corporate America.

With its revelations about DDT, the poison eagerly promoted by the chemical industry, Rachel Carson's *Silent Spring* set the stage for gnawing questions about the relationship of big business to the general welfare. Her reserved personality and her early death, however, also left the stage open for a charismatic figure, one who could further articulate the country's doubts and channel them into a full-fledged reform movement. It had been done before, during the Progressive heyday of swashbuckling, magnetic Teddy Roosevelt. The Depression administration of Franklin Delano Roosevelt repeated earlier drives for justice and reform. And now it was about to happen again, in the mid-1960s, the Age of Aquarius. Always, despite the enthusiasm of the moment, the results are only partially successful. And often the heroes, perceived as larger than life in the public mind, are bound to suffer with the general realization that these leaders are, after all, only men.

Washington, of course, constantly swarms with "kooks, dreamers, utopian schemers, chicken littles, and political alchemists ready to turn the dross of contemporary America into golden utopia," as Capital observer Laurence Leamer sees it. Armed with shopping bags and tattered briefcases stuffed with plans of their latest inventions or blueprints for social reconstruction, "they prowl the public passages in search of that one attentive ear that they think will open doors to them and their ideas." Many of them are sincere, some brilliant, but most are shunted aside by White House guards or politely discouraged by congressmen's patient secretaries.

Before his testimony in the State Caucus Room propelled him into such arbiters of fame as *Time* and *Newsweek,* Ralph Nader was just another "kook." Arriving at Princeton University from small-town Connecticut, he branded himself a nonconformist by refusing to wear white buck shoes. Once he donned a bathrobe for his classes to protest the unofficial college dress code of the 1950s. The Phi Beta Kappa railed, ineffectually, when workmen sprayed campus trees with DDT. Harvard Law School, for him, was a "high-priced tool factory," turning out parts that neatly fit the requirements of status-quo corporate America.

Nevertheless, Harvard granted him a law degree, with distinction; he set off to roam Europe, Latin America, and Africa as a free-lance journalist. In 1964, Daniel Patrick Moynihan rescued Nader from a desultory legal practice in Hartford. Impressed by the attorney's independent researches on auto safety, the Assistant Secretary of Labor installed him in his department as a consultant. While expanding his studies into a book, Nader also fed information to Senator Ribicoff's traffic-safety subcommittee. Thus, unlike a host of fellow messiahs, Nader had an entree into Washington's circle of power. With the GM hearing, fate yanked the unknown lawyer out of the ranks and sat him blinking in the glare of nationwide TV.

"He's just like Jesus," croons one woman, after Nader — lean, rumpled, earnest — ends a speech in Cleveland. Others use less sanguine epithets: "ambulance chaser," "a high-minded crackpot," "a Lenin or a Hitler." Whatever the various judgments, Ralph Nader remains one of the most trusted men in the nation. After twenty years of crisscrossing the country with his messages, he is still a favorite on the lecture circuit — something of a phenomenon in a country that characteristically demands glittering novelty from a succession of short-lived celebrities.

Yet Nader's asceticism makes him stand out, sets him apart from the horde of Barnum-and-Bailey politicians, gurus, and starlets clamoring for the nation's attention. When the GM Keystone Cops episode launched him on his career as America's ombudsman, a term he probably introduced into the language, the Harvard graduate, who could converse in Arabic, Chinese, Portuguese, Spanish, and Russian, was living in a $20-a-week rooming house. He clothed his lanky six-foot-four-inch frame in baggy blue suits, didn't smoke, rarely drank and worked eighteen hours a day.

Despite the fame — the fact that many people equate his name with the consumer movement, that one glance from Nader can make a corporate head tremble — he has remained much the same. He owns, it is rumored, only one ancient narrow tie; apparently, his only concession to the flesh is an occasional double order of strawberry shortcake. He explains that marriage would distract him from the central causes of his life. To use the words of Nader observer Charles McCarry, there is "a whiff of sackcloth and ashes" about this man dedicated to nothing less than restoring "the original humanism of America" by ferreting out the evils in its structure. For many concerned Americans, Nader is a selfless, forthright, and incorruptible rock in an increasingly chaotic and corrupted nation. If one reviews his renown in this light, Nader reflects the country's lingering romanticism grafted to its residual puritanism. There has always been a place in the country for a John Brown, a Lone Ranger.

There is, of course, much more to the story of Nader's ascendancy. His description of the hot dog as "America's most dangerous missile" was not mere flippancy. He lectured students that they were being "taught the freedom to roam in their cages." Years ago, he warned the country that "if people knew what the facts were and if they had to choose between nuclear power and candles, they would choose candles." This was not simple hyperbole. Nader was tonguing the abscessed teeth, capitalizing on the growing introspection and uneasiness of the late '60s, which were swelling the ranks of civil rights organizations, of anti-war and environmental groups. In the following years, Watergate, illegal CIA tactics, the disaster of Three Mile Island seemed to bear him out, to confirm the country's gut-level qualms about its direction. In a time of change, Nader was promoting change. And he knew how to play on the fears of political conservatives as well: "Unless the challenge of corporate reform is undertaken, this country will be headed toward a choice between a corporate state or a socialist state."

Nader had another key to fame. He understood reporters; his remarks contrasted with the frustrating double talk they heard from what they were labeling "The Establishment." Given the apprehensive mood of the nation, what he said was almost always newsworthy. Journalists deemed it a privilege to receive calls from insider Ralph — frequently in the wee hours, thus heightening the mystery — to get tips on his next exposé. To top it off, again in McCarry's words, the calm voice on the other end of the line represented "a reporter's dream because he not only had accurate, and sometimes sensational, information, but he knew how to present it to a newsman in a way that often saved the reporter from having to do much work. The facts were straight, the quotes were vivid, and the substance was a declaration of conscience." It became a kind of conspiracy. Nader passed on the hot copy about the latest corporate skulduggery; reporters deflected attacks from Nader enemies. As will be seen, however, with a shift in the zeitgeist this chummy relationship also changed.

Nader pyramided his gains. He organized, he expanded his attacks. Nagged by a Nader suit for invasion of privacy, GM settled out-of-court, reportedly anteing up $425,000. Into the pot went the burgeoning royalties from *Unsafe At Any Speed,* his lecture fees, foundation grants, and private contributions. For himself, the nation's foremost consumer advocate took only enough to support his monkish needs. The rest of the kitty went into the formation of Public Citizen, Inc., an umbrella organization which funds more than a dozen other Nader creations.

Critics point out that he has spawned a conglomerate as unwieldy, diffuse, and sometimes as secretive as the government agencies and corporations he condemns. In response, Nader asserts that his goal is "nothing less than the qualitative reform of the industrial revolution," a task requiring a complex attack. His groups do research, write books, and lobby in the pursuit of former Supreme Court Justice Louis Brandeis' maxim that "sunlight is the best disinfectant." The famed Nader's Raiders, for instance, is a yearly gathering of students, summertime shock troops whose investigations have probed the workings of the Federal Trade Commission or studied pollution in the Gulf of Mexico. Lawyers of another organization, the Public Interest Research Group, have ranged widely to unearth irregularities in the Office of Management and Budget, support property-tax reform, or do ghostwriting for sympathetic congressmen.

Besides their unifying philosophy of reform, the Nader groups hold other features in common. Their offices — used furniture, bare floors — verge on the ramshackle. Critics also like to mention the staffs. Largely volunteer, at best underpaid, they tend to attract hyperactive and youthful idealists from the upper economic stratum. Notable for its roster of graduates of Yale, MIT, and Stanford, the ranks of former workers include, for example, wealthy Edward Cox, who became Richard Nixon's son-in-law. However, there is nothing sinister in the selection of young, sometimes well-to-do people who turn, if only tem-

The automobile. Does it symbolize "the better life" or–as Ralph Nader suggests–is it the nemesis of America? Here traffic chokes the Walt Whitman Bridge across the Delaware River at South Philadelphia. Dick Swanson, courtesy of EPA—Documerica

porarily, to activism. Nader's requirements are enthusiasm, brilliance, and, often, the ability to pay one's way.

As to the one-man, single-minded drive behind the organizations, it might be posited that any reformer is an extremist, a departure from the norm. Ralph Nader argues the case differently. "I don't consider myself abnormal. I consider the auto industry abnormal — people who, for great profit, sell cars with built-in defects that they

know will kill people. That, to me, is real abnormality." He
has a point, and a look at his background lends support to a
view of Nader as a product of America's traditional
idealism — an idealism that has generated conflicts
throughout the country's history because it is frequently
at odds with political and economic realities.

"If everyone knew my father," says the advocate's sister
Laura, "there would be no reason to wonder why Ralph is
the way he is." In 1912 when Nadra Nader sailed past the
Statue of Liberty, he brought with him the mental bag-
gage of many a poverty-stricken immigrant. Behind lay a
Lebanon ruled by Turkish potentates — a country of
hunger, corruption, and repression. His only hope was to
leave, a hope fulfilled when he stepped off the boat with
twenty dollars in his pocket.

America's youth soon adjust to the differences between
ideals touted in civics classes and the ways they are carried out in government and business. But like many a man
who has sacrificed all to follow his dream, Nadra held onto
the dream. As he worked at menial jobs in New Jersey, it
soon became evident to the newcomer that America was
not a land of milk and honey, of justice for all. Yet in his
mind, the reality was no reason why the country should
not strive for ideal goals. He saved his money, went back to
the old country, and returned with a Lebanese bride, Rose
Bouziane.

Seeking a "better life" — the standard American pursuit — the couple eventually escaped polluted New Jersey
and settled in Winsted, a town idyllically nestled among
the green, rounded Berkshire Mountains of northwestern
Connecticut. On one of Winsted's main streets, they
opened a restaurant, the Highland Arms. They bought a
spacious white house perched on Hillside Avenue. Their
four children grew up mopping floors and washing dishes
to support the family business, while looking ahead to
Princeton and the University of California. They were

comfortably middle-class, with upward-mobile ideas.

Except for Nadra's intense streak of idealism. At the Highland Arms, people got "10 cents worth of coffee and a dollar's worth of conversation," remarks one steady customer fondly. Another Winsted resident recalls with some annoyance that "Mr. Nader would never let anything alone." Nadra was a colorful, sometimes trying, small-town Socrates; he kept town meetings lively by extending Constitutional principles to, say, the debate over installing parking meters on Main Street. "Never tip your hat and never look down on anyone," the father drummed into his brood. Parental principles wore off on the children, especially on Ralph, born in 1934. Perhaps because he arrived when the family's prosperity already was assured, he received the greatest emphasis on ideas. Nadra and Rose had a special dictum for their youngest: "We made Ralph understand that working for justice in the country is a safeguard of our democracy." In brief, Ralph took his father seriously.

The ideals that form a sacred legacy from Ralph Nader's childhood are broad, simplistic. The price of liberty may be eternal vigilance, but constant watchfulness is impossible for most humans. Just as Winsted's citizens wearied of Nadra Nader's perennial carpings, the American public, materially well-off despite injustices, tires of prolonged tirades. Ralph Nader himself has glimpsed the flaw: "We ask people to think, instead of asking them to believe. And history has always gone to those who ask people to believe."

Nader targets the large, monopolistic corporations as the prime enemies of the public weal. His goal is to replace the profit motive with justice. By uniting the citizenry, according to Laurence Leamer, he wants "to drive the corporate moneychangers from the temple of democracy" — as if once purged the temple will remain pure. Beyond that well-intentioned urge, Nader has offered few designs for a better system. It comes as some surprise to Nader's many conservative detractors that, at the beginning of his fame, he proclaimed allegiance to free enterprise. According to Nader, this system is a will-o'-the-wisp, one that big business has never allowed to function. More recently, reflecting the thinking of economist John Kenneth Galbraith, he has spoken in terms of a decentralized socialism that will promote cooperatives and local control. Yet whatever the shifts in the reformer's thinking, his theories present few clear-cut beliefs. Also, his broad frontal attacks have added to the confusion. Nader spurs his Raiders into assaults on so many windmills — the dangers of rock 'n' roll deafness as well as the hazards of nuclear reactors — that people are sometimes left wondering just what it is he wants. Is he, after all, simply a malcontent, a chronic complainer?

Post-Vietnam and post-Watergate cynicism has not been kind to reformers; a distrustful nation now demands that public figures subject their personal lives to unusually harsh scrutiny. In the process, personal quirks sometimes become magnified out of proportion to accomplishments. Furthermore, Nader once appeared saintlike, and because he has not solved problems with saintly dispatch, his reputation has suffered. Sensing that their readers want sensationalism mixed with retribution, reporters who once respected his privacy have concentrated on shirt-sleeve psychology for Nader copy.

As might be expected, they have found nothing scandalous; but Nader's life is cryptic enough to be of gossipy interest. And while discovering supposed flaws, journalists have raised some valid questions about Nader's future effectiveness. Living out his high principles, Nader can be brusque, unintentionally cruel. Dashing through an airport, habitually late, jaw set, clutching his mound of files, he brushes aside autograph seekers as foolish time-wasters. He has been known to make a scene in a restaurant over a dead fly in his salad — as if the speck were evidence of corporate America's malfeasance and the embarrassed waiter a party to the crime. Nader is not like the rest of us in other ways. He expects followers to share his zeal absolutely, to stick it out eighteen hours a day, seven days a week, forsaking wives, children, comfort. Few can take the pace. Hays Gorey passes on a telling incident in *Nader and the Power of Everyman*. Striding through a Washington park, a young aide, father of two children and living on his wife's income, dared ask his preoccupied boss for the weekend off:

"What for?"

"To lie on the beach and rest in the sun."

"Here — help me pull this bench into the sun. There. Now lie on the bench, pretend you're at the beach, and rest in the sun."

Ralph was serious, of course.

Novelist Gore Vidal has urged that Nader run for President, but the man from Winsted, Connecticut, remains the ascetic loner. Though now middle-aged, sometimes he proceeds as if he were still the young abused lawyer single-handedly tweaking the nose of General Motors. The constant negative homilies, the overextension of issues, the rickety structure of his organizations, the inability to accommodate shifts in the country's moods — all cast shadows on his prospects. Titles of recent magazine articles sum up his position: "Is Nader Losing His Clout?"; "How Far Can a Lone Ranger Ride?"

What often gets overlooked is that Nader has already ridden far. Still a relatively young man, Ralph Nader has left an indelible mark on the nation, one that is so broad that he often fails to receive the credit. The nation can thank his organizations for major laws promoting traffic safety and regulating food additives; for legislation designed to curb the oil giants, improve mental health services, combat air pollution, and stop the Forest Service from overcutting the country's timberlands.

Thousands of ordinary Americans can look forward to more secure retirements because Nader unearthed swindles in pension funds, then put Congress on the spot until it passed reforms. Nonsmokers can thank Nader for their own sections on airlines, a small but significant gain. During the Watergate upheavals, it was Nader lawyers who rushed to court after the "Saturday Night Massacre," to stop President Nixon from further trampling the democratic process. A series of Nader-sponsored "sunshine laws" has forced elected officials closer to the ideal of serving their constituents.

One wonders how many Senators — how many Presidents, for that matter — have left a comparable record of benefit to others. Without a political machine and without traditional financial backing, private citizen Nader has taken on the medusal corporations and government agencies of a complex, trillion-dollar economy. In view of the odds, he has been a phenomenal success.

Few Nader students have grasped his larger impact: his example has armed other activists, conservationists included, with hope. *Washington Post* writer William Greider rightly emphasizes that this angry man from Winsted, Connecticut, "who drew his nourishment from constant outrage rather than Fritos and Cokes," has again sparked "the romanticism of America's self-image." He has helped rekindle the American belief that ordinary people can work together to bring about significant changes. And no matter how cyclical and ephemeral this belief has been or how often it has failed over the course of American history, its periodic rebirth has always been a necessary precedent of practical reform.

Amory Lovins. He foresees utility bills going down instead of up, to the benefit of consumers as well as of utility companies. No wonder that the New Englander is heralded as a "Messiah" by some observers. Friends of the Earth

Chapter 16

Amory Lovins:
Elephants and Pumpkins

Every high school seems to have at least one, the budding genius who bounds through the halls behind his thick glasses, fascinated by the marvels of computers, oblivious to the joys of rock 'n' roll. He goes off to Harvard or MIT. Years later, former classmates see him grinning back at them from the pages of the local newspaper. Happily lost in his theoretical world, he's on the research staff of some distant electronics firm or working on a complicated government project.

In the case of Amory Lovins, the stereotype holds some truth. However, he did not follow his fascinations into a narrow if satisfying obscurity. Instead, Wall Street gurus, members of Congress — not to mention United Nations agencies and prime ministers — tug at his sleeve as the young physicist jets about recommending energy strategies for the future. The same man also gives piano recitals, ties knots for a hobby, and writes poetry. One admiring colleague summarizes Lovins' Renaissance energy: "He has been consultant to many of the world's think tanks, has debated in many countries, testified before governments, working his way meanwhile through a calendar crowded with conferences, manuscript deadlines, mountains of reading, and mountains, too, to climb and photograph, with musical interludes." The counsel that world leaders eagerly seek from Lovins is anchored in scientific research, but it also has strong psychological appeal.

Confronted with the Arab oil embargo of several years ago, the industrialized nations trembled like addicts suddenly faced with a waning supply of fixes. Since then prospects have grown steadily bleaker. The price of gasoline soars, home heating oil becomes scarce. The once-touted dream of unlimited power from nuclear plants has turned into the bizarre nightmare of radioactive clouds floating across the nation. The addiction must end, but the withdrawal, nations fear in their industrialized hearts, will be painful, perhaps even fatal.

Not so, says Lovins. In his view, the United States has abundant energy. He foresees utility bills going down instead of up, to the benefit of consumers as well as of utility companies. There will be no freezing in the dark, or no slow sulfur-dioxide and radioactive Armageddon — if the world will exercise a little ingenuity. No wonder that this New Englander is heralded as a "Messiah" by the *Washington Post,* the "Whiz Kid Energycologist" by *New Times,* and a "Wunderkind" in the pages of *Science.* Although public enthusiasm belies the difficult choices that Lovins insists face the world in the coming years, essentially he bears a novel message of good news.

Lovins' unusual personality and a chance encounter with a famous environmentalist steered him away from a traditional career. "I was brought up as a normal, healthy technocrat," reflects Amory, who as a child entertained himself by tinkering with clocks. His father was an engineer in Washington, D.C., his mother a social worker and editor. In 1960 they moved to western Massachusetts

with their thirteen-year-old son. South Amherst's vistas
of wooded hills and rolling cow pastures presented the boy
with a harmonious perspective of man and nature, a view
central to the lives of fellow New Englanders Benton
MacKaye and Frederick Law Olmsted.

Further, as with MacKaye's Shirley Center or Olmsted's Hartford, South Amherst matches rural grace with
a cultural heritage unusual for a town its size. Within a
half hour's drive lie ivy-covered Amherst College, Smith,
Mt. Holyoke; and the area includes innovative Hampshire
College and the more pedestrian University of
Masachusetts. Enriched by the intellectual climate, in
high school Lovins was "the resident whiz kid," as Ellen
Frank depicts him in the *New Times,* "a scrawny guy with
a huge Adam's apple, thick glasses and an ever-present
weighty briefcase that swung wildly as he careened
around the corridors." Some Lovins observers notice a
physical resemblance to Woody Allen, but the energy
"Messiah" has few of the anxieties and phobias of the
failure-prone comic. During high school, Lovins won
prizes at international science fairs, took part in a production of *The Mikado,* and entertained friends with his
antics and piano playing. Equally important, teachers
recognized his genius and encouraged him to take courses
at Amherst College.

Despite early successes, his truncated university career
is an indication of a freewheeling brilliance that insists on
its own development. Racing ahead of his professors,
young Lovins soon wearied of the fare at Harvard and left
Massachusetts for Oxford, England, to pursue a Ph.D. in
experimental physics. The scholars at Oxford were impressed by their candidate. They made him a research
fellow — the youngest in the University's long history.
But restlessness again plagued him; M.A. degree in hand,
he left in 1971.

"I was willing to jump off and try something else," ex-

plains the scientist to interviewer Ellen Frank, but there
was much more to Lovins' break with academe than a
simple urge to branch out. He spent school holidays
exploring the countryside afoot. Enthralled by tramps
into Wales, he and a friend composed a book-length manuscript on the Eryri Mountains of Snowdonia National
Park, a craggy, lonesome place of mists and eagles. Lovins'
search for a publisher led to a meeting in 1970 with fellow
American David Brower.

In the preceding year, Brower's unrestrained zeal for
conservation reform had set off a furor within the Sierra
Club, followed by his forced resignation as executive
director. Undaunted, Brower was in England to place his
own recently founded organization, Friends of the Earth,
on international footing. Events moved quickly after the
young physicist and the renegade environmentalist,
thirty-five years his senior, made friends. *Eryri, the
Mountains of Longing* (1971) became an early offering in
FOE's series of lavish-format books. The volume combined
passion with logical arguments, urging the public to demand that one of Great Britain's last wild corners be
spared careless mineral and hydroelectric development.
Further, not only did Lovins find a publisher, he acquired
a job and a new direction to his life as FOE's London-based
British representative.

Writers have tried to pin down the ability of Brower —
articulate, charismatic, his white shock of hair flying
fashionably — to move individuals to unexpected and
sustained activism. Brower watchers characterize him
variously as the "archdruid" of the environmental movement and "the father of zealots." It would be inaccurate to
say that the Californian worked a conversion on intellectually independent Lovins. Better stated, the optimistic druid crystallized the thinking of a youthful
genius, who was stewing at the age of twenty-three because "it wouldn't make much difference to anyone

whether I solved the problems of the world in the laboratory."

FOE's representative plunged into solving Britain's immediate environmental ills. Lobbying, writing, organizing, Lovins scuttled another planned invasion of Snowdonia, this time an open-pit copper mine. He served on the Royal Commission on Environmental Pollution and publicized his efforts with *Open-Pit Mining* (1973) and *Non-Nuclear Futures* (1975). Thus he moved through a spectrum of issues to tackle what he came to view as the overriding environmental crisis: decreasing energy supplies in a growing world.

Multi-talented, politically adroit, Lovins is an expert at the lightning attack, the master stroke. The small group of world leaders and would-be world leaders which reads *Foreign Affairs* expects to find pronouncements by such figures as Arthur M. Schlesinger, Jr. and Walter Mondale. When prime ministers and industrialists picked up the October 1976 issue, however, they turned to "Energy Strategy: The Road Not Taken?" by Amory B. Lovins, not yet thirty, a mere boy in contrast to his graying fellow authors. He peered from the photo insert, baby-faced behind dark-rimmed glasses. His tentative grin, if widened just a bit, might be about to break out with "What, me worry?" Energy salvation was at hand, the article said.

Critics lambasted his thesis as "a piece of crap" or praised it as "the most influential single work on energy policy written in the last five years." *Foreign Affairs* found itself deluged with requests for reprints that broke a thirty-year record. *Electric Perspectives*, an organ of the United States utility industry, marshaled an entire issue into an attack of Lovins' article. More than anything else, the *Foreign Affairs* piece launched the FOE staff member into international limelight. There, while he dodges brickbats with apparent ease, his fame promises to grow as energy problems worsen.

Amory Lovins protests that he is not so much an original thinker as a "roving synthesizer and gadfly." Expanded in *Soft Energy Paths* (1977), his ideas draw heavily on the innovative thinking of such men as E. F. Schumacher, of *Small Is Beautiful* fame. Foremost in Lovins' approach, the industrialized world suffers not from energy want, but from energy waste. His first emphasis, then, is on conservation, on "mining the inefficiencies in the present system." He points to the typical American refrigerator as an example, so badly designed that the motor uses about half its power to cool itself — in contrast to more efficient pre-World War II models. Lovins reasons that with the technology now available — weatherstripping, insulation, solar heating, and more efficient motors and lighting — the country could cut energy demands by about two thirds. He goes on to chide those who equate high energy use with prosperity: "Some people feel that civilization in the U.S. would be inconceivable if we used, say, half as much electricity as we do now. Yet that is what we did use in 1963, when Americans were at least half as civilized as they are now."

The *Foreign Affairs* article began with the well-known quotation from Robert Frost about two roads diverging in a wood. As Lovins sees it, the world needs to abandon what he calls the "hard path" for the "soft path." The present hard path has led us into a centralized, capital intensive, complex, inefficient, dangerous, inappropriate, and non-renewable thicket. The soft path takes the opposite direction, toward a placid, decentralized, inexpensive, uncomplicated, efficient, safe, appropriate, and renewable glade. Lovins places nuclear reactors and typically gargantuan fossil-fuel generating plants in the first category. He contrasts them with solar, wind, geothermal, and biomass energy sources — environmentally benign alternatives tailored to meet local needs. He points to the enormous waste of nuclear plants, which create temperatures of trillions of degrees to light 100-watt bulbs. "That is," he grins, "like cutting butter with a chainsaw."

Lovins is a realist. Unlike many theorists who fail to bridge the gaps between solutions and everyday problems, he focuses on the economic carrot of the profit motive. He notes the plight of economically flagging utilities, faced on the one hand by customers gnashing their teeth over rising bills and on the other by financiers reluctant to invest in a troubled industry. He wants to encourage them to participate in the transition from the hard to the soft path in ways that would benefit both buyers and sellers of energy. For example, he suggests a program of industry-sponsored loans:

> Say you've just borrowed $2,000 from the utility to weatherstrip and insulate your house and maybe another $1,000 to solarize it. All of that saves you, say $300 a year off your utility bill. Then you pay it back at $300 a year or a little less, so that your bill is the same as if you had done nothing. You therefore get a house that's cheaper to run without paying any more. Meanwhile, when the loan's paid off, say in 10 years or so, your bill goes down because, of course, you're using less. And the utility also benefits, because it saves money and improves its cash flow and avoids bankruptcy.

It is just such thinking that wins Lovins friends among entrepreneurs, politicians, and conservationists.

Hard-path nuclear power is an "economic turkey" in the free-enterprise system, requiring huge subsidies by the government because it can't attract sufficient capital on its own; but beyond economic and environmental problems lies another danger, that of a "friendly Fascism." The nuclear industry, for instance, means loss of traditional freedoms because it must protect itself with guards, secrecy, and censorship. As a Jeffersonian democrat, Lovins fears the power of "an alien, remote and perhaps humiliatingly uncontrollable technology run by a faraway, bureaucratized technical elite."

Again echoing a theme from Schumacher, he feels that only local control and local ingenuity can be flexible enough to devise economically feasible and environmentally sane soft paths. He observes in a *New Roots* interview that "to work their best, most renewable energy systems have to be tailored to local climatic and cultural conditions, but the Exxons of this world can't do that. They can only make cookie-cutter technologies." People working on the local level "can solve most of their energy problems themselves, providing they have the incentive and the opportunity." Individual inventors, he reminds his detractors, have led the way to alternative energy sources with homemade solar collectors. Yet grassroot innovations may easily be strangled if Washington persists in granting subsidies favoring large business interests.

Such broad suggestions might be dismissed as the pipings of a day-dreamer if they weren't backed by Lovins' thorough research. "Amory is the only person I know," commented a friend at a solar conference, "who can write a one-column letter to *Science* magazine and follow it with *two* columns of footnotes." The attention to detail keeps his critics scrambling. Lovins claims that "It's numbers. That's what makes them mad. I'm using their own figures against them. It's not the eloquence of my arguments. It's just that their way costs too much."

As is the case in any debate on a complex issue, Lovins' proposals have sincere, intelligent critics. Some of them accuse him of bending their own facts to suit his purposes. Yet his well-documented arguments are winning increasing support in the scientific community. Writing for *Science,* Allen L. Hammond carefully picks his way through Lovins' proposals and concludes that the New Englander's message "is easily the most comprehensive and technically sophisticated attempt to put together an energy program compatible with environmental values."

If comprehensiveness and professional sophistication have thrust the young physicist to the fore of the energy debate, his good nature sustains his leadership in the environmental movement. A friend from high-school days comments: "He has never let his intelligence get in the way of friendship. It's like an autonomous product, a computer tucked in his pocket." Nonetheless, Lovins can be a deadly combatant. Another admirer describes him as an "artful spider spinning his web, waiting for his prey to step unsuspectingly across the threads, coming closer, close enough for Amory to deliver the fatal sting...." But for Lovins, trapping opponents is an intellectual exercise. Once it is completed, he puts aside competitive instincts in favor of warm concern for others.

Author and activist Alexis Parks provides a picture of Lovins, like all good leaders attentive to practical details as well as to the feelings of those around him: "In the midst of a speech to a crowd of some six hundred, a speech I was recording from my front-row seat, Amory, without a break in his stride, as if it were merely some sort of punctuation (a comma for example) looked at me, pointed to my tape recorder on the floor to remind me that the tape needed turning over (he had heard the click, I hadn't), and continued on. In Austria, working on the ECO-Salzberg papers, he manned the typewriters with the rest of the staff, typing at faster speeds than most of us, often with an apple or chunk of bread in his mouth."

Faced with what they see as life-and-death issues, environmentalists can easily burn themselves out with their seriousness. Not Lovins. His breezy humor combines with self-confidence to leaven what can be a gloomy business. Noting the failing economics of nuclear reactors, he characterizes the industry as "beginning to turn into a pumpkin and roll away." Using another metaphor, he advises fellow environmentalists to be careful with the electric industry: "With the utilities we are in the position of somebody stuck in a narrow alley with a blind elephant. You want to be very careful if you're in that position and lead it gently by the nose — to make sure you keep one step ahead of it." Rushing to a meeting with a state governor, he digs out a necktie and quips to a reporter about putting on his "camouflage."

Michael Kernan describes Lovins for readers of the *Washington Post* as darting "around the world like a waterbug with address book and toothbrush, sleeping on friends' living room floors, eating on his feet, living what someone has called an elegantly spartan life. He wears a calculator and a compass on his belt. He talks fast. He mentions a fiancee in Europe who sounds like a patient person." But Lovins' life is not all work. Each summer he escapes to the White Mountains of southern Maine. At Camp Winona, dressed in his well-worn lederhosen, the scientist counsels boys and leads them on climbs. The break also gives him a chance to indulge his love for photography, an avocation that served him well during his long-gone days as a student at Oxford. Since the Eryri book, Lovins' camera work has appeared in another FOE volume, *New England's White Mountains: At Home in the Wild* (1978).

Still relatively young, the physicist sees the world making the necessary shift from the hard to the soft path — with or without his efforts. To him the issue is one of lessening the trauma of a change that will come through necessity. "It's going to happen anyway. If we don't start it now, when the price runup does come, it will come faster and go higher. But if you do it on a pre-announced schedule, so people can take it into account, you can absorb the shock." Lovins, then, feels that countries already hold the answers to their energy troubles; the question is how soon they will implement them.

Partly because of this view, he's ready to move on. Also, for some time Lovins has worked on his solutions with the help of Hunter Sheldon, an assistant director of the California Conservation Project. He credits her background in the social sciences with broadening his perspectives. In 1979 they were married, and their combined interests are leading Lovins into new, even more complex, challenges. As he puts it, "I'm becoming more involved with food, land and water issues, not just with energy. The more we look at the ways of using energy efficiently, the more in the long run it seems that energy isn't a terribly interesting problem. It's not nearly as difficult as we thought. Problems like peace and social justice and food are going to be much more difficult and complicated, and we really ought to be getting on with those." Perhaps. But however easy the solutions to energy problems may appear to a mind racing far ahead of the present, implementing the cures continues to plague a system hooked on habits born of cheap energy. In acknowledgment of this, the Lovinses' most recent books, *Energy War: Breaking the Nuclear Link* and *Brittle Power*, document, not so much how easy, but how necessary, is the shift away from the prevailing mania for bigness and waste.

Chapter 17

Reassembling the Parts:
Sleek for the Long Flight

Diplomat, revolutionary, zoo keeper, physicist, President — such are the occupations of the figures included in this book. We tend to forget that up until recently there were few professional environmentalists. Only in the last decade or so, with the country's sharpened sense of ecological crisis, has conservation become a large profession in its own right. Before government funding, industry, and volunteer organizations made this the case, conservation for the most part — like poetry or painting — had the status of an avocation; however, as in the case of a Ralph Nader or a Rachel Carson, it often took precedence over the normal, breadwinning functions of an individual's life.

And one might argue that conservation, demanding commitment, was better off as a result. One wonders what would happen to an environmental movement led by professionals who emerge from the nation's universities armed with B.S. degrees, expecting to find jobs — and regular paychecks — waiting for them in the bureaucracy. Certainly, professionals are needed and should be welcomed. On the other hand, they might pale by comparison with the depth of a George Perkins Marsh, who could bring the whole force of the philosophy, literature, history, and linguistics of his day to bear in writing *Man and Nature*. Or with a Frederick Law Olmsted, whose vision of preservation was supported by experience as a sailor on the China Seas, as a frontiersman, farmer, and editor. Such a broad-gauged life is nearly impossible today. We are, it is often lamented, all becoming either managers or technicians in an age of specialization.

Though such fears certainly have their base, they are precipitously morose as far as the present conservation movement is concerned. Government agencies and industries, spurred by political and economic considerations, may frustrate the goals of the conservationists they employ. Yet the main thrust of environmentalism does not lie there. The movement's resiliency and creativity remain with the grassroots organizations — the Sierra Club, Audubon Society, Friends of the Earth — whose memberships consist of ordinary but deeply concerned citizens. As volunteers, free of employment considerations, they can raise a hue and cry when an oil slick floats toward their beaches or when radioactive clouds come bubbling out of a supposedly harmless Three Mile Island reactor.

This is, of course, coming back full circle to the diversity mentioned in Chapter 1, which gives the movement its fiber — and to the complexity of ecology, which makes its study a pursuit of limitless variety, change, and frustration. For ecology is "subversive" in more ways than we might expect — or perhaps would care it to be.

For instance, French peasants had many good reasons to detest the landed aristocracy for whose pleasures they labored. One of them concerned the forests surrounding their villages. In the nobleman's scheme, woodlands existed for his enjoyment. Often hungry, cold, poorly housed, the peasants suffered severe restrictions on the use of nature's bounty. Among many other scores, that one was enthusiastically settled during the chaos of the French Revolution. With their oppressors on the run or beheaded, the peasants declared the estates liberated. Vengefully they surged into the forests to kill game and cut timber with abandon. That seemed a proper action at the time. It also permanently damaged some of France's finest forests.

That is an extreme example in illustration of a vastly more complex world situation: what seems right today may result in unforeseen disaster tomorrow. Skepticism lies at the heart of the twentieth century's new knowledge and awareness of the human condition. And we should remember that environmentalism, for all its good intentions, carries with it that burden.

Lovers of irony might compile volumes on the subject. Some examples have been at least touched on in this one. Teddy Roosevelt strained to create the U.S. Forest Service as the protector of America's timberlands. Yet in the eyes of such critics as Jack Shepherd the agency has become a forest-killing arm of the government. T.R. also glowed over his dam-building schemes, elaborately designed to make deserts bloom for the benefit of society. But his followers carried his vision to extremes. The overdraft on the earth's resources helped create the dust bowls that his cousin Franklin Delano Roosevelt strove to combat twenty years after the completion of T.R.'s first dam. Similarly, Benton MacKaye's idea of excluding through traffic from towns seemed a positive suggestion in its time; yet the freeways his notions fostered have become the bane of our cities.

And there are more subtly disarming examples. The love of wild America in the hearts of Robert Marshall and Howard Zahniser resulted in the Wilderness Act of 1964. In a society craving the "wilderness experience," however, lands protected under such legal status often become magnets by virtue of the designation. They must withstand the millions of visitors each year that the lure of such labels as "wilderness" or "national park" attract. In his poetic book on mountaineering, Galen Rowell sums up the irony with a reflection on a trip to little visited Hetch-Hetchy, a valley just a few miles away from famed Yosemite. Early in the century, conservationists suffered a loss of heart. They lost the long battle to stop the dam they thought would "ruin" Hetch-Hetchy with a man-made lake. Yet perched atop one of the spires overlooking the reservoir, Rowell now muses that he "saw no roads, no buildings, no campfires or smoke; heard no horns, motors, or voices. Below me was only a 'narrow body of monotonous water' whereas if I had been in Yosemite Valley, the same site would have been occupied by Curry Village, fifty motor homes, a dozen tour buses, and the Valley tram car — all dubious benefits of national park status."

One might project similar doubts into the issues of energy, population, insect control, pollution — in fact into any of the areas in which man tampers with the myriad functions of this pulsing, fragile planet. And of course he tampers everywhere. Being a tool-maker, an inventor of arrows, wheels and wagons, ballistae, detergents, aluminum beer cans, off-shore drilling rigs, and atom bombs, man is by definition, by his very existence, nature's disturber, a tamperer. "You can never do nothing," warn ecologists.

What, then, can concerned people do other than palpitate with the knowledge that any act — even doing nothing — may be the one that triggers our undoing, ten, thirty, a hundred years down the ecological road? Are we, the "new conservationists," as Frank Graham, Jr. calls us — struggling with the issues of life itself but aware of our fallibility at every turn — to muddle along, hamstrung, victims of our own knowledge that we can know nothing absolutely? Perhaps, first of all, we can take heart in that twenty years ago the question wasn't even asked by most people. Reviewing *Silent Spring* in 1962, *Time* magazine dismissed some of Rachel Carson's warnings as "nonsense." In contrast, newscasts now report the latest oil spill and the most recent nuclear faux pas. We know much better now. We have a deeper sense of our own mortality.

Still, what should we do? In his classic statement of a land ethic, *A Sand County Almanac,* Aldo Leopold outlined the approach as far back as 1949. He begins by emphasizing that "the land is one organism. Its parts, like our own parts, compete with each other and co-operate with each other. The competitions are as much a part of the inner workings as the co-operations. You can regulate them — cautiously — but not abolish them." Then, since we are to be regulators to one degree or another, Leopold provides the key to sane regulation: "the less violent the man-made changes, the greater the probability of successful readjustment in [nature's] pyramid."

Unfortunately, violence has gone hand-in-hand with the development of technology. The incautious industrialized world has spent much of its energies ransacking the house of nature in which we all live, making off with its shingles, its window frames, digging under its foundations, until the structure seems ready to collapse. If that is true, as many ecologists believe, one aspect of conservationists' job is clear, and it is directly in the tradition of Olmsted, Burroughs, Zahniser: reverse the violent trend, choosing what least disrupts natural processes — mass transit over freeways, solar energy over fossil fuel, natural foods over chemical diets. Only by taking such care can we assure a decent heritage for our children.

One of Leopold's favorite themes concerns the complexity of the universe, "all interlocked in one humming community, one biota." Since we are to be disturbers of its mechanisms, whether through choice or otherwise, he offers another dictum for conservationists: "who but a fool would discard seemingly useless parts? To keep every cog

and wheel is the first precaution of intelligent tinkering."
Ignorant as we are, we never can know what apparently
insignificant gear may be the essential, irreplaceable
element in the heap of a dismantled clock.

This thought rarely occurred to early activists. Their
task brought satisfaction, a sense of finality, for they had
what now seems a simple approach. To them the dedication of a new park or national forest meant so much more
ecological money in the bank. We can thank them for the
land they preserved. But our more recent view of an interrelated and infinitely complex world brings a sense of
urgency along with knowledge. We must preserve all the
abused parts that are left — the whooping crane, the
grizzly bear, the wolf, the redwoods. As lovers of the earth,
we love them for themselves. But if one needs justification
beyond that, who knows what obscure vole or flower now
quietly moving toward extinction may be the unrecog-
nized linchpin that holds our world together? The question
is not hyperbolic, given the bewilderingly complicated
scheme of nature.

So in this sense the job seems clear. Yet saving all the
parts isn't enough; we must go beyond that to reassemble
them as best we can, to re-create the diversity of the earth
that once gave it ecological stability. That was the idea
behind establishing national forests from worn-out and
abandoned farm lands in the East. It was the idea behind
Benton MacKaye's "reinvasion" by nature. It was
Franklin Delano Roosevelt's goal on his own Hyde Park
estate, enlarged and projected into the Tennessee Valley
Authority and the Soil Conservation Service. Today the
rebuilding continues in the national parks and in preserves established by the Audubon Society and the Nature
Conservancy.

Yet fueled by economics and out of control, the destruction goes on at a far faster pace than the intense but
limited efforts at restoration. At times the picture looks

bleak. Perhaps the passenger pigeon was that forever-lost and essential linchpin, and we already are doomed, wasting our time with our ecological busyness; but we would at least like to know the odds. At times it would seem to make sense amidst the chaos to eat, drink, etc., as one Greek sect advised in far simpler times.

This way of life would also, as John Donne pointed out, make us less human. Olaus Murie, conservationist, writer, and artist, was no Pollyanna. He worked through the thick of doubt piled onto bureaucratic frustration. His wife Margaret explains the existential buoyancy that kept him painting, writing, lobbying. "He believed that even with the very worst forecast possible for the future, it was more fun to take part in the battle for what you believed in than just to stand on the sidelines wringing your hands." That we don't know our chances for survival may be frustrating, yet it also makes the game more fascinating. "Death is the mother of beauty," one poet said. And Leopold the scientist echoed the sentiment — not as gloomy as it might at first seem — with, "It must be poor life that achieves freedom from fear." That humans can never have that kind of freedom we now know. So here we are on this planet, stripped of our hubris, at last sharing with all animals the fears for survival that keep them alert, their bodies sleek for the long flight into the unknown. It should be an exciting journey.

Selected Bibliography

Chapter 1 Wild America and "The Gobble Gobble School of Economics"

Brooks, Paul. *The View from Lincoln Hill: Man and the Land in a New England Town*. Boston: Houghton Mifflin, 1976.

Clepper, Henry, ed. *Leaders of American Conservation*. New York: The Ronald Press, 1971.

Coyle, David C. *Conservation: An American Story of Conflict and Accomplishment*. New Brunswick, New Jersey: Rutgers University Press, 1957.

Fleming, Donald. "Roots of the New Conservation Movement." *Perspectives in American History*, v. 6, Cambridge, Massachusetts: Harvard University Press, 1972.

Foerster, Norman, *Nature in American Literature*. New York: Macmillan, 1923.

Frome, Michael. *Battle for the Wilderness*. New York: Praeger, 1974.

_____. *Whose Woods These Are: The Story of the National Forests*. Garden City, New York: Doubleday, 1962.

Glacken, Clarence J. "The Origins of the Conservation Philosophy." *Journal of Soil and Water Conservation*, 11 (March 1956), 63-66.

230

Graham, Frank, Jr. *The Adirondack Park: A Political History*. Alfred A. Knopf, 1978.

———. *Man's Dominion: The Story of Conservation in America*. New York: M. Evans, 1971.

Keller, Jane Eblen, "Olympics Illuminate the Long War over Future of the Adirondacks." *Smithsonian*, 10 (February 1980), 42-51.

Matthiessen, Peter. *Wildlife in America*. New York: Viking, 1959.

Nash, Roderick, ed. *The American Environment: Readings in the History of Conservation*. 2nd ed. Reading, Massachusetts: Addison-Wesley, 1976.

———. *The Call of the Wild: 1900-1916*. New York: George Braziller, 1970.

———. *The Nervous Generation: American Thought, 1917-1930*. Chicago: Rand McNally & Company, 1970.

———. *Wilderness and the American Mind*. rev. ed. New Haven: Yale University Press, 1982.

Reiger, John F. *American Sportsmen and the Origins of Conservation*. New York: Winchester Press, 1975.

Shepard, Paul. *Man in the Landscape: A Historic View of the Esthetics of Nature*. New York: Alfred A. Knopf, 1967.

Smith, Frank E. *The Politics of Conservation*. New York: Pantheon Books, 1966.

Smith, Herbert A. "The Early Forestry Movement in the United States." *Agricultural History*, 12 (October 1938), 326-46.

Stewart, George R. *American Ways of Life*. Garden City, New York: Doubleday, 1954.

Taft, Robert. *Artists and Illustrators of the Old West; 1850-1900*. New York: Charles Scribner's Sons, 1953.

Tocqueville, Alexis de. *Democracy in America*. Richard D. Heffner, ed. New York: New American Library, 1956.

Trefethen, James B. *An American Crusade for Wildlife*. New York: Winchester Press and the Boone and

Crockett Club, 1975.

Udall, Stewart. *The Quiet Crisis*. New York: Holt, Rinehart and Winston, 1963.

Wallace, Edward S. *The Great Reconnaissance: Soldiers, Artists, and Scientists on the Frontier, 1848-1861*. Boston: Little, Brown, 1955.

Weslager, C. A. *The Log Cabin in America*. New Brunswick, New Jersey: Rutgers University Press, 1969.

Woodward, William E. *The Way Our People Lived*. New York: Washington Square Press, 1965.

Worster, Donald. *Nature's Economy: The Roots of Ecology*. San Francisco: Sierra Club, 1977.

Chapter 2 George Perkins Marsh: The Prophet from Vermont

Bancroft, George. "Our Literary Diplomats: Part III." *The Book Buyer*, 21 (August 1900), 38-40.

Beck, Richard. "George P. Marsh and Old Icelandic Studies." *Scandinavian Studies*, 17 (May 1943), 195-203.

"Culture and Progress." Review of *Man and Nature*. *Scribner's Monthly*, 9 (November 1874), 119-21.

Curtis, Jane. *The World of George Perkins Marsh, America's First Conservationist*. Woodstock, Vermont: The Woodstock Foundation, 1982.

Glacken, Clarence J. "The Origins of the Conservation Philosophy." *Journal of Soil and Water Conservation*, 11 (March 1956), 63-66.

Kliger, Samuel. "George Perkins Marsh and the Gothic Tradition in America." *The New England Quarterly*, 19 (December 1946), 524-31.

Lowell, James Russell. Review of *Man and Nature*. *North American Review*, 99 (July 1864), 318-20.

232

Lowenthal, David. "George Perkins Marsh and the American Geographical Tradition." *The Geographical Review*, 43 (April 1953), 207-13.

———. "George Perkins Marsh: The Magnificent Amateur." *American Forests*, 83 (September 1977), 8-11, 44-48.

———. *George Perkins Marsh: Versatile Vermonter*. New York: Columbia University Press, 1958.

———. "On the Author of *Man and Nature*." *American Forests*, 83 (September 1977), 6.

March, F. A. "George Perkins Marsh." Review of *Life and Letters of George Perkins Marsh*. *Nation*, 47 (September 6, 1888), 213-15.

Marsh, Caroline. *Life and Letters of George Perkins Marsh*. 2 vols. New York: Charles Scribner's Sons, 1888. (Volume 2 was never printed.)

Marsh, George Perkins. "Agriculture in Italy." *Nation*, 2 (February 8, 1866), 183-84.

———. "The Aqueducts of Ancient Rome." *Nation*, 32 (March 3, 1881), 147-48.

———. "The Biography of a Word." *Nation*, 32 (February 10, 1881), 88-89.

———. *The Camel: His Organization, Habits and Uses, Considered with Reference to his Introduction into the United States*. Boston: Gould and Lincoln, 1856.

———. "The Catholic Church and Modern Civilization." *Nation*, 5 (September 19, 1867), 229-31.

———. "A Cheap and Easy Way to Fame." *Nation*, 1 (December 21, 1865), 778.

———. *A Compendious Grammar of the Old Northern or Icelandic Language: Compiled and Translated from the Grammars of Rask*. Burlington, Vermont: H. Johnson and Company, 1838.

———. *The Earth as Modified by Human Action: A Last Revision of Man and Nature*. New York: Charles Scribner's Sons, 1885.

———. *The Earth as Modified by Human Action: A New*

Edition of Man and Nature. New York: Scribner, Armstrong and Company, 1874.

———. "The Education of Women." *Nation*, 3 (August 30, 1866), 165-66.

———. *The Goths in New-England: A Discourse Delivered at the Anniversary of the Philomathesian Society of Middlebury College, August 15, 1843*. Middlebury, Vermont: J. Cobb, Jr., 1843.

———. *Irrigation: Its Evils, the Remedies, and the Compensations*. Washington: U.S. Government Printing Office, 1875. (In U.S. Department of Agriculture *Report*, 1874, pp. 362-81.)

———. *Lectures on the English Language*. New York: Charles Scribner, 1860.

———. *Man and Nature*. David Lowenthal, ed. Cambridge, Massachusetts: Harvard University Press, 1965.

———. *Man and Nature: Or, Physical Geography as Modified by Human Action*. New York: Charles Scribner, 1864.

———. *Medieval and Modern Saints and Miracles. Not ab uno e Societate Jesu*. New York: Harper and Brothers, 1876.

———. "Old English Literature." *Nation*, 1 (December 21, 1865), 778.

———. *The Origin and History of the English Language, and of the Early Literature it Embodies*. New York: Charles Scribner, 1862.

———. "Pruning Forest Trees." *Nation*, 1 (November 30, 1865), 690-91.

———. *Report Made under Authority of the Legislature of Vermont, on the Artificial Propagation of Fish*. Burlington, Vermont: Free Press Print, 1857.

"Notes." *Nation*, 35 (August 3, 1882), 94.

Randall, Charles Edgar. "George Perkins Marsh: Conservation's Forgotten Man." *American Forests*, 71 (April 1965), 20-23.

"Rockefeller Home Designated Historic Landmark." *Parks and Recreation*, 2 (August 1967), 23, 48.

Russell, Franklin. "The Vermont Prophet: George Perkins Marsh." *Horizon*, 10 (Summer 1968), 16-23.

Sargent, Charles Sprague. "Notes." *Nation*, 35 (August 17, 1882), 136.

Smith, Herbert A. "The Early Forestry Movement in the United States." *Agricultural History*, 12 (October 1938), 326-46.

Stillman, William James. "The Late George P. Marsh." *Nation*, 35 (October 12, 1882), 304-05.

Trauth, Mary Philip. *Italo-American Diplomatic Relations, 1861-1882: The Mission of George Perkins Marsh, First American Minister to the Kingdom of Italy*. Washington, D. C.: The Catholic University of America Press, 1958.

Chapter 3 Frederick Law Olmsted: "Emerson with a Hoe"

Barlow, Elizabeth. *Frederick Law Olmsted's New York*. New York: Praeger, 1972.

Davis, Douglas. "Prophet in the Park." *Newsweek*, 80 (November 6, 1972), 77.

"Environmental Legacy." *Nation*, 214 (March 13, 1972), 326.

Fabos, Julius Gy., Gordon T. Melde, and V. Michael Weinmayr. *Frederick Law Olmsted, Sr.: Founder of Landscape Architecture in America*. Amherst: The University of Massachusetts Press, 1968.

Fein, Albert. *Frederick Law Olmsted and the American Environmental Tradition*. New York: George Braziller, 1972.

Heidrich, Robert W. "'A Village in a Park': Riverside Illinois." *Historic Preservation*, 25 (April-June 1973),

28-33.

Jones, Holway R. *John Muir and the Sierra Club: The Battle for Yosemite*. San Francisco: Sierra Club, 1965.

Kaufmann, Edgar, Jr. *The Rise of an American Architecture*. New York: Praeger, 1970.

Kelly, Bruce. *Art of the Olmsted Landscape*. New York: Arts Publisher, 1981.

Martin, John Stuart. " 'He Paints with Lakes and Wooded Slopes....' " *American Heritage*, 15 (October 1964), 14-19.

Mitchell, Broadus. *Frederick Law Olmsted: A Critic of the Old South*. Baltimore: Johns Hopkins University Press, 1924.

Mitchell, John G. "The Re-greening of Urban America." *Audubon*, 80 (March 1978), 29-52.

Moses, Robert. "Frederick Law Olmsted: An Appreciation and an Appraisal." *National Review*, 25 (May 25, 1973), 580-81.

Mumford, Lewis, ed. *Roots of Contemporary American Architecture*. New York: Reinhold, 1952.

Olmsted, Frederick Law. *Civilizing American Cities: A Selection of Frederick Law Olmsted's Writings on City Landscapes*. S. B. Sutton, ed. Cambridge, Massachusetts: M.I.T. Press, 1971.

_____. *The Cotton Kingdom: A Traveler's Observations on Cotton and Slavery in the American Slave States*. 2 vols. New York: Mason Brothers, 1861.

_____. *Frederick Law Olmsted: Landscape Architect, 1822-1903*. Frederick Law Olmsted, Jr., and Theodora Kimball, ed. rpt. New York: Benjamin Blom, Inc., 1970. (This collection of Olmsted's professional papers was first published in two volumes, 1922 and 1928.)

_____. *A Journey in the Back Country*. New York: Mason Brothers, 1860.

_____. *A Journey in the Seaboard Slave States*. New York:

Dix and Edwards, 1856.

_____. *A Journey through Texas: Or, a Saddle-trip on the South-western Frontier*. New York: Dix and Edwards, 1857.

_____. *The Papers of Frederick Law Olmsted. The Formative Years: 1822 to 1852*. Charles Capen McLaughlin, ed. Baltimore: Johns Hopkins University Press, 1977. (Letters, articles, unpublished writings. Seven volumes are planned.)

_____. "Parks." In *Appleton's New American Cyclopedia*. New York: D. Appleton and Company, 1861, 768-75.

_____. "Parks, Parkways and Pleasure-Grounds." *Engineering Magazine*, 9 (May 1895), 253-60.

_____. *Public Parks and the Enlargement of Towns*. Cambridge, Massachusetts: The Riverside Press, 1870.

_____. *Walks and Talks of an American Farmer in England*. New York: G. P. Putnam, 1852.

_____. "The Yosemite Valley and the Mariposa Big Trees: A Preliminary Report, 1865." *Landscape Architecture*, 43 (October 1952), 17, 20-23.

"The Prescient Planner." *Time Magazine*, 100 (December 11, 1972), 98-99.

Reed, Henry, and Sophia Duckworth. *Central Park: A History and a Guide*. New York: Clarkson N. Potter, Inc., 1967.

Roper, Laura Wood. *F L O: A Biography of Frederick Law Olmsted*. Baltimore: Johns Hopkins University Press, 1973.

Sax, Joseph L. "America's National Parks: Their Principles, Purposes, and Prospects." *Natural History*, 85 (October 1976), 57-88.

Schickel, Richard. "Frederick Law Olmsted, Creator of 'The Central Park.'" *New York Times*, December 31, 1972, Sec. 6, pp. 12-14, 16-19.

Stevenson, Elizabeth. *Park Maker: A Life of Frederick Law Olmsted*. New York: Macmillan, 1977.

Streatfield, David C. "The Evolution of the California Landscape." *Landscape Architecture*, 66 (March 1976), 117-26, 170.

Tatum, George B. "The Emergence of an American School of Landscape Design." *Historic Preservation*, 25 (April-June 1973), 34-41.

van Rensselaer, M. G. "Frederick Law Olmsted." *The Century*, 46 (October 1893), 860-67.

Wurman, Richard, Alan Levy, and Joel Katz. *The Nature of Recreation*. Cambridge, Massachusetts: M.I.T. Press, 1972.

Chapter 4 Carl Schurz: A Sharp Tongue vs. A Profligate Nation

"Carl Schurz." *New York Times*, May 15, 1906, p. 8.

Donald, David. "The Senator with a Conscience." Review of *Charles Sumner. Saturday Review of Literature*, 34 (June 16, 1951), 46.

Easum, Chester Verne. *The Americanization of Carl Schurz*. Chicago: University of Chicago Press, 1929.

Fuess, Claude Moore. *Carl Schurz: Reformer*. New York: Dodd, Mead, 1932.

Hacker, Louis M. "Carl Schurz." Review of *Carl Schurz: Reformer. Nation*, 134 (May 18, 1932), 575-76.

Howells, W. D. "Carl Schurz." *Harper's Weekly*, 50 (May 26, 1906), 728.

Morgan, Bayard Quincy. *Carl Schurz*. Berlin: Vereinigung Carl Schurz, 1938.

Reynolds, Robert L. "A Man of Conscience." *American Heritage*, 14 (February 1963), 20-23, 83-91.

Schafer, Joseph. *Carl Schurz: Militant Liberal*. Madison: State Historical Society of Wisconsin, 1930.

Schurz, Carl. *Abraham Lincoln: An Essay*. Boston and New York: Houghton Mifflin, 1891.

238

———. *Annual Report of the Secretary of the Interior on the Operations of the Department for the Fiscal Year Ended June 30, 1877*. Washington: U.S. Government Printing Office, 1877, (III), XV-XX. (In subsequent reports Schurz expands on his concerns about America's land policies.)

———. *The Autobiography of Carl Schurz*. Wayne Andrews, ed. New York: Charles Scribner's Sons, 1961.

———. *Charles Sumner*. Arthur Reed Hogue, ed. Urbana: University of Illinois Press, 1951.

———. *Intimate Letters of Carl Schurz*. Joseph Schafer, ed. Madison: State Historical Society of Wisconsin, 1928.

———. *Lebenserinnerungen, bis zum jahre 1850*. Edward Manley, ed. Boston: Alyn and Bacon, 1913.

———. *Life of Henry Clay*. 2 vols. Boston and New York: Houghton Mifflin, 1887.

———. *The Reminiscences of Carl Schurz*. 3 vols. New York: The McClure Company, 1907-1908.

———. *Speeches, Correspondence and Political Papers of Carl Schurz*. Frederic Bancroft, ed. 6 vols. New York: G. P. Putnam's Sons, 1913. (See especially "The Need of a Rational Forest Policy," v. 6, pp. 22-33, an address to the American Forestry Association.)

———. *Speeches of Carl Schurz*. Philadelphia: J. B. Lippincott, 1865. "Schurz, the Orator and Patriot — Part I." Review of *Speeches, Correspondence and Political Papers of Carl Schurz*. *Nation*, 97 (September 18, 1913), 261-63.

"Schurz, the Orator and Patriot — Part II." Review of *Speeches, Correspondence and Political Papers of Carl Schurz*. *Nation*, 97 (September 25, 1913), 286-87.

Trefethen, James B. "Carl Schurz: Forestry's Forgotten Pioneer." *American Forests*, 67 (September 1961), 24-27.

Trefousse, Hans Louis. *Carl Schurz: A Biography*. Knoxville: University of Tennessee Press, 1982.

Twain, Mark. "Carl Schurz, Pilot." *Harper's Weekly*, 50 (May 26, 1906), 727.

Villard, Oswald Garrison. "A Patriotic American." Review of *Carl Schurz: Reformer*. *Saturday Review of Literature*, 8 (April 9, 1932), 645, 649-50.

Chapter 5 John Burroughs: The Harvest of a Quiet Eye

Barrus, Clara. *John Burroughs Boy and Man*. Garden City, New York: Doubleday, Page and Company, 1920.

_____. *The Life and Letters of John Burroughs*. 2 vols. Boston: Houghton Mifflin, 1925.

_____. *Our Friend John Burroughs*. Boston: Houghton Mifflin, 1914.

_____. *Whitman and Burroughs Comrades*. Boston: Houghton Mifflin, 1931.

Burroughs, John. *Accepting the Universe*. Boston: Houghton Mifflin, 1920.

_____. *Bird and Bough*. Boston: Houghton Mifflin, 1906.

_____. *Birds and Poets with Other Papers*. New York: Hurd and Houghton, 1877.

_____. *The Breath of Life*. Boston: Houghton Mifflin, 1915.

_____. *Camping with President Roosevelt*. Boston: Houghton Mifflin, 1906. (In 1907 the book was reprinted with additional material and with the title *Camping and Tramping with Roosevelt*.)

_____. *Far and Near*. Boston: Houghton Mifflin, 1904.

_____. *Field and Study*. Boston: Houghton Mifflin, 1919.

_____. *Fresh Fields*. Boston: Houghton Mifflin, 1884.

_____. *The Heart of Burroughs's Journals*. Clara Barrus, ed. Boston: Houghton Mifflin, 1928.

_____. *Indoor Studies*. Boston: Houghton Mifflin, 1889.

_____. *John Burroughs' America*. Farida Wiley, ed. New York: Devin-Adair, 1951.

_____. *John Burroughs and Ludella Peck*. New York: Harold Vinal, 1925. (Letters.)

_____. *John James Audubon*. Boston: Small, Maynard and Company, 1902.

_____. *The Last Harvest*. Boston: Houghton Mifflin, 1922.

_____. *Leaf and Tendril*. Boston: Houghton Mifflin, 1908.

_____. *The Light of Day*. Boston: Houghton Mifflin, 1900.

_____. *Literary Values and Other Papers*. Boston: Houghton Mifflin, 1902.

_____. *Locusts and Wild Honey*. Boston: Houghton, Osgood and Company, 1879.

_____. *My Boyhood*. Garden City, New York: Doubleday, Page and Company, 1922.

_____. *Notes on Walt Whitman as Poet and Person*. New York: American News Company, 1867.

_____. *Pepacton*. Boston: Houghton Mifflin, 1881.

_____. *Riverby*. Boston: Houghton Mifflin, 1894.

_____. *Signs and Seasons*. Boston: Houghton Mifflin, 1886.

_____. *The Summit of the Years*. Boston: Houghton Mifflin, 1913.

_____. *Time and Change*. Boston: Houghton Mifflin, 1912.

_____. *Under the Apple-Trees*. Boston: Houghton Mifflin, 1916.

_____. *Under the Maples*. Boston: Houghton Mifflin, 1921.

_____. *Wake-Robin*. New York: Hurd and Houghton, 1871.

_____. *Ways of Nature*. Boston: Houghton Mifflin, 1905.

_____. *Whitman: A Study*. Boston: Houghton Mifflin, 1896.

_____. *Winter Sunshine*. New York: Hurd and Houghton, 1875.

_____. *With John Burroughs in Field and Wood*. Elizabeth Burroughs Kelley, ed. South Brunswick, New Jersey: A. S. Barnes, 1969.

"Careful, Mr. Burroughs." *American Heritage*, 14 (February 1963), 2.

Davis, Millard C. "The Influence of Emerson, Thoreau, and Whitman on the Early American Naturalists — John Muir and John Burroughs." *The Living Wilderness*, 30 (Winter 1966-1967), 18-23.

Dreiser, Theodore. "John Burroughs in His Mountain Hut." *The New Voice*, 16 (August 19, 1899), 7, 13.

Firestone, Harvey S. *Men and Rubber: The Story of Business*. Garden City, New York: Doubleday, Page and Company, 1926. (See Chapter 13, "Camping with Edison, Ford, and Burroughs," pp. 188-201, and Chapter 14, "Camping Through the Smoky Mountains and the Shenandoah Valley," pp. 202-19.)

Foerster, Norman. *Nature in American Literature*. New York: Macmillan, 1923. (See Chapter 9, "Burroughs," pp. 264-305.)

Gilborn, Craig. "A. F. Tait: Artist in the Adirondacks." *Conservationist*, 29 (June-July 1975), 20-26.

Hicks, Philip M. *The Development of the Natural History Essay in American Literature*. Philadelphia: University of Pennsylvania Press, 1924.

Howells, William Dean. Review of *Wake-Robin*. *Atlantic Monthly*, 28 (August 1871), 254.

Huyck, Dorothy Boyle. "Over Hill and Dale with Henry Ford and Famous Friends." *Smithsonian*, 9 (June 1978), 88-95.

James, Henry. Review of *Winter Sunshine*. *Nation*, 22 (January 27, 1876), 66.

Kelley, Elizabeth Burroughs. *John Burroughs: Naturalist*. New York: Exposition Press, 1959.

Komarek, Connie. "In Burroughs' Footsteps." *Conservationist*, 27 (December-January 1972-1973), 13-20.

Perry, Bliss. *The Praise of Folly*. Boston and New York: Houghton Mifflin, 1923. (See "John Burroughs," pp. 63-72.)

Sharp, Dallas Lore. *The Seer of Slabsides*. Boston: Houghton Mifflin, 1921.

Shatraw, Harriet Barrus. "The Magic of John Burroughs." *Conservationist*, 28 (June-July 1974), 20-21.

Westbrook, Perry D. *John Burroughs*. New York: Twayne Publishers, 1974.

_____. "John Burroughs and the Transcendentalists." *Emerson Society Quarterly*, no. 55, part 2 (2nd Quarter, 1969), 47-55.

_____. "John Burroughs: New York's Early Defender of the Environment." *Conservationist*, 25 (August-September 1970), 30-32.

Chapter 6 George Bird Grinnell: Western Frontiersman, Eastern Editor

Bunzel, Ruth L., and Margaret Mead. *The Golden Age of American Anthropology*. New York: George Braziller, 1960.

Chittenden, Hiram Martin. *The Yellowstone National Park*. Cincinnati: Robert Clark, 1905.

"Dr. G. B. Grinnell, Naturalist, Dead." *New York Times*, April 12, 1938, p. 23.

Fisher, Albert Kenrick. "In Memoriam: George Bird Grinnell." *Auk*, 56 (January 1939), 1-12.

Forest and Stream. (August 14, 1873 to December 30, 1911). 77 vols.

Goetzmann, William H. *Exploration and Empire: The Explorer and the Scientist in the Winning of the West*. New York: Alfred A. Knopf, 1966.

Graham, Frank, Jr. *The Adirondack Park: A Political History*. Alfred A. Knopf, 1978.

Grant, Madison. *Early History of Glacier National Park Montana*. Washington, D. C.: U.S. Government Printing Office, 1919.

Grinnell, George Bird, ed. *American Big Game and Its Haunts*. New York: Forest and Stream Publishing

Company, 1904.

———, ed. *Audubon Magazine*, 1 (February 1887-January 1888).

———. *Audubon Park: The History of the Site of the Hispanic Society of America and Neighboring Institutions*. New York: Hispanic Society of America, 1927.

———. *Blackfoot Lodge Tales: The Story of a Prairie People*. New York: Charles Scribner's Sons, 1892.

———, ed. *A Brief History of the Boone and Crockett Club*. New York: Forest and Stream Publishing Company, 1910.

———. *The Cheyenne Indians: Their History and Ways of Life*. 2 vols. New Haven: Yale University Press, 1923.

———. "The Crown of the Continent." *Century Magazine*, 62 (September, 1901), 660-72.

———. *The Fighting Cheyennes*. New York: Charles Scribner's Sons, 1915.

———. *Jack, the Young Ranchman: Or a Boy's Adventures in the Rockies*. New York: F. A. Stokes Company, 1899.

———. "The Last of the Buffalo." *Scribner's*, 12 (September 1892), 267-86.

———. "An Old-Time Bone Hunt." *Natural History*, 23 (1923), 329-36.

———. "Recollections of Audubon Park." *Auk*, 37 (July 1920), 372-80.

———. "Sketch of Professor O. C. Marsh." *Popular Science Monthly*, 13 (September 1878), 612-17.

———. "Tenure of Land Among the Indians." *American Anthropologist*, 9 (January-March 1907), 1-11.

———. *When Buffalo Ran*. New Haven: Yale University Press, 1920.

———, and Charles Sheldon, eds. *Hunting and Conservation*. New Haven: Yale University Press, 1925.

———, and Charles Sheldon, eds. *Hunting and Conservation*. New Haven: Yale University Press, 1925.

——, and Theodore Roosevelt, eds. *American Big-Game Hunting*. New York: Forest and Stream Publishing Company, 1901.

——, and Theodore Roosevelt, eds. *Hunting in Many Lands*. New York: Forest and Stream Publishing Company, 1895.

——, and Theodore Roosevelt, eds. *Trail and Camp-Fire*. New York: Forest and Stream Publishing Company, 1897.

Hough, Emerson. *Getting a Wrong Start: A Truthful Autobiography*. New York: Macmillan, 1915.

Ise, John. *Our National Park Policy: A Critical History*. Baltimore: Johns Hopkins University Press, 1961.

Lanham, Url. *The Bone Hunters*. New York: Columbia University Press, 1973.

Ludlow, William. *Report of a Reconnaissance from Carroll, Montana Territory, on the Upper Missouri, to the Yellowstone National Park, and Return, Made in the Summer of 1875*. Washington, D. C.: U.S. Government Printing Office, 1876.

Reiger, John F. *American Sportsmen and the Origins of Conservation*. New York: Winchester Press, 1975.

——. "A Dedication to the Memory of George Bird Grinnell, 1849-1938." *Arizona and the West*, 21 (Spring 1979), 1-4.

——. "George Bird Grinnell." *National Wildlife*, 10 (February-March 1973), 12-13.

——. "George Bird Grinnell and the Development of American Conservation, 1870-1901." dissertation, Northwestern University, 1970.

——. *The Passing of the Great West: Selected Papers of George Bird Grinnell*. New York: Winchester Press, 1972.

Saveth, Edward N. "The American Patrician Class: A Field for Research." *American Quarterly*, 15 (Summer 1963), 235-52.

Trefethen, James B. *An American Crusade for Wildlife*. New York: Winchester Press and the Boone and Crockett Club, 1975.

Chapter 7 Theodore Roosevelt: Leading the Charge for Conservation

Blum, John M. *The Republican Roosevelt*. 2nd ed. Cambridge, Massachusetts: Harvard University Press, 1977.

Brooks, Chester L., and Ray H. Mattison. *Theodore Roosevelt and the Dakota Badlands*. Washington: National Park Service, 1958.

Burroughs, John. *Camping with President Roosevelt*. Boston: Houghton Mifflin, 1906. (In 1907 the book was reprinted with additional material under the title *Camping and Tramping with Roosevelt*.)

Burton, David H. *Theodore Roosevelt*. New York: Twayne Publishers, 1972.

Chessman, G. Wallace. *Theodore Roosevelt and the Politics of Power*. Boston: Little, Brown, 1969.

Cutright, Paul Russell. *Theodore Roosevelt the Naturalist*. New York: Harper, 1956.

Dannen, Kent. "Teddy You're a Bear." *Backpacker Magazine*, 3 (Fall 1975), 34-36, 77-78.

Eliot, J.L. "T.R.'s Wilderness Legacy." *National Geographic*, 162 (September, 1982), 340-63.

Fausold, Martin L. *Gifford Pinchot: Bull Moose Progressive*. Syracuse: Syracuse University Press, 1961.

Greeley, William B. *Forests and Men*. rpt. New York: Arno Press, 1972.

Hagedorn, Hermann. *Roosevelt in the Badlands*. Boston: Houghton Mifflin, 1921.

Harbaugh, William H. *The Life and Times of Theodore Roosevelt*. rev. ed. New York: Collier Books, 1963.

Hays, Samuel P. *Conservation and the Gospel of Efficiency: The Progressive Conservation Movement, 1890-1920*. Cambridge, Massachusetts: Harvard University Press, 1959.

Lorant, Stefan. *The Life and Times of Theodore Roosevelt*. Garden City, New York: Doubleday, 1959.

McGeary, Martin Nelson. *Gifford Pinchot: Forester-Politician*. Princeton: Princeton University Press, 1960.

Merriam, C. Hart. "Roosevelt, the Naturalist." *Science*, 75 (February 12, 1932), 181-83.

Mowry, George E. *Theodore Roosevelt and the Progressive Movement*. Madison: University of Wisconsin Press, 1946.

Pinchot, Gifford. *Breaking New Ground*. New York: Harcourt, Brace, 1947.

Pinkett, Harold T. *Gifford Pinchot: Private and Public Forester*. Urbana: University of Illinois Press, 1970.

Pringle, Henry F. *Theodore Roosevelt*. New York: Harcourt, Brace, 1931.

Puter, Stephen A. *Looters of the Public Domain*. rpt. New York: Arno Press, 1972.

Richardson, Elmo R. *The Politics of Conservation: Crusades and Controversies, 1897-1913*. Berkeley: University of California Press, 1962.

Roosevelt, Kermit, and Theodore Roosevelt. *East of the Sun and West of the Moon*. New York: Charles Scribner's Sons, 1926.

———. *Trailing the Giant Panda*. New York: Charles Scribner's Sons, 1929.

Roosevelt, Theodore. *African Game Trails*. New York: Charles Scribner's Sons, 1910.

———. *A Book-lover's Holidays in the Open*. New York: Charles Scribner's Sons, 1916.

———. *Hunting Tales of the West*. New York: The Current Literature Publishing Company, 1907.

_____. *Outdoor Passtimes of an American Hunter*. New York: Charles Scribner's Sons, 1903.

_____. *Ranch Life and the Hunting-Trail*. New York: The Century Company, 1888.

_____. *The Rough Riders*. New York: Scribner, 1898.

_____. *Stories of the Great West*. New York: The Century Company, 1909.

_____. *Theodore Roosevelt: An Autobiography*. New York: Macmillan, 1913.

_____. *Through the Brazilian Wilderness*. New York: Charles Scribner's Sons, 1914.

_____. *The Winning of the West*. 6 vols. New York: G. P. Putnam's Sons, 1889-1896.

Thayer, William Roscoe. *Theodore Roosevelt: An Intimate Biography*. Boston and New York: Houghton Mifflin, 1919.

White, Edward G. *The Eastern Establishment and the Western Experience: The West of Frederic Remington, Theodore Roosevelt and Owen Wister*. New Haven, Connecticut: Yale University Press, 1968.

Wilson, R. L. *Theodore Roosevelt: Outdoorsman*. New York: Winchester Press, 1971.

Chapter 8 William T. Hornaday: Warrior for Wildlife

"Dr. Hornaday." *The Commonweal*, 25 (March 19, 1937), 583.

"Dr. Hornaday's Plea for Its Conservation." Review of *Wild Life Conservation in Theory and Practice. New York Times Book Review*, March 7, 1915, p. 80.

"Dr. W. T. Hornaday Dies in Stamford." *New York Times*, March 7, 1937, Section 2, p. 9.

Forbes, John Ripley. *In the Steps of the Great American Zoologist, William Temple Hornaday*. Mystic, Connecticut: Natural Science for Youth Foundation,

1976.

———. "The Museum Goes to the Little Red Schoolhouse." *Nature Magazine*, 38 (August-September 1945), 374-76.

———. "W. T. Hornaday." *National Wildlife*, 9 (April-May 1971), 24-25.

Graham, Frank, Jr. *Man's Dominion: The Story of Conservation in America*. New York: M. Evans and Company, 1971. (See Chapters 17-20 for material on Hornaday.)

"A Great Naturalist." *The World's Work*, 11 (December 1905), 7017.

Hornaday, William T. *The American Natural History: A Foundation of Useful Knowledge of the Higher Animals of North America*. New York: Charles Scribner's Sons, 1904.

———. *Awake! America: Object Lessons and Warnings*. New York: Moffat, Yard and Company, 1918.

———. "Behind the Scenes in a Great Zoo." *The Mentor*, 15 (August 1927), 1-13.

———. *Camp-Fires in the Canadian Rockies*. New York: Charles Scribner's Sons, 1906.

———. *Camp-Fires on Desert and Lava*. New York: Charles Scribner's Sons, 1908.

———. *The Extermination of the American Bison*. Washington, D.C.: U.S. Government Printing Office, 1889.

———. *Free Rum on the Congo, and What it is Doing There*. Chicago: Woman's Temperance Publication Association, 1887.

———. *The Lying-Lure of Bolshevism*. New York: American Defense Society, 1919.

———. *The Man Who Became a Savage: A Story of Our Own Times*. Buffalo, New York: The P. Paul Book Company, 1896.

———. "Masterpieces of American Bird Taxidermy." *Scribner's*, 78 (September 1925), 261-73.

_____. *The Minds and Manners of Wild Animals*. New York: Charles Scribner's Sons, 1922.

_____. "My Fifty-Four Years with Animal Life." *The Mentor*, 17 (May 1929), 1-11.

_____. The New York Plan for Zoological Parks." *Scribner's*, 46 (November 1909), 590-606.

_____. *Old-Fashioned Verses*. New York: Clark and Fritts, 1919.

_____. *Our Vanishing Wild Life: Its Extermination and Preservation*. New York: New York Zoological Society, 1913.

_____. *The Preservation of Health in Cuba: Things Worth Knowing, Gleaned from Experiences in the Tropics*. New York: Sears and White, 1898.

_____. "Prohibition that Prohibits." *Collier's*, 48 (November 11, 1911), 17.

_____. *Save the Sage Grouse from Extinction: A Demand from Civilization to the Western States*. New York: New York Zoological Park, 1916.

_____. *A Searchlight on Germany: Germany's Blunders, Crimes and Punishment*. New York: American Defense Society, 1917.

_____. *The Statement of the Permanent Wild Life Protection Fund: 1913-1914*. New York: The Fund, 1915.

_____. *Tales from Nature's Wonderlands*. New York: Charles Scribner's Sons, 1924.

_____. *Taxidermy and Zoological Collecting*. New York: Charles Scribner's Sons, 1891.

_____. *Thirty Years War for Wild Life: Gains and Losses in the Thankless Task*. New York: Charles Scribner's Sons, 1931.

_____. *Two Years in the Jungle: The Experiences of a Hunter and Naturalist in India, Ceylon, the Malay Peninsula and Borneo*. New York: Charles Scribner's Sons, 1885.

_____. *Wild Animal Interviews and Wild Opinions of Us*.

New York: Charles Scribner's Sons, 1928.

———. *A Wild-Animal Round-Up: Stories and Pictures from the Passing Show*. New York: Charles Scribner's Sons, 1925.

———. "Wild Animals We Never See Alive." *Scribner's*, 82 (November 1927), 584-95.

———. *Wild Life Conservation in Theory and Practice*. New Haven, Connecticut: Yale University Press, 1914.

Osborn, Fairfield. "Obituary: William Temple Hornaday." *Science*, 85 (May 7, 1937), 445-46.

Preble, Edward A. "William Temple Hornaday: An Appreciation." *Nature Magazine*, 29 (May 1937), 303-04.

Trefethen, James B. *An American Crusade for Wildlife*. New York: Winchester Press and the Boone and Crockett Club, 1975.

———. *Crusade for Wildlife: Highlights in Conservation Progress*. Harrisburg, Pennsylvania: The Stackpole Company, and New York: the Boone and Crockett Club, 1961.

Chapter 9 Benton MacKaye: The Reinvasion by Nature

"Benton MacKaye: A Tribute." *Living Wilderness*, 75 (January-March 1976), 6-34. (Reminiscences of MacKaye by nine friends. Includes "A Benton MacKaye Bibliography.")

Brower, David. "FOE Books and the World Heritage." *Not Man Apart*, 8 (mid-October-November 1978), 12-14.

Bryant, Paul Thompson. "The Quality of the Day: The Achievement of Benton MacKaye." dissertation, University of Illinois, 1965.

Fisher, Ronald M. *The Appalachian Trail*. Washington, D. C.: National Geographic Society, 1972.

Floyd, Tom. "Volunteers on the Appalachian Trail." *Na-*

tional Parks and Conservation Magazine, 53 (February 1979), 20-22.

Frank, Bernard. "Benton MacKaye." *Journal of Forestry*, 45 (April 1947), 295-96.

Frome, Michael. *Whose Woods These Are: The Story of the National Forests*. Garden City, New York: Doubleday, 1962. (See Chapter 5, "Mount Washington and Friends.")

Johnson, Hugh B. "In Memory of Benton MacKaye, 'Father of the Appalachian Trail.' " *Journal of the American Institute of Architects*, 65 (February 1976), 68.

Long, John E. "Benton MacKaye: The Verdant Prophet." *American Forests*, 70 (July 1964), 16-19.

Lubove, Roy. *Community Planning in the 1920's: The Contribution of the Regional Planning Association of America*. Pittsburgh: University of Pittsburgh Press, 1963.

MacKaye, Benton. "An Alaska-Siberia 'Burma Road.' " *The New Republic*, 106 (March 6, 1943), 292-94.

_____. "The Appalachian Trail: A Guide to the Study of Nature." *Scientific Monthly*, 34 (April 1932), 330-42.

_____. "An Appalachian Trail: A Project in Regional Planning." *Journal of the American Institute of Architects*, 9 (October 1921), 325-30.

_____. "The Challenge of Muscle Shoals." *Nation*, 136 (April 19, 1933), 445-46.

_____. "Dam Site vs. Norm Site." *Scientific Monthly*, 71 (October 1950), 241-47.

_____. *Employment and Natural Resources*. U.S. Department of Labor, Office of the Secretary, 1919.

_____. *Expedition Nine: A Return to a Region*. Washington, D. C.: The Wilderness Society, 1969.

_____. *From Geography to Geotechnics*. Paul T. Bryant, ed. Urbana: University of Illinois Press, 1968.

_____. "Making New Opportunities for Employment."

Monthly Labor Review, 8 (April 1919), 1067-85.

———. "A New England Recreation Plan." *Journal of Forestry*, 27 (December 1929), 927-30.

———. *The New Exploration: A Philosophy of Regional Planning*. rpt. Urbana: Illinois University Press, 1962.

———. "The New Exploration: Charting the Industrial Wilderness." *The Survey*, 54 (May 1, 1925), 192, 194.

———. "The New Northwest Passage." *Nation*, 122 (June 2, 1926), 603-04.

———. "Our Iron Civilization." *Saturday Review*, 6 (November 2, 1929), 342-43.

———. "The Soldier, the Worker, and the Land's Resources." *Monthly Labor Review*, 6 (January 1918), 48-56.

———. "The Townless Highway." *New Republic*, 62 (March 12, 1930), 93-95.

———. "Townless Highways for the Motorist." *Harper's*, 163 (August 1931), 347-56.

———. *A Two Year Course in Geotechnics*. Shirley Center, Massachusetts: privately printed, 1972.

———. "War and Wilderness." *The Living Wilderness*, 6 (July 1941), 7-8.

———. "Why the Appalachian Trail?" *The Living Wilderness*, 1 (September 1935), 7-8.

———. "A Wilderness Philosophy." *The Living Wilderness*, 11 (March 1946), 1-4.

———, and Lewis Mumford. "Regional Planning." *Encyclopedia Britannica*, 14th ed., 1928.

———, eds. *The Survey*, 54 (May 1, 1925). (A special issue on regional planning edited by MacKaye and Mumford.)

MacKaye, Percy. *Epoch: The Life of Steele MacKaye*. New York: Boni and Liveright, 1927.

Stallings, Constance L. "The Last Interview with Benton MacKaye." *Backpacker Magazine*, 4 (April 1976),

54-55, 57, 81-85.

Sutton, Ann, and Myron Sutton. *The Appalachian Trail.* Philadelphia and New York: J. B. Lippincott, 1967.

Whitley, Penny. "Long, Long Trail Awinding." *American Forests,* 77 (February 1971), 16-18, 59-60.

Chapter 10 Robert Marshall: Last of the Radical Bureaucrats

Adler, Cyrus. *Louis Marshall: A Biographical Sketch.* New York: The American Jewish Committee, 1931.

Ahern, George Patrick. *Deforested America.* Washington, D. C.: U.S. Government Printing Office, 1929.

_____, et al. "A Letter to Foresters." *Journal of Forestry,* 28 (April 1930), 456-58.

Broome, Harvey. "Origins of the Wilderness Society." *The Living Wilderness,* 5 (July 1940), 13-15.

Carson, Russell M. L. *Peaks and People of the Adirondacks.* Garden City, New York: Doubleday, 1928.

Collier, John. *From Every Zenith: A Memoir.* Denver: Alan Swallow, 1963.

_____. "The Indians and Their Lands." *Journal of Forestry,* 31 (December 1933), 905-10.

_____. "Wilderness Now on Indian Lands." *The Living Wilderness,* 3 (December 1937), 3-4.

Frome, Michael. *Battle for the Wilderness.* New York: Praeger, 1974.

_____. *The Forest Service.* Praeger, 1971.

Graham, Frank, Jr. *Man's Dominion: The Story of Conservation in America.* New York: M. Evans and Company, 1971. (See Chapter 25, "The Spirit.")

Marshall, George. "Bibliography of Robert Marshall, 1901-1939." *The Living Wilderness,* 16 (Autumn 1951), 20-23.

_____. "Bibliography of Robert Marshall: A Supplement."

The Living Wilderness, 19 (Summer 1954), 31-35.

———. "Bob Marshall and the Alaska Arctic Wilderness."
The Living Wilderness, 34 (Autumn 1970), 29-32.

———. "On Bob Marshall's Landmark Article." *The Living
Wilderness*, 40 (October-December 1976), 28-30.

———. "Robert Marshall as a Writer." *The Living Wilderness*, 16 (Autumn 1951), 14-20.

Marshall, Louis. *Louis Marshall, Champion of Liberty:
Selected Papers and Addresses*. Charles Reznikoff,
ed. Philadelphia: Jewish Publications Society of
America, 1957.

Marshall, Robert. *Arctic Village*. New York: Harrison
Smith and Robert Haas, 1933.

———. *Arctic Wilderness*. George Marshall, ed. Berkeley:
University of California Press, 1956. (Rptd. 1970
with the title *Alaska Wilderness*.)

———. "Forest Devastation Must Stop." *Nation*, 129 (August 28, 1929), 218-19.

———. "The Forest for Recreation." In *A National Plan for
American Forestry*. 73rd Cong., 1st Sess., Senate Doc.
12, 2 vols. (Washington, 1933), I, 463-87.

———. *The High Peaks of the Adirondacks*. Albany: The
Adirondack Mountain Club, 1922.

———. "Impressions from the Wilderness." *The Living Wilderness*, 16 (Autumn 1951), 10-13. (Also in *Nature
Magazine*, 44 (November 1951), 481-84.

———. "Mountain Climbing." *The Living Wilderness*, 19
(Summer 1954), 30.

———. *The People's Forests*. New York: Harrison Smith
and Robert Haas, 1933.

———. "A Plea for the Old Wilderness." *New York Times*,
April 25, 1937, Magazine Section, pp. 16-17.

———. "Precipitation and Presidents." *Nation*, 124 (March
23, 1927), 315-16.

———. "Priorities in Forest Recreation." *American Forests*,
41 (January 1935), 11-13, 30.

_____. "The Problem of the Wilderness." *Scientific Monthly*, 30 (January to June 1930), 141-48.

_____. "A Proposed Remedy for Our Forestry Illness." *Journal of Forestry*, 28 (March 1930), 273-80.

_____. "Public Forestry or Private Devastation?" *New Republic*, 79 (June 27, 1934), 176-78.

_____. "Recreational Limitations to Silviculture in the Adirondacks." *Journal of Forestry*, 23 (February 1925), 173-78.

_____. "Should We Settle Alaska?" *New Republic*, 102 (January 8, 1940), 49-50.

_____. *The Social Management of American Forests*. New York: League for Industrial Democracy, 1930.

_____. "The Universe of the Wilderness Is Vanishing." *Nature Magazine*, 29 (April 1937), 235-40.

Mencken, H. L. "Utopia in Little." Review of *Arctic Village. American Mercury*, 29 (May 1933), 124-26.

Nash, Roderick. "The Strenuous Life of Bob Marshall." *Forest History*, 10 (October 1966), 18-25.

_____. *Wilderness and the American Mind*. rev. ed. New Haven: Yale University Press, 1973.

Reed, Franklin, "Reviews." Review of *The People's Forests. Journal of Forestry*, 32 (January 1934), 104-07.

Rosenstock, Morton. *Louis Marshall, Defender of Jewish Rights*. Detroit: Wayne State University Press, 1965.

Schaefer, Paul. "Bob Marshall, Mount Marcy, and — the Wilderness." *The Living Wilderness*, 30 (Summer 1966), 6-10.

"A Summons to Save the Wilderness." *The Living Wilderness*, 1 (September 1935), 1-2.

Wolff, Meyer H. "The Bob Marshall Wilderness Area. *The Living Wilderness*, 6 (July 1941), 5-6.

Wright, Sam. "To Jump Three Thousand Years." *American West*, 8 (March 1971), 21-27.

Chapter 11 Franklin Delano Roosevelt: The Debt Falls Due

Berkman, Richard L., and W. Kip Viscusi. *Damming the West: Ralph Nader's Study Group Report on the Bureau of Reclamation*. New York: Grossman, 1973.

Bonnifield, Paul. *The Dust Bowl: Men, Dirt, and Depression*. Albuquerque: University of New Mexico, 1979.

Brink, Wellington. *Big Hugh: The Father of Soil Conservation*. New York: Macmillan, 1951.

Brough, James, and Elliot Roosevelt. *An Untold Story*. New York: G. P. Putnam's Sons, 1973.

Burns, James MacGregor. *Roosevelt: The Lion and the Fox*. New York: Harcourt Brace, 1956.

———. *Roosevelt: The Soldier of Freedom*. New York: Harcourt Brace Jovanovich, 1970.

Freidel, Frank. *Franklin D. Roosevelt: The Apprenticeship*. Boston: Little, Brown, 1952.

———. *Franklin D. Roosevelt: Launching the New Deal*. Boston: Little, Brown, 1973.

———. *Franklin D. Roosevelt: The Triumph*. Boston: Little, Brown, 1956.

———. *Franklin D. Roosevelt: The Triumph*. Boston: Little, Brown, 1956.

Friedrich, Otto, "F.D.R.'s Disputed Legacy." *Time Magazine*, 119 (February 1, 1982), 20-26, 30, 33-38, 43.

Hopkins, Harry Lloyd. *Spending to Save: The Complete Story of Relief*. Seattle: University of Washington Press, 1972.

Ickes, Harold L. *The Autobiography of a Curmudgeon*. New York: Reynal and Hitchcock, 1943.

———. *The Secret Diary of Harold L. Ickes*. 3 vols. New York: Simon and Schuster, 1953-1954.

Johnson, Vance. *Heaven's Tableland: The Dust Bowl Story*. New York: Farrar, Straus, 1947.

Leopold, Aldo. *A Sand County Almanac and Sketches*

Here and There. New York: Oxford University Press, 1949.

Leuchtenburg, William E. *Franklin D. Roosevelt and the New Deal, 1932-1940*. New York: Harper and Row, 1963.

Lilienthal, David E. *TVA: Democracy on the March*. New York: Harper and Brothers, 1944.

Miller, Nathan. *FDR: An Intimate Biography*. Garden City, New York: Doubleday, 1983.

Riesch, Anna Lou. "Conservation under Franklin D. Roosevelt." dissertation, University of Wisconsin, 1952.

Roosevelt, Franklin D. *Franklin D. Roosevelt and Conservation: 1911-1945*. 2 vols. Edgar B. Nixon, ed. Hyde Park, New York: Franklin D. Roosevelt Library, 1957.

———. *Nothing to Fear: The Selected Addresses of Franklin Delano Roosevelt, 1932-1945*. B. D. Zevin, ed. Boston: Houghton Mifflin, 1946.

Salmond, John A. *The Civilian Conservation Corps, 1933-1942: A New Deal Case Study*. Durham, North Carolina: Duke University Press, 1967.

Schlesinger, Arthur M., Jr. *The Age of Roosevelt: The Coming of the New Deal*. Boston: Houghton Mifflin, 1959.

———. *The Age of Roosevelt: The Crisis of the Old Order, 1919-1933*. Boston: Houghton Mifflin, 1956.

———. *The Age of Roosevelt: The Politics of Upheaval*. Boston: Houghton Mifflin, 1960.

Tate, Cassandra. "Ambivalent TVA Roles in Energy and Conservation." *Smithsonian*, 10 (January 1980), 94-103.

Wallace, Henry A. *New Frontiers*. New York: Reynal and Hitchcock, 1934.

Warne, William E. *The Bureau of Reclamation*. New York: Praeger, 1973.

Wallace, Henry A. *New Frontiers*. New York: Reynal and Hitchcock, 1934.

Watkins, T.H. "The Terrible-Tempered Mr. Ickes." *Audubon*, 86 (March, 1984), 93-104.

Worster, Donald. *Dust Bowl: The Southern Plains in the 1930s*. New York: Oxford University Press, 1979.

Chapter 12 Howard Zahniser: Genial Man behind the Wilderness Act

"A Circle That Took Us In." *American Forests*, 70 (June 1964), 8-9.

Frome, Michael. *Battle for the Wilderness*. New York: Praeger, 1974. (Includes complete text of the Wilderness Act in Appendix A.)

"Howard Zahniser." *Washington Post*, May 9, 1964, Sec. A., p. 8.

"Howard Zahniser, 58, Is Dead: A Leader in U.S. Conservation." *New York Times*, May 6, 1964, p. 47.

"Howard Zahniser Memorial Fund." *The Living Wilderness*, 31 (Spring-Summer 1967), 1.

The Living Wilderness, number 86 (Spring-Summer 1964). (A special issue with articles explaining the history and interpreting the content of the Wilderness Act of 1964. Includes complete text of the legislation.)

McCloskey, Michael. "The Wilderness Act of 1964: Its Background and Meaning." *Oregon Law Review*, 45 (1966), 288-321.

Mercure, Delbert V., Jr., and William M. Ross. *Congress and the Environment*. Seattle: University of Washington Press, 1970. (See Chapter 4, "The Wilderness Act: A Product of Congressional Compromise.")

Nash, Roderick. *Wilderness and the American Mind*. rev.

ed. New Haven: Yale University Press, 1973.

"1906 — Howard Clinton Zahniser — 1964." *The Living Wilderness*, 85 (Winter-Spring 1964), 3-6.

Oehser, Paul H. "Nature in Print." *Nature Magazine*, 45 (February 1952), 58-59.

_____. "Remembering Zahnie: Nature Was His God." *Backpacker Magazine*, 5 (February 1977), 35.

Pomeroy, Kenneth B. "Built-In Lobbies." *American Forests*, 63 (July 1957), 7.

_____. "Exclusive Use or Multiple Use?" *American Forests*, 63 (April 1957), 6-7, 65.

Schwartz, William, ed. *Voices for the Wilderness*. New York: Ballantine Books, 1969.

Stegner, Wallace, ed. *This Is Dinosaur: Echo Park Country and Its Magic Rivers*. New York: Alfred A. Knopf, 1955.

Zahniser, Ed. "Elder of the Tribe: Howard Zahniser." *Backpacker Magazine*, 5 (February 1977), 32-35, 66-67, 69-70.

Zahniser, Howard. "How Much Wilderness Can We Afford to Lose?" *Wildlands in Our Civilization*, David Brower, ed. San Francisco: Sierra Club, 1964.

_____. "Lake Solitude Sermon." *The Living Wilderness*, 85 (Winter-Spring 1964), 1.

_____. "Need for Wilderness Areas." *Congressional Record*, 84th Cong., 1st Sess., 101 (June 1, 1955), A3809.

_____ "Shall We Dam Our National Park System?" *Congressional Record*, 84th Cong., 1st Sess., 101 (April 19, 1955), 4691-95.

_____. "To Harry C. James After Receiving from Him and Reading a Gift Copy of *The Divine Comedy of Dante Alighieri as Translated into English Verse by Melville Best Anderson*." (poem.) *The Living Wilderness*, 84 (Summer-Fall 1963), 14.

_____. "The Wilderness Bill and Foresters." *American Forests*, 63 (July 1957), 6, 51-54.

_____. "Wilderness Forever." In *Wilderness: America's Living Heritage*, David Brower, ed. San Francisco: Sierra Club, 1961.

_____, and Michael Nadel. "Parks and Wilderness." *America's Resources*. Charles H. Callison, ed. New York: The Ronald Press, 1967.

Chapter 13 Rachel Carson: The Issue Becomes Life Itself

"Are We Poisoning Ourselves?" *Business Week*, 1723 (September 8, 1962), 36, 38.

Bates, Marston. "Man and Other Pests." Review of *Silent Spring*. *Nation*, 195 (October 6, 1962), 202-03.

Briggs, Shirley A. "Remembering Rachel Carson." *American Forests*, 76 (July 1970), 8-11.

Brooks, Paul. *The House of Life: Rachel Carson at Work*. Boston: Houghton Mifflin, 1972.

Carson, Rachel. *The Edge of the Sea*. Boston: Houghton Mifflin, 1955.

_____. "Rachel Carson Answers Her Critics." *Audubon*, 65 (September-October 1963), 262-65, 313-15.

_____. *The Sea Around Us*. New York: Oxford University Press, 1951.

_____. *The Sense of Wonder*. New York: Harper and Row, 1965.

_____. *Silent Spring*. Boston: Houghton Mifflin, 1962.

_____. *Under the Sea-Wind*. New York: Simon and Schuster 1941.

_____. "Undersea." *Atlantic Monthly*, 160 (September 1937), 322-25.

Darby, William J., "Silence, Miss Carson." *Chemical & Engineering News*, 40 (October 1, 1962), 60, 62-63.

Davis, Kenneth S. "The Deadly Dust: The Unhappy History of DDT." *American Heritage*, 22 (February

1971), 44-47, 92-93.

Diamond, Edwin. "The Myth of the 'Pesticide Menace.'" *Saturday Evening Post*, 33 (September 28, 1963), 16, 18.

Eiseley, Loren. "Using a Plague to Fight a Plague." Review of *Silent Spring. Saturday Review*, 34 (September 29, 1962), 18-19, 34.

Gartner, Carol B. *Rachel Carson*. New York: Frederick Ungar, 1983.

"The Gentle Storm." *Life*, 53 (October 12, 1962), 105-06, 109-10.

Graham, Frank, Jr. *Since Silent Spring*. Boston: Houghton Mifflin, 1970.

Kenyon, Richard L. "Assault on Nature." *Chemical & Engineering News*, 40 (July 23, 1963), 5.

"Many a Spring." *Time Magazine*, 83 (April 24, 1964), 73.

Milne, Lorus, and Margery Milne. "There's Poison All Around Us Now." Review of *Silent Spring. New York Times Book Review*, September 23, 1962, pp. 1, 26.

"Miss Carson Goes to Congress." *American Forests*, 69 (July 1963), 20-23, 49, 51-53.

"Obituary Notes." *Publishers Weekly*, 185 (April 7, 1964), 63-64.

"Pesticides: The Price for Progress." *Time Magazine*, 80 (September 28, 1962), 45-46, 48.

"Rachel Carson." *American Forests*, 70 (May 1964), 8.

Shanks, Bernard. "Fish and Wildlife Service: Growth and Contradiction." *High Country News* (Lander, Wyoming), November 2, 1979, pp. 6-7.

Udall, Stewart. "The Legacy of Rachel Carson." *Saturday Review*, 47 (May 16, 1964), 23, 59.

van den Bosch, Robert. *The Pesticide Conspiracy*. Garden City, New York: Doubleday, 1978.

Vogt, William. "On Man the Destroyer." Review of *Silent Spring. Natural History*, 72 (January 1963), 3-5.

262

Chapter 14 Barry Commoner: Science and Social Duty

Anderson, Alan, Jr. "Scientist at Large." *New York Times*, November 7, 1976, Magazine Section, pp. 58-60, 62, 66, 68, 74, 76.

Boffey, P. M. "Commoner Defies Damoclean Sword." *Science*, 191 (February 13, 1976), 545.

Chisholm, Anne. *Philosophers of the Earth*. New York: E. P. Dutton, 1972.

"A Clash of Gloomy Prophets." *Time Magazine*, 97 (January 11, 1971), 56.

"Cleaning Up the National Mess: How Great the Cost? Who Will Pay?" *Time Magazine*, 95 (February 2, 1970), 60-61.

Coffman, Bob. "The Man Who Says You Use Too Much Fertilizer." *Farm Journal*, 96 (February 1972), 28-29, 45.

Commoner, Barry. "By Using Nature as a Lab." *Saturday Review*, 49 (May 7, 1966), 68-69.

———. *The Closing Circle: Nature, Man, and Technology*. New York: Alfred A. Knopf, 1971.

———. "Ethanol." *New Yorker*, 59 (October 10, 1983), 124, 126, 128-38, 141-53.

———. "Frail Reeds in a Harsh World." *Natural History*, 78 (February 1969), 44-45.

———. "Government Research Grants: Effect of the New Procedures on the Individual Investigator." *Science*, 140 (June 7, 1963), 1048, 1051, 1053.

———. "How Poverty Breeds Overpopulation (And Not the Other Way Around)." *Ramparts*, 13 (August 1975), 21-25, 58-59.

———. "In Defense of Biology." *Science*, 133 (June 2, 1961), 1745-48.

———. *The Politics of Energy*. Alfred A. Knopf, 1979.

———. *The Poverty of Power: Energy and the Economic*

Crisis. New York: Alfred A. Knopf, 1976.

_____. Reflections: The Solar Transition — Part I." *New Yorker*, 55 (April 23, 1979), 53-54, 57-60, 63-64, 66, 69-70, 72, 77-78, 80, 82-84, 86-90, 92, 95-98.

_____. "Reflections: The Solar Transition — Part II." *New Yorker*, 55 (April 30, 1979), 46-48, 51-54, 57-58, 60, 65-66, 68, 73-74, 76, 81-82, 84-88, 90-93.

_____. *Science and Survival*. New York: Viking, 1966.

_____. "Technology and the Natural Environment." *Architectural Forum*, 130 (June 1969), 68-73.

_____. "Trains into Flowers." *Harper's*, 247 (December 1973), 78-80, 82, 85-86.

"The Commoner Cancer Screen." *Time Magazine*, 106 (August 11, 1973), 45, 47.

Crichton, Michael. Review of *The Closing Circle*. *New York Times Book Review*, October 17, 1971, pp. 7, 34.

Dahlin, Robert. "Commoner Takes on Carter and the Energy Act in a June Book Knopf Rushes to Publication." Review of *The Politics of Energy*. *Publishers Weekly*, 215 (March 19, 1979), 64.

Ehrlich, Paul R. *The Population Bomb*. 2nd ed. New York: Ballantine, 1971.

"Fighting to Save the Earth from Man." *Time Magazine*, 95 (February 2, 1970), 56-57, 59-63.

Francis, David R. "New Light on Birthrates in Struggling Lands." *Christian Science Monitor*, March 5, 1979, p. 14.

Gillette, Robert. "Breeder Reactor Debate: The Sun Also Rises." *Science*, 184 (May 10, 1974), 650-54.

Herrera, Philip. "Learning the Three Es." Review of *The Poverty of Power*. *Time Magazine*, 107 (May 31, 1976), 67-68.

Holden, Constance. "Ehrlich versus Commoner: An Environmental Fallout." *Science*, 117 (July 21, 1972), 745-47.

Lang, Daniel. "When Science Shoots the Works." Review

of *Science and Survival. New York Times Book Review*, November 6, 1966, pp. 3, 58.

"The Last Ball Game." Review of *The Closing Circle. Newsweek*, 78 (November 1, 1971), 95-96.

"Latter Day Wizard of Oz." *Forbes*, 118 (July 1, 1976), 26-27.

Mamdani, Mahmood. *The Myth of Population Control.* New York: Monthly Review Press, 1972.

Mesthene, Emmanuel G. "Our Threatened Planet: The Technological Plague." Review of *Science and Survival. Science*, 166 (January 27, 1967), 441-42.

Passell, Peter. Review of *The Poverty of Power. New York Times Book Review*, May 23, 1976, pp. 8, 10, 12.

"Paul Revere of Ecology." *Time Magazine*, 95 (February 2, 1970), 5-8.

"The Pentagon Has the Money." *Nation*, 213 (August 1971), 100.

"The Price of Progress." Review of *The Closing Circle. Time Magazine*, 98 (November 1, 1971), 79.

Review of *Science and Survival. New Yorker*, 42 (November 26, 1966), 244, 246.

Roth, Henry. *Call It Sleep.* rpt. Paterson, New Jersey: Pageant Books, 1960.

"Science Beware Science." Review of *Science and Survival. Times Literary Supplement*, (February 9, 1967), 112.

Watson, James D. *The Double Helix.* New York: Atheneum, 1968.

Weschler, Laurence. "An Interview with Barry Commoner," *Rolling Stone* (May 1, 1980), 44-48.

Chapter 15 Ralph Nader: Slayer of Corvairs

Anderson, Patrick. "Ralph Nader, Crusader: Or, the Rise of A Self-Appointed Lobbyist." *New York Times*, October 29, 1967, Magazine Section, pp. 25, 103-04, 106, 108, 110-12.

Armstrong, Richard. "The Passion that Rules Ralph Nader." *Fortune*, 83 (May 1971), 144-47, 219, 220, 224, 226, 228.

"Auto Safety: Nader Again." *Newsweek*, 69 (February 20, 1967), 85-86.

Baldwin, Deborah. "Environmentalism Goes Underground." *Environmental Action*, 10 (December 2, 1978), 4-5.

———. "Wheeling and Dealing in Washington." *Environmental Action*, 9 (March 25, 1978), 4-8.

Barney, Daniel R. *The Last Stand: Ralph Nader's Study Group on the National Forests*. New York: Grossman Publishers, 1974.

Buckhorn, Robert F. *Nader: The People's Lawyer*. Englewood Cliffs, New Jersey: Prentice-Hall, 1972.

Burt, Dan. *Abuse of Trust*. Chicago: Regnery-Gateway, 1982.

"Business Lobbying: Threat to the Consumer Interest." *Consumer Reports*, 43 (September 1978), 526-31.

Cox, Edward Finch, Robert C. Fellmeth, and John E. Schulz. *The Nader Report on the Federal Trade Commission*. New York: R. W. Baron, 1969.

De Toledano, Ralph. *Hit & Run: The Rise – And Fall? – Of Ralph Nader*. New Rochelle, New York: Arlington House, 1975.

Esposito, John C. *Vanishing Air: The Ralph Nader Study Group Report on Air Pollution*. New York: Grossman Publishers, 1970.

Gates, David. "Nader the Raider Marches On." *Newsweek*, 103 (February 20, 1984), 9, 10.

Gorey, Hays. *Nader and the Power of Everyman*. New York: Grosset and Dunlap, 1975.

Green, Mark J. *The Closed Enterprise System: Ralph Nader's Study Group Report on Antitrust Enforce-

ment. New York: Grossman Publishers, 1972.

Greider, William. "How Far Can a Lone Ranger Ride?" *Ramparts*, 12 (March 1974), 21-23, 52-55.

Holsworth, Robert D. *Public Interest Liberalism and the Crisis of Affluence: Reflections on Nader, Environmentalism, and the Politics of a Sustainable Society*. Boston: G.K. Hall, 1980.

Ignatius, David. "Stages of Nader." *New York Times*, January 18, 1976, Magazine Section, pp. 8-9, 44-45, 51-52, 54.

"Investigations: The Spies Who Were Caught Cold." *Time Magazine*, 87 (April 1, 1966), 79.

"Is Nader Losing His Clout?" *U.S. News and World Report*, 83 (December 19, 1977), 18.

Lapp, Ralph Eugene. *Nader's Nuclear Issues: A Critique*. Greenwich, Connecticut: Fact Systems, 1975.

Leamer, Laurence. *Playing for Keeps in Washington*. New York: Dial Press, 1977. (See Chapter 6, "The Raider.")

"Lobbyists." *Time Magazine*, 90 (December 15, 1967), 28-29.

McCarry, Charles. *Citizen Nader*. New York: Saturday Review Press, 1972.

———. "The Public Ways of the Private Nader. *Saturday Review*, 55 (February 12, 1972), 32-36.

"Meet Ralph Nader." *Newsweek*, 71 (January 22, 1968), 65-67, 70, 73.

Michael, James R. *Working on the System: A Comprehensive Manual for Citizen Access to Federal Agencies*. New York: Basic Books, 1974.

Miller, James Nathan. "What Makes Ralph Nader Run?" *Reader's Digest*, 102 (June 1973), 113-18.

"Nader on Nader." *Time Magazine*, 97 (May 10, 1971), 18.

Nader, Ralph. *Beware*. New York: Law-Arts, 1971.

———, ed. *The Consumer and Corporate Accountability*. New York: Harcourt Brace Jovanovich, 1973.

_____. *Unsafe at Any Speed*. rev. ed. New York: Grossman Publishers, 1972.

_____, and Michael Fortun, eds. *Eating Clean: Food Safety and the Chemical Harvest*. Washington, D.C.: Center for Responsive Law, 1982.

_____, and Claire Nader. *The White House*. New York: Viking Press, 1979.

_____, and Donald Ross. *Action for a Change: A Student's Manual for Public Interest Organizing*. New York: Grossman Publishers, 1971.

_____, and John Abbotts. *The Menace of Atomic Energy*. New York: Norton, 1977.

_____, and Kate Blackwell. *You and Your Pension*. New York: Grossman, 1973.

_____, and Mark Green, eds. *Verdicts on Lawyers*. New York: Crowell, 1976.

_____, et al. *Ralph Nader Congress Project*. 6 vols. New York: Viking, 1975.

_____, et al, eds. *Who's Poisoning America?* San Francisco: Sierra Club Books, 1981.

_____, Kate Blackwell, and Peter J. Petkas, eds. *Whistle Blowing: The Report of the Conference on Professional Responsibility*. New York: Grossman Publishers, 1972.

_____, Lowell Dodge, and Rolf Hotchkiss. *What to Do with Your Bad Car: An Action Manual for Lemon Owners*. New York: Grossman Publishers, 1971.

_____, Mark Green, and Joel Seligman. *Taming the Giant Corporation*. New York: Norton, 1976.

"Nader Samurai." *Time Magazine*, 97 (February 1, 1971), 72-73.

"Nader: Success or Excess?" *Time Magazine*, 110 (November 14, 1977), 76.

"Nader v. G.M. (Contd.)." *Time Magazine*, 96 (August 24, 1970), 29.

"Nader's Raiders on Reagan's Ruling Class." *Newsweek*,

100 (September 6, 1982), 18-19.

"Nibbling at the Nader Myth." *Time Magazine*, 108 (September 6, 1976), 20.

Nicholson, Tom. "Ralph Nader: An 'Abuse of Trust'?" *Newsweek*, 99 (April 19, 1982), 74, 79.

"Private Eyes and Public Hearings." *Newsweek*, 67 (April 4, 1966), 77-78.

Ridgeway, James. "The Dick." *New Republic*, 154 (March 12, 1966), 11-13.

Sanford, David. *Me & Ralph: Is Nader Unsafe for America?* Washington, D. C.: New Republic Book Company, 1976.

Shrum, Robert. "Is Ralph Nader Obsolete?" *New Times*, 10 (April 3, 1978), 22-25, 29-31.

"The Spartan Life." *Newsweek*, 68 (November 28, 1966), 88, 90.

Stang, Alan. "Ralph Nader: The Autocrat and the Establishment." *American Opinion*, 18 (January 1975), 35-37, 39, 41, 43, 45, 47-48, 91-94.

Starr, Paul. *The Discarded Army: Veterans after Vietnam: The Nader Report on Vietnam and the Veterans Administration.* New York: Charterhouse, 1974.

Townsend, Claire. *Old Age: The Last Segregation. Ralph Nader's Study Group Report on Nursing Homes.* New York: Grossman Publishers, 1971.

Turner, James S. *The Chemical Feast: The Ralph Nader Study Group Report of Food Protection and the Food and Drug Administration.* New York: Grossman Publishers, 1970.

"The U.S.'s Toughest Customer." *Time Magazine*, 94 (December 12, 1969), 89-92, 94, 96, 98.

Vidal, Gore. "The Best Man/'72." *Esquire*, 75 (June 1971), 102-05.

Welford, Harrison. *Sowing the Wind.* New York: Grossman Publishers, 1972.

Whiteside, Thomas. *The Investigation of Ralph Nader:*

General Motors Vs. One Determined Man. New York: Arbor House, 1972.

———. "Profiles: A Countervailing Force — Part I." *New Yorker*, 49 (October 8, 1973), 50-52, 54, 56, 59-60, 65, 67-68, 71-72, 74, 78, 80, 82, 84, 89-90, 92, 94, 99, 100-02, 105-08, 110-11.

———. "Profiles: A Countervailing Force — Part II." *New Yorker*, 49 (October 15, 1973), 46-48, 50, 55-56, 58, 60, 62, 65-66, 68, 70, 72, 75, 77-78, 80, 82, 84, 86, 88, 90, 92-93, 96, 98, 100-01.

Zimmerman, Fred L. "Ralph Nader Plans to Expand His Crusades by Opening Firm to Lobby for the Public." *Wall Street Journal*, October 31, 1967, pp. 34, 25.

Zwick, David R., and Marcy Benstock. *Water Wasteland: Ralph Nader's Study Group Report on Water Pollution*. New York: Grossman Publishers, 1971.

Chapter 16   Amory Lovins: Elephants and Pumpkins

Brower, David. "The Most Important Issue We've Ever Published." *Not Man Apart*, 6 (mid-November 1976), 1. (The issue includes a reprint of Lovins' *Foreign Affairs* article, 3-13.)

Copeland, Jeff B. "Energy: A U.S. Achilles' Heel." *Newsweek*, 99 (May 24, 1982), 67-69.

Electric Perspectives, number 3 (1977). (The entire issue of this industry-sponsored publication is devoted to critiques of Lovins' *Foreign Affairs* article.)

Florman, Samuel C. "Small May Be Beautiful, But It Doesn't Really Work Very Well." *Los Angeles Times*, July 24, 1977, Part 7, p. 3.

Frank, Ellen. "A True Friend of the Earth." *San Francisco Chronicle*, (November 18, 1978), 13.

———. "The Whiz Kid Energycologist." *New Times*, 2 (August 21, 1978), 36-38, 40, 42, 44, 46.

270

Hammond, Allen L. " 'Soft Technology' Energy Debate: *Limits to Growth* Revisited?" *Science*, 196 (May 27, 1977), 959-61.

"An Interview with Amory Lovins, Soft Energy's Answer Man." *New Roots*, 7 (September-October 1979), 18-23.

Kernan, Michael. "The Soft Energy Messiah." *Washington Post*, May 3, 1978, Section D, pp. 1, 11.

Lovins, Amory. "The Case against the Fast Breeder Reactor." *Science and Public Affairs*, 29 (March 1973), 29-35.

_____. "The Case for Long-Term Planning." *Bulletin of the Atomic Scientists*, 30 (June 1974), 38-49.

_____. "Energy Strategy: The Road Not Taken?" *Foreign Affairs*, 55 (October 1976), 65-96.

_____. *Eryri, the Mountains of Longing*. San Francisco: Friends of the Earth, 1971.

_____. *Openpit Mining*. London: Earth Island, 1973.

_____. "The Soft Energy Path." *Center Magazine*, 11 (September 1978), 32-45.

_____. *Soft Energy Paths: Toward a Durable Peace*. San Francisco: Friends of the Earth, 1977.

_____. "Statement of Amory B. Lovins, British Representative, Friends of the Earth, Inc." In *Alternative Long-Range Energy Strategies*. Washington: U.S. Government Printing Office, 1977. (Lovins' rebuttal to critics of his *Foreign Affairs* article, given before a joint hearing of the Senate Select Committee on Small Business and the Committee on Interior and Insular Affairs, 94th Congress, 2nd Session, 153-85.)

_____, ed. *The Stockholm Conference: Only One Earth*. London: Earth Island, 1972.

_____. "Thorium Cycles and Proliferation." *Bulletin of the Atomic Scientists*, 35 (February 1979), 16-22.

_____. "World Energy Strategies." *Bulletin of the Atomic Scientists*, 30 (May 1974), 14-32.

_____. *World Energy Strategies: Facts, Issues, and Options*. San Francisco: Friends of the Earth, 1975.

_____, and L. Hunter Lovins. *Brittle Power*, Andover, Massachusetts: Brick House, 1982.

_____, and L. Hunter Lovins. *Energy War: Breaking the Nuclear Link*. New York: Harper and Row, 1981.

_____, and John H. Price. *Non-Nuclear Futures: The Case for an Ethical Energy Strategy*. San Francisco: Friends of the Earth, 1975.

Lyons, Stephen, ed. *New England's White Mountains: At Home in the Wild*. San Francisco: Friends of the Earth, 1978. (Photography by Amory Lovins, et al.)

McPhee, John. *Encounters with the Archdruid*. New York: Farrar, Straus and Giroux, 1971.

Mayer, Allan J. "Thinking Soft." *Newsweek*, 90 (November 14, 1977), 108, 112, 114.

Nash, Hugh, ed. *The Energy Controversy: Soft Path Questions and Answers by Amory B. Lovins and His Critics*. San Francisco: Friends of the Earth, 1979.

Parisi, Anthony J. " 'Soft' Energy, Hard Choices." *New York Times*, (October 16, 1977), Section 3, pp. 1, 7.

Parks, Alexis. "Amory Lovins Brings Good News." *High Country News* (Lander, Wyoming), November 3, 1978, pp. 1, 6.

Schumacher, E. F. *Small Is Beautiful*. New York: Harper and Row, 1973.

Snyder, Theodore A., Jr. "Our Energy Future: A Time to Choose." *Sierra: The Sierra Club Bulletin*, 64 (September-October 1979), 4-5.

" 'Soft Energy' Promoted as U.S. Solution." *Los Angeles Times*, April 26, 1978, Part 1-B, p. 6.

von Hoffman, Nicholas. "America: Trying to Kick the Oil Habit." *Washington Post*, March 17, 1977, Section D, p. 17.

Chapter 17 Reassembling the Parts: Sleek for the Long Flight

Graham, Frank, Jr. *Man's Dominion: The Story of Conservation in America*. New York: M. Evans, 1971.

Harding, Jim. "The Transient That Came to Dinner." *Not Man Apart*, 9 (May 1979), 5-6.

Leopold, Aldo. *Round River: From the Journals of Aldo Leopold*. Luna Leopold, ed. New York: Oxford University Press, 1953.

———. *A Sand County Almanac and Sketches Here and There*. New York: Oxford University Press, 1949.

Murie, Margaret. "Inner Ingredients Inspire Others." *High Country News* (Lander, Wyoming), September 23, 1977, p. 3.

"Pesticides: The Price for Progress." *Time Magazine*, 80 (September 18, 1962), 45-46, 48.

Rowell, Galen. *High and Wild: A Mountaineer's World*. San Francisco: Sierra Club, 1979.

Shepherd, Jack. *The Forest Killers: The Destruction of the American Wilderness*. New York: Weybright and Talley, 1975.

Index

Massachusetts Institute of Technology, 200, 209
Mayflower, 7
McCarry, Charles, 198-99
McCarthy, Joseph, 186
McKay, Douglas, 172
McKinley, William, 85
McClain Bird Protection Bill, 63, 104
Mead, Margaret, 69
Melville, Herman, 30
Men and Rubber: The Story of Business, 55
Mencken, H. L., 134
Mexican-American War, 18
Michtom, Morris, 81
Middle East, 16, 19
Middletown, 134
Mikado, The, 211
Mission Mountains, Montana, *127*
Mississippi, 44
Missouri River, 70
Mondale, Walter, 213
Montana, 8, 68
Montreal, Quebec, 40
Moran, Thomas, 11
Morgan, J. P., 83-84
Moynihan, Daniel Patrick, 197
Mt. Holyoke, Massachusetts, 211
Mt. Katahdin, Maine, 111
Mt. Tom, Vermont, xii, 15
Muir, John, 1, 6, 11, 38, 49, 56, 91, 100, 109, 133, 153, 169
Muller, Dr. Paul, 167-68
Mumford, Lewis, 16, 112-13, 115
Murie, Margaret, 227
Murie, Olaus, 227
Muscle Shoals, 145
Mussolini, 138

Nader and the Power of Everyman, 305
Nader, Laura, 202
Nader, Nadra, 202-03
Nader, Ralph, xiv, 135, *194*, 195, 206, 221
Nader, Rose Bouziane, 202-03
Nancy, France, 88
Naples, Italy, 167
Nash, Roderick, 124, 135, 155, 161
Nation, 48, 125, 134
National Association of Manufacturers, 111
National Energy Plan, 191
National Forest Commission, 88
National Forestry School, 88
National Museum, Washington, D.C., 97-98
National Park Act, 8
National Park Service, 38, 77, 124, 131, 161
National Resources Board, 146

National Trails System Act, 120
National Zoo, Washington, D.C., 39
Nature Conservancy, 226
Nature Magazine, 125, 154
Nebraska, 67-68
New England, xi, 5-7, 28-29, 33, 37-38, 59, 107-08, 114-15, 117-18, 210-11, 217
New England's White Mountains: At Home in the Wild, 219
New Exploration, The, 118
New Hampshire, 17, 107
New Jersey, 59, 134, 184, 202
New Mexico, 124
New Republic, 124
New Roots, 216
New Times, 210-11
New York, 10, 19, 21, 29, 31, 34, 45, 56-57, 59-60, 62, 65, 68, 76-78, 81-83, 91, 98, 117, 126, 139-41, 170
New York City, New York, 30, 38, 70, 81, 88, 109, 117, 125, 139
New York Evening Post, 48
New York State College of Forestry, 126
New York Times, 30, 100, 125, 134, 182
New York Tribune, 19
New York Zoological Society, 98, 100-02
New Yorker, 183, 187-88
New Zion, 4
Newcomb Cleveland Prize, 185
Newsweek, 34, 197
Niagara Falls, 38
Nixon, President Richard, 200, 206
Nobel Prize, 187
Non-Nuclear Futures, 213
North America, 108
North Carolina, 88
North Dakota, 86
Northern Pacific Railroad, 68
Northern Rocky Mountain Experiment Station, Missoula, Montana, 127
Norwich Academy, 17
Notes on Walt Whitman, 60

Oehser, Paul, 159
Office of Indian Affairs, 127
Office of Management and Budget, 200
Ohio, 185
Olmsted, Frederick Law, 6-7, 11, *26*, 27-40, 49, 67, 88, 113-14, 119, 124, 211, 222, 225
Olmsted, Frederick Law, Jr., 38
Olmsted, John, 38
Open-Pit Mining, 213
Origin and History of the English Language, The, 21
Our Vanishing Wildlife, 102
Oxford University Press, 171